DIVIDED WE STAND

A History of the Continuing Anglican Movement

Douglas Bess

TRACTARIAN PRESS
Riverside, CA

Copyright © 2002, Douglas Bess

All rights reserved

Cover and book design: Jonathan Gullery

ISBN: 0-9719636-0-6
LCCN: 2002104268

Without limiting the rights under copyright reserved above, no part of the publication may be reproduced, stored in or introduced into a retrieval system, or transmitted, in any form or by any means (electronic, mechanical, photocopying, recording or otherwise), without the prior written permission of both the copyright owner and the above publisher of this book.

TABLE OF CONTENTS

	Introduction 5
1	The Decline of the Episcopal Church 15
2	The Anglican Orthodox Church 41
3	The American Episcopal Church and Other Early Continuing Groups 61
4	Traditionalist Dissidents in the Early 1970s 81
5	The St. Louis Congress 97
6	The Dallas Synod 121
7	The Formation of the Anglican Catholic Church 135
8	Indianapolis and Hot Springs 155
9	The Phalanx Strikes Back 175
10	1984-1987 201
11	1988-1991 215
12	1992 – 1996 233
13	1997 – 2001 241
	Conclusion – The Status and Future of Continuing Anglicanism 259
	Appendix A The Affirmation of St. Louis 265
	Appendix B The Southern Phalanx 279
	Notes 283

INTRODUCTION

This book examines the history of a relatively small movement of Episcopalian dissidents who, during the last decades of the 20th century, withdrew from the institutional church in order to form independent ecclesiastical bodies. These Episcopalian sects were developed during various waves of traditionalist and orthodox discontent, which began in the 1950s, increased during the 1960s, and reached their peak in the 1970s. Although the first twenty years were relatively optimistic periods for these ecclesiastical rebels, based in large part on the belief that a substantial reservoir of sympathetic churchmen would soon be willing to join them, by the 1980s the sectarians were forced to confront a more disappointing reality. Their movement had not shaken the Episcopal Church to its knees, nor had it succeeded in gaining large numbers of adherents, since the total membership in the movement numbered in the tens of thousands, rather than the hundreds of thousands or millions, as had initially been hoped for. This book chronicles the controversies within the Episcopal Church that led to the formation of traditionalist dissent, and eventually to traditionalist schism, but focuses most of its attention on the internal history of the ecclesiastical bodies formed by those who broke away from the Episcopal Church.

The traditionalists did not initially see themselves as sectarians, but insisted instead that the leadership of the institutional Episcopal Church had abandoned traditionalist churchmen in the pursuit of radical, trendy, and even heretical theological and liturgical exploration. Thus most of the dissenting traditionalists accepted the term "Continuing Anglican" to describe their movement since they claimed to be maintaining the true teachings of the

Episcopal Church. One of the great ironies of the Continuing Movement, and perhaps its greatest weakness, was that the exact parameters that constituted the "true teachings" of the Episcopal Church were not as easy to define as had been imagined by many of the earliest Continuers. The theological ambiguity that lay at the heart of Anglicanism, which paradoxically claims to be both Protestant and Catholic, would establish itself anew after the formation of the Continuing bodies. Although each of the Continuing bodies had been formed in reaction to a perceived state of heresy within the Episcopal Church (either for espousing political or theological radicalism, ordaining women to the priesthood, or for improperly revising the 1928 Prayer Book), each would eventually have to confront the fact, in terms of theology and doctrine, that there was a greater divide within their own ranks than they had assumed. The old animosities between High, Low, and Broad-Church Episcopalians, which could be smoothed over when confronting the changes within the Episcopal Church that they agreed were in error, could not be ignored once the Continuers were isolated in the jurisdictions of their own creation.

A good portion of this study deals with the two conflicting visions that separated the Continuers as to what constituted a genuinely purified Episcopal Church. The Broad-Church party was the most likely to embrace the designation of "Continuing Anglican" for the Movement, and tended to stress that the Episcopal Church was relatively orthodox until its recent forays into radical theology and practice in the post-World War II period. These Broad-Church Continuers were generally Low-Church in their theology, assuming that authentic Episcopalian doctrine was essentially Protestant in nature, thus stressing the sufficiency of the Bible for establishing doctrine, the symbolic understanding of the Body of Christ in the Eucharist, a generally low opinion in regard to the scope of the authority of the bishops within the Church, and so on. What separated them from more consistently Low-Church Continuers was their relative tolerance of certain High-Church teachings and practices, so long as these were contained at the level of the local parish or the individual churchman, and not imposed on the Church at large. The High-Church party tended to view the Episcopal Church as having been in need of a major overhaul, both in doctrine and practice, in the direction of ancient Catholicism, from its very beginning, extending back to the period of the English Reformation itself. The High-Church party tended to view itself in a historical context, as constituting an essential reforming block within the Episcopal Church, and as having elected to remain within the church only so long as it retained its minimum standards of Catholic identity, such as the Apostolic Succession of bishops. The High-Church Continuers stressed that the Bible should be interpreted only in conjunction with the Tradition of the ancient Church and its Ecumenical Councils, that the Body of Christ was really present in the Eucharistic elements, and that bishops should possess much more authority than they previously had in the Anglican tradition. These differing understandings of just how the Episcopal Church was to be "continued" would strain the Continuing Movement from the very beginning.

  This interpretation, focusing as it does on the doctrinal and churchmanship disagreements within the Continuing Movement, is in many ways revisionist in terms of how it will be viewed by many contemporary Continuing churchmen. The reason for this is that the Movement has had no comprehensive, serious history written about it. Much of the story of the Continuing Movement can only be found in isolated and controversy-shy printings of small parish and diocesan newsletters, as well as by word of mouth and gossip between individual Continuing churchmen. The majority of the sources that achieved the level of a national distribution and scope were tainted as historical records by the varying degrees of bias on the part of the small clique of Continuing churchmen who funded and manned them. The churchmen behind these national publications were generally in favor of the Low-Church interpretation of the Continuing Movement, though they often denied both that they had chosen sides and that they were Low-churchmen. Still, their actions (usually unrecorded in their publications) often spoke louder than their claims of neutrality toward disputes within the Movement.

The most prevalent interpretation of the Continuing Movement has been that it was greatly hindered, if not harmed, by the selfish actions of the Movement's bishops, who tore the movement apart in order to aggrandize more power and prestige for themselves, with theological and churchmanship issues being of only secondary importance. Though the questionable actions of some Continuing bishops certainly played an important role in limiting the success and/or harmony of the Movement, this book gives equal weight to the role that wealthy and influential laymen played in bringing disharmony into the Movement. In this regard, this book pays special attention to a group that I call the Southern Phalanx, an association of Broad and Low-Churchmen, mostly from the South, who used their wealth and polemical talents to spread their message through a national distribution of periodicals and journals that they either created, controlled, or influenced. It was this Southern Phalanx, of which much will be said throughout, that promulgated the above-mentioned "standard" view that has largely been accepted within the Continuing Movement itself.[1]

In researching this work, many obstacles developed which greatly hindered the overall effectiveness of the project. To begin with, there are many sources that would no doubt greatly illuminate the Movement, but which remain outside of the reach[2] of all but the most diligent, wealthy, or well connected of scholars. As a young doctoral student (read: semi-employed) with a wife and two children, I do not have the resources to travel to the scattered locations that contain all of the Movement's materials. This work is essentially a private project, which has been undertaken only out of frustration that no history has been written of the Movement, and thus with a reluctant sense of mission. I have had to rely on those resources that are available locally (Claremont School of Theology and Cal State Fullerton), one research trip to the Graduate Theological Library at Berkeley, and the generosity of individual Continuing churchmen who loaned me those materials that they have collected over the years. The sources available on the internet offered little more help since most Continuing Movement websites offer only the most generic and hagiographic accounts of their own histories. It is my hope that in the future a more professional and thorough history of the Continuing Movement will be written by a scholar with better access to resources than myself.

    Another problem in constructing this history has been the hesitancy that most Continuing churchmen have shown toward the project. Although I attempted to contact (by telephone, mail, and the internet) most of the Continuers that played important roles in the Movement's history, few of them responded to my inquiries. Of those who did respond, many seemed to be suspicious of my motives. I was left with the impression that many Continuers do not relish the thought of having their Movement's, and perhaps their particular denomination's, history revealed to a wider audience. Problematically, many of those who did respond to my enquiries spoke only on conditions of anonymity, supposedly due to fears of ecclesiastical repercussions and even lawsuits.2 Despite these limitations, there were Continuing churchmen who were generous enough to offer their help and insights. Of these I especially wish to thank the recently deceased Fr. Walter Buerger, and his wife Mary, Fr. Clifford Bulloch, Fr. Thomas McDonald, Fr. Anthony Rasch, Fr. Gregory Wilcox, Dr. Donald Gerlach, Bishop Huron C. Manning, Bishop Charles E. Morley, Fr. Mark Clavier, Bishop Walter Grundhorf, and many laymen and clergy who chose to be labeled as anonymous when being cited in this study.

Another difficulty in constructing a thorough history of the Continuing Movement is the number of groups that have proliferated with each passing decade. Whereas before 1980 the historian only had to examine a handful of Continuing church bodies, as of 2002 there are well over 30 groups claiming some kind of connection to the Continuing Anglican Movement. The historian is presented with the problem of deciding which groups are "authentically" Continuing bodies, which groups are large enough to deserve attention, and so forth. My general approach aims to avoid trying to distinguish between the claims of legitimacy by the assorted groups, and to try to include as many of their stories as possible. However, the lack of sources for constructing a history of the Movement in general (mentioned above is amplified when applied to some of the numerically smaller Continuing bodies. The few sources that discuss these smaller groups (especially their own websites) usually give little information that is of historical value. For instance, a typical website for one of the smaller Continuing bodies stated simply that the group had been formed in the 1990s in order to bring unity to the world of traditionalist Anglicans. When I contacted the group's leading bishop for more concrete information, such as whether or not the group had previously been associated with any other groups, he informed me that he would have to pass my request along to his College of Bishops in order to get permission to release such information. Such walls of secrecy regarding basic historical information practically beg the historian to exclude these kinds of Continuing groups from this study.

Another problem is that some of these smaller groups (more usually their bishops) have engaged in such bizarre behavior that they frighten away all but the most courageous historian. For instance, one of the founding bishops of the Continuing Episcopal Church (formed in 1984), Colin James III, has been thoroughly attacked on the internet during recent years by an Archbishop Montgomery Griffith-Mair, who as far as I can tell is either now, or once was, associated with another of the smaller groups, the Anglican Rite Synod of America. Griffith-Mair, writing under the name Father Monty, accuses James of assorted scandalous and unchristian behaviors, and of legally harassing him. Father Monty's internet missives give the impression that Bishop James is making similarly scandalous claims regarding the behavior of Griffith-Mair against him. Thus each prelate is accusing the other of either unchristian, harassing, or illegal behavior. I for one am not inclined to try and decipher these allegations, since a series of lawsuits seems to be flying between them, and therefore I am neither inclined to give either of these groups much attention in this study. For what its worth, Griffith-Mair was reported to have been arrested in October of 2001 for raping a young man in Arkansas. He also reportedly explained to police that the relationship was mutual, rather than criminal, which would seem odd for a supposedly traditionalist Anglican bishop whose internet writings frequently rail against the evil behaviors of his enemies (usually other traditionalists/Continuing churchmen).[3]

Beyond the difficulties associated with insufficient sources and/or the eccentric behavior of certain bishops within these smaller bodies, a further problem arises in that many of these groups seem to be structurally rather amorphous. That is, their very smallness leaves them susceptible to frequent transferences of allegiance and/or intercommunion, which are then often just as frequently revoked. For example, in trying to construct the history of the Southern Episcopal Church (SEC) (discussed more assuredly in Chapter 2) the story became very confused after the initial period of its founding in the mid-1960s. Although I interviewed the current Presiding Bishop, Huron C. Manning, and two SEC laymen who were enthusiastic about the project, it became apparent that these well-intentioned people were suffering some genuine memory loss regarding certain important developments. For example, Bishop Larry Shaver was said to have become an SEC bishop when the SEC's original Presiding Bishop (B.H. Webster) became ill sometime prior to his death in 1991. None of my interviewees seemed to be able to positively remember which group Bishop Shaver was associated with at the time (perhaps the United Episcopal Church), but they claimed that Shaver seemed to have assumed that the SEC was going to be incorporated into another group (the United Episcopal Church?). There was then apparently some kind of falling out which resulted in Shaver, some newly consecrated bishops, and some other SEC churchmen joining the Anglican Rite Jurisdiction in the Americas. What is apparent is that there was some kind of ecclesiastical controversy that occurred within the SEC, but unfortunately, few within the SEC (that were willing to speak to myself) seem to have fully grasped, or to have remembered, the reasons for the eventual split.

It is difficult to construct an historical account on such sketchy information. Thus, out of necessity more than any other motive, this study focuses most of its attention on the larger Continuing groups which at least benefit from having more sources from which to piece together a coherent narrative from otherwise frequently conflicting versions of key events and controversies. A similar editorial decision had to made in regard to the foreign Continuing Anglican bodies that are currently such an important component of the future of the Continuing Movement. Continuing groups from Canada, Australia, England, and other regions of the world are discussed in relation to American events due not to any prejudice, but to the simple facts of limited access to resources combined with space constraints.

Chapter 1

THE DECLINE OF THE EPISCOPAL CHURCH

The Protestant Episcopal Church (PECUSA) experienced one of its greatest periods of numerical growth and vitality during the decade and a half that followed World War II. Whereas in 1900 there was one Episcopalian communicant for every one hundred Americans, by 1950 the ratio was one to ninety-two, and by 1960 the ratio was one to eighty-six.[4] During this period the number of clergy rose to its highest level in the church's history, and some observers noted that it was a challenge to construct parish buildings fast enough to meet the demands produced by increased attendance. However, this impressive growth would prove to be a temporary phenomenon, and by the late 1960s PECUSA began a decline in membership that would continue for more than twenty years. The 3.4 million Episcopalians in 1960 had dwindled to 1.6 million by 1994.[5]

Although many scholars and other observers have offered a variety of explanations as to why PECUSA experienced such a sharp decline in membership after the 1960s peak, these play no part in this historical study. For within the world of the traditionalists Episcopalians who would later become the first Continuing churchmen, there was really only one explanation for the decline of PECUSA: their church had been infected with an immoral and heretical spirit. If one wishes to understand why these traditionalist Episcopalians formed smaller church bodies that are independent of the national church and the worldwide Anglican communion, then one needs to have a knowledge of the ideas, events, and changes that occurred within PECUSA from the 1950s until the largest split which occurred in 1977, and how these were viewed by traditionalists. These changes were often interpreted by traditionalists as either somewhat confusing devolutions from a simpler and purer past or, more often than not, as blatant desertions of authentic faith and morality by ecclesiastical authorities. It was within the context of a "church in crisis" mentality that the evolution of Continuing Anglicanism took place. The crisis tended to be an amorphous problem that did not lend itself to easy categorization or analysis, but most traditionalists understood the nature of the problem at an instinctual level, and they proceeded to identify it as best they could while organizing to combat the forces that they interpreted as intending to harm their beloved church. The crisis was interpreted by traditionalists as infecting the church from within, as a result of spiritual weakness, and from without by way of attacks from the "ungodly secular spirit of the age."

One of the first controversies to develop within PECUSA, according to the traditionalist churchmen, was its increasing involvement with the Federal, National, and World Councils of Churches. These organizations had originally been formed as a way for the Protestant denominations to pool their resources in order to facilitate more effective evangelization, and to address what were perceived to be assorted social problems. However, almost from their institutional formation, these organizations quickly became associated with the kind of political ideology and activism that many traditionalist churchmen interpreted as transgressing the symbolic line that appropriately separated the spheres of church and state. As each year passed, these church councils issued statements and became involved in political actions that increasingly dismayed traditionalist churchmen.

In 1952, and then again in 1955, the National Council of Churches (NCC) issued resolutions expressing their disapproval of universal military training and service for young men.[6] In 1953 the NCC published the first of a six-volume study on the problems of American economic policy. The general thesis of the study had been described as a proposal maintaining that, "welfare economics (the welfare state under another name) was the best, if not the only, solution to the problem of finding a balance between the individual and the economic group."[7] After criticisms of this position intensified, the NCC issued a statement that was more critical of "collectivist solutions," but still reminded its readers that there was a misconception "held by sincere Christians, that a maximum of individual economic freedom will by itself create the economic conditions that contribute to a good society. On the contrary, the weight of evidence shows that some use of government in relation to economic activities is essential to provide the environment in which human freedom can flourish."[8] The NCC would criticize both the South African *and* American governments for the perpetuation of apartheid in 1963, to argue for recognition of communist China in 1966, and to propose a guaranteed income for every American in 1968, to name just a few of their pronouncements that were viewed by many traditionalists as being either too political, un-Christian, or un-American.[9]

During the early 1950s, when Cold War concerns about the possible infiltration of international Communism into the United States were at their peak, the atmosphere was rife with accusations that the NCC had been tainted with Communism and/or radicalism. The NCC had replaced the Federal Council of Churches in 1950, and the Federal Council had already made itself suspect in the eyes of many political conservatives, including many traditionalist churchmen, when it began to criticize the Constitutionality of the House Un-American Activities Committee (HUAC) in 1948.[10] The NCC continued the Federal Council's position as one of the most consistent and prominent critics of the HUAC investigations. Many churchmen shared the suspicions of other conservative Americans that the NCC's attacks on HUAC were proof that the organization was sympathetic to Communism or radicalism. The accusations against the NCC were taken so seriously by many Americans at the time that Methodist Bishop G. Bromley Oxnam, former president of the Federal Council, appeared before HUAC in 1953 at his own request in order to answer the charges that Communists had infiltrated America's churches. Episcopalians paid special attention to these developments since their Presiding Bishop at the time, Henry Knox Sherrill, was the acting president of the NCC. Unfortunately, Oxnam's defiant and mocking performance on national television tended to actually intensify the suspicions of many churchmen. It was only the general discrediting of those who searched for Communist infiltration of American institutions (what came to be known by the epithet of "red baiting") by the media and the nation's establishment that led to a lessoning of pressure on the NCC by traditionalist churchmen. Nevertheless, even though fewer churchmen were willing to transgress the symbolic line demarcating respectability, and therefore to be vocal anti-Communists of the old stripe, the number of churchmen who continued to have serious misgivings about PECUSA's involvement with the NCC remained significant. As late as 1960 a scandal developed in which the Air Force published a training manual warning that the NCC was a subversive organization that was tainted with "Communist influence." Although the Air Force quickly retracted and repudiated the manual amidst the ensuing controversy, many churchmen could not help but suspect that the NCC was an organization that their church should not be supporting. Conservative (some would label them "right wing") Christian writers continued to assail the National and World Councils of Churches throughout the 1960s and beyond.[11]

While the accusations of radicalism in the NCC were dealt with effectively enough by its apologists to ease the suspicions of most churchmen, developments within PECUSA itself were pushing many churchmen to look closer to home for the creeping influence of radicalism in their own church. It is important to remember that during the 1950s and 1960s many traditionalist churchmen equated political activism by the church with political radicalism. The very entry of the church into the realm of political activism was deemed by many to be a radical position. The political activism of PECUSA during this period was most pronounced, and most controversial for some traditionalists, in the realm of what is known today as the Civil Rights Movement. At first the push for civil rights and racial equality by the institutional church was mild and rather genteel. Beginning in the late 1940s, a movement had begun in order to desegregate all PECUSA dioceses. In 1954 South Carolina became the last diocese to remove race as a determining factor in selecting representatives to church conventions. PECUSA also made a powerful symbolic statement of sympathy with the Civil Rights Movement when it moved its 1955 General Convention from Houston, Texas, which could not guarantee that all facilities would be open to non-whites, to Honolulu, Hawaii. However, the involvement of PECUSA in the cause of civil rights would eventually begin to mirror the wider Civil Rights Movement in its transition toward more radical demands for the immediate remedy of the social and economic grievances of black Americans.

In 1958 the Episcopal Society for Cultural and Racial Unity (ESCRU) was formed to be a civil rights activism outlet for Episcopalians. One of its earliest actions, and most successful in terms of publicity, was the Prayer Pilgrimage, an interracial junket of traveling priests designed to educate the church and society about racial discrimination. The "Pilgrimage" began its journey in New Orleans and then made confrontational stops in assorted Southern cities on its way to the 1961 General Convention in Detroit, Michigan. The Executive Director of ESCRU, John B. Morris, stated that everyone participating in the Pilgrimage should be prepared to go to jail, and go to jail they did. In Jackson, Mississippi, fifteen priests were arrested for attempting to sit in a "whites-only" restaurant. The convention delegates in Detroit passed a resolution that approved of the Pilgrimage's mission, but refused to endorse their law-breaking activities. This cautious approach would soon give way to calls for increased intensity in the struggle for civil rights. Presiding Bishop Arthur Lichtenberger, who had served a term as Chairman of the National Council of Churches' Commission of Religion and Race, issued a statement in 1963 that supported overt political action by Episcopalians in the cause of civil rights. Lichtenberger stated, "It is not enough for the church to exhort men to be good...[People] today are risking their livelihood and their lives in protesting for their rights. We must support and strengthen their protest in every way possible."[12] PECUSA moved closer to officially adopting Lichtenberger's position when the 1964 General Convention stated its support for those who gave material and moral aid to activists involved in conflicts related to questions of civil rights. Perhaps more importantly, the 1964 General Convention also elected Bishop John Hines of Mississippi to be PECUSA's next Presiding Bishop. Presiding Bishop Hines would become the symbol, in the eyes of many traditionalists, of the church's errant venture into inappropriate political involvement in the cause of racial justice.

In 1967 Hines announced his plan to establish the General Convention Special Program (GCSP), a church program designed to "empower" blacks and other minorities. This empowerment was to be accomplished by way of grants that would be made directly to groups that were controlled by minorities in order to facilitate their "self-determination" in overcoming the "oppression" that they suffered in the American "system." Another key component of the program's provisions, and an eventual thorn in the side of many of its supporters, was that no church monies were to be given to any group that advocated or engaged in violence. The convention approved the program with little opposition, but a member of the Program and Budget Committee, J.L. McFadden of Texas, objected in a dissenting opinion that it appeared that $500,000 was to be given to groups that advocated what was known as "black power." As it turned out, McFadden's warning proved to be prophetic, but most of his fellow Episcopalians were content to trust the motivations and common sense of their church leadership. Unfortunately, few of the convention delegates seemed to realize at the time that the rhetoric of "empowerment" and "self-determination" were the catch-phrases and guiding vocabulary of the newly emerging militant black-power-wing of the Civil Rights Movement. It was not until numerous scandalous reports appeared regarding some of the groups that had received church grants that many churchmen began to question the legitimacy of the GCSP, and to understand that J.L. McFadden was not simply a mere obscurantist stick-in-the-mud.[13]

Although many of the grants went to groups whose goals appear, in retrospect, to have been rather harmless and/or naïve, (such as an organization called Southern

Media that proposed to produce low-budget films in order to help blacks achieve an improved sense of self-esteem), some of the money went to organizations whose agendas were deadly serious and often quite violent. One of the first grants was awarded to a group called the Citywide Citizens Action Committee of Detroit. This group had been implicated as one of the primary organizers of the riots that had erupted in Detroit in 1966 and 1967. In 1969 money was sent to an organization called Malcolm X Liberation University in North Carolina, and funds were also given to a group that wished to distribute a documentary film that glorified Black Panther Party leader, and suspected cop killer, Huey Newton. In 1970 a grant was given, despite the opposition of the local bishops, to a group in South Carolina (the Black Awareness Coordinating Committee) that had seized the campus of PECUSA's Voorhees College by forcibly removing its occupants at gunpoint. Several of the group's leaders had previously been convicted by predominantly black juries of assorted crimes, and local civil rights groups had even criticized the radical organization for its strong-arm tactics, such as intimidating local blacks to join in their cause. However, the grant that drew the most attention and controversy was that made to a small group in New Mexico, the Alianza Federal de Mercedes (AFM), that had announced its intentions of seizing self-determination for Hispanics by revolting against the governments of the southwestern United States. The story of the AFM grant is not only important for what it reveals about the increased radicalism of PECUSA's political activism, but also for an understanding of the increasing divide between the church's leadership and many of the more traditionally-inclined laity.

  In 1963, Reies Lopez Tijerina organized the AFM in order to force the return of all Spanish and Mexican land grants to those Hispanics who were alleged to be the descendents of the "rightful" holders of the grants. Once this confiscated land was returned to its "rightful owners," it was to become a republic in which Hispanics could be free of white oppression. In 1966, Tijerina and four of his followers attacked two forest rangers in New Mexico's Carson National Forest. In 1967, the AFM tried to organize a meeting in Northern New Mexico, but they were prevented from drawing a large crowd due to the probably illegal actions of local law enforcement officials who "discouraged" local residents from attending the meeting by stressing that radical provocateurs would be encouraging violence. This conclusion by the police was drawn largely from their having read a manifesto, published in a local newspaper, in which the AFM had stated that it would consider any efforts to stop their campaign to be an act of war, and that those who opposed them would be put on trial and executed. A few days after the failed organizing meeting, Tijerina lead an AFM attack upon the courthouse of Tierra Amarilla, the county seat of Rio Arriba County, New Mexico. The stated purpose of the AFM action was to place the District Attorney under citizen's arrest for allegedly violating the civil rights of AFM when the police had earlier intimidated local citizens into not attending the AFM meeting. Tijerina lead 150 men into the courthouse, surprising a state police officer, and then shooting him in the chest. An elderly unarmed jailor attempted to climb out of a window, but was shot in the face by Tijerina, and then shot again. The AFM mob next pistol-whipped the sheriff, and then held twenty people hostage for two hours before escaping with stolen goods and money. Tijerina was finally captured in 1969 along with six followers. The elderly jailor testified in a preliminary hearing that it was Tijerina who had shot him, but the witness was later mysteriously beaten to death before he could testify at the trial. The State Chief of Police described the attack at the most severe beating that he had seen in his thirty-year career. Other local residents also claimed to have been intimidated by the AFM into not testifying at Tijerina's trial. Nonetheless, Tijerina and four of his accomplices were convicted, although Tijerina would only serve six months of his original ten-year sentence.

The AFM had applied for a GCSP grant in March 1969, in order to help develop the internal structure of their organization. The GCSP investigator assigned to the case, John Davis, went to New Mexico to interview the leaders of the AFM and the bishop with jurisdiction, Lester Kinsolving. The Screening and Review Committee met in New York in November to consider the recommendation of the GCSP staff that the AFM receive a grant of $40,000. After the AFM leaders had presented their case, Bishop Kinsolving and those opposed to the grant presented theirs. Kinsolving noted that the Standing Committee of the Diocesan Council, the clergy conference, and most of the vestries and bishop's committees had all opposed the awarding of the grant to the AFM due to its advocacy of violence. A report presented by the opponents of the grant noted seven separate occasions in which there was documentation of Tijerina and the AFM initiating violent activity, and sixteen cases of speeches and written references in which AFM spokesmen had urged their followers to commit acts of violence against the government. Toward the end of the meeting, at which Presiding Bishop Hines attended, the AFM representatives were given a short rebuttal period, during which they countered that whatever violence they had committed had been defensive in nature and justified due to the violent nature of the American system that had "oppressed" them. A question period followed in which the Committee reserved all of its sharp and hostile questions for the opponents of the grant. When one of the opponents, John W. Ellison, stated that the whole meeting seemed to be a moot point since the 1967 Seattle resolution that had established the GCSP specifically forbid the dispensing of funds to groups that advocated violence, the head of the GCSP, Leon Modest, contradicted him. Modeste claimed that the wording of the resolution had stated that no money should be given to organizations *advocating* violence. Modeste wryly asked the AFM representatives if they advocated violence "*at this time*", and they responded that they did not currently advocate violence. The final report issued by the Committee intimated that, if anything, it was the AFM that had been the victims of violence and discrimination, and that this had compelled them to "employ confrontation tactics." The grant was approved over the opposition of most of the clergy and laity of the Diocese of New Mexico and Southwest Texas.[14]

Controversial grants such as that given to the AFM resulted in a groundswell of resentment and retaliatory activism by those who opposed the political agenda of the GCSP, irregardless of whether they would describe themselves as traditionalists or political conservatives. Many parishes and dioceses began to withhold portions of the money that would normally be sent to assist in the work of the national church. However, the incident that really sharpened the criticism of the kind of radical political activism that was increasingly being associated with the GCSP and the national church was the way in which PECUSA handled what was known at the time as the Black Manifesto. This radical document had been created in 1969 by James Foreman, with the backing of hundreds of representatives from assorted radical black groups, during a meeting of the Black Economic Development Conference (BEDC) in Detroit. The meeting had been sponsored by the Interreligious Foundation for Community Organization, the most generously endowed recipient of GCSP funds. The Manifesto called on the churches and synagogues of America to pay blacks (really the radical groups who claimed to speak for all blacks) $500 million in compensation for black suffering in American history. This sum would later be increased to $3 billion. Manifesto-wielding activists then began interrupting the worship services and national offices of various Protestant denominations to demand payment of what were called "reparations" to black Americans.

Foreman, leader of the Student Non-Violent Coordinating Committee, and a former Black Panther Party member, first unveiled the Manifesto when he interrupted the services of PECUSA's Riverside Church in New York. PECUSA officials later agreed to meet with a group of black activists who demanded that the church pay them $60 million and sixty percent of the church's proceeds annually. PECUSA's Executive Council, which was in charge of giving final approval to any GCSP grant, rejected the demands made by the activists, who seemed to be making-up monetary demands arbitrarily and with little consistency, but insisted that the church was still effecting the same outcome by way of the GCSP. However, the activists who advocated reparations by way of the Black Manifesto were not finished in their harassment of church officials, and they would strike their most controversial blow against the church at what was termed a "Special General Convention" in South Bend, Indiana in 1969.

Also known as General Convention II, this "additional" Special Convention had been called in order to allow for "other voices" to be heard within PECUSA on the controversial issues that were gripping the nation's attention at the time. These "other voices" included women, assorted non-whites, war protestors, a group generally referred to as "youth," and assorted activist groups who were not even members of PECUSA. The South Bend gathering quickly descended into a carnival-like atmosphere. For example, a demonstration organized by the Episcopal Peace Fellowship, as well as Clergy and Laymen Concerned About

Vietnam, began with several protestors interrupting the scheduled activities by positioning themselves at different areas in the auditorium in order to read aloud the names of those who had been killed in the war. A demonstrator then took control of the main podium and asked everyone who was "concerned about peace" to join in a recital of the Lord's Prayer. A small number of delegates joined in this symbolic action. Later, during scheduled speeches given by "youth" that addressed the war, Bishop Kilmer Myers of California took the podium and announced that two AWOL soldiers would be entering the auditorium. A peace procession, replete with psychedelically decorated signs containing anti-war slogans, escorted the men to the platform. A speech was given that encouraged the church to give "sanctuary" to such war protestors, and, after the AWOL soldiers had also given short speeches, people were then asked to show their support for their rebellious action by standing behind them in a show of mass solidarity. About half of those present in the gallery followed suit.[15] However, the most serious controversy centered on the decisions made at South Bend regarding the GCSP and the Black Manifesto.

    The South Bend Convention began somewhat ominously when Presiding Bishop Hines stated in his opening address that those who opposed the GCSP were a "small group of pietistic isolationists" who were either supporting a racist system or were just misinformed about the church's support for racial justice. This dismissal of his critics turned out to be severely misconceived when it became apparent to many delegates that PECUSA had capitulated to the demands of the Black Manifesto. The process began rather innocently, with the Executive Council giving limited recognition to the BEDC as a movement which "shows promise" for helping black Americans. However, the Executive Council stopped short of agreeing with the ideas expressed in the Black Manifesto, and asserted that no church funds would go to the BEDC as a result of threats or intimidation. Reaching its decision prior to the official opening of the Special Convention, the Executive Council had concluded its evaluation of the BEDC demands by describing the Black Manifesto as "Marxist, anti-Christian, and anti-Semitic," and required the BEDC to go through the same application process (through the GCSP) as any other group seeking church funds. However, this requirement angered many of the activists at South Bend who were seeking the church's recognition of the Black Manifesto.

The first session of the Special Convention was disrupted by Fr. Paul Washington and Muhammed Kenyatta, two black activists from Philadelphia, both wearing dark sunglasses though they were indoors, who took over the podium in order to demand the immediate examination of the Executive Council report regarding the funding of the BEDC. Hines tried to restore order, but Washington and Kenyatta refused to yield their place on stage. Kenyatta demanded that the Convention immediately agree to pay $200,000 to the BEDC directly out of church funds, rather than out of the GCSP budget. When Dr. John Coburn, president of the House of Deputies, explained that the Executive Council's recommendations would have to be evaluated through the proper channels and committees, Washington and Kenyatta led their supporters in a walk-out of the convention in order to plan their next move. The leadership of the Special Convention decided overnight to delay the next day's scheduled business so that the demands of Washington and Kenyatta could be debated.

A host of supporters of the BEDC gave speeches on its behalf, with Kenyatta condescendingly explaining that the BEDC program was designed to liberate both the master and the slave. Undoubtedly, many less radical churchmen were surprised to learn that blacks in America were still in a state of slavery, and that whites were still their masters. The Convention thus proceeded to defeat the proposal to give funds to the BEDC outside of the normal process of applying to the GCSP. However, the black activists became enraged at this rebuff of their agitations. Fr. Junius Carter attacked the decision of the delegates, stating, "I'm sick of you…you've just crucified every black priest in this church," before melodramatically walking out of the auditorium. The next day the delegates, mostly out of guilt-induced badgering, acquiesced to the pressure applied by the black clergy, and approved the proposal that had been defeated the previous day. It was agreed that BEDC would receive its $200,000 indirectly, by way of a grant to an interdenominational and ecumenical group known as the National Committee of Black Clergy. However, it was clearly explained that the money would go to the BEDC. The president of the Union of Black Clergy, Fr. Frederick Williams, called the resolution a "copout," since it didn't give the BEDC and the Black Manifesto the symbolic recognition that the black activists had been seeking. However, to the national media, and more importantly, to the many traditionalist churchmen who were already agitated over the direction of PECUSA's political activism, the resolution was interpreted as an acceptance of the Black Manifesto's demands for reparations.[16]

Reactions from churchmen across the country were immediate and mostly negative. A Chicago priest likened the scene at South Bend to that of early Rome, in which the "Christians were thrown to the lions." A priest from Indiana declared, "What was it like to be a priest or lay deputy at Notre Dame? It was sheer agonythe most painful five days of my whole priesthood. The House of Deputies was threatened, insulted, scorned, and (figuratively) spit on by hurt, angry blacks, by self-righteous pacifists, and by the most extreme hippies. On several occasions, had not the Deputies practiced extraordinary restraint and humility, there would have been the scandal of open fighting at the convention center."[17] Fr. Carrol Simcox, editor of the oldest, and at that time, largely traditionalist magazine for Episcopalians, *The Living Church*, editorialized that he felt as though there had been much hateful talk at South Bend, but that he was simply dismissed by supporters of the activists with assurances that they were just "telling it like it is." He expressed the opinion of many when he noted, "That many white people have exploited many black people is true: that is history. That white people as such (including all of them) have exploited black people as such is a distortion of history. It is also a distortion of moral theology. A 'race,' or any other collectivity, cannot sin or repent, any more than a committee can think. Many at South Bend had been so indoctrinated. That any such historic and social wrong as blacks have suffered at the hands if whites can be set right by paying money to self-appointed agents of the aggrieved group, when these step forward to demand 'reparations,' is unsupportable by history, morals, human nature, or common sense."[18]

In the immediate aftermath of the Special Convention, parishes and dioceses across the United States began to step-up the movement to withhold funds from the national church in order to protest its radical political activities. This occurred despite the fact that many of the more "progressive" leaders in the church tried to pacify exasperated churchmen by emphatically insisting that PECUSA had not capitulated to the radicals' demands for reparations. Nonetheless, giving to the national church decreased so greatly that half of the staff at the Episcopal Church Center in New York was eventually let go in 1971. This grassroots movement by concerned churchmen would also eventually succeed in forcing the church to decrease its funding of the GCSP so sharply that it was finally disbanded in 1974. However, before this move toward responsibility occurred, traditionalist churchmen would have to endure repeated criticisms and slurs from their Presiding Bishop and other church leaders.

Presiding Bishop Hines issued a statement that denigrated the opposition to the GCSP, contrasting the generous donations made to a Biafra Hunger Appeal with the decrease in funds being given to his pet project, "It may mean that a need which costs us nothing more than money...fares much better with us than a need which threatens not our money, but our traditional assumptions, or our prejudices."[19] Leon Modeste, whom Hines had appointed to head the GCSP, admitted that most of the people that he had hired to run the program respected Hines, but not PECUSA or most of its members. Even worse, Modeste further disturbed many churchmen when he proclaimed in his 1970 Annual Report on the GCSP, "For Christ's sake, let's crucify the church." He clarified his meaning by eschewing any symbolic reading of his words, "I have used the word crucifixion deliberately and not abstractly. The church, the temporal, institutional, body of Christ, must be willing to suffer and die in the name of Him who paid the price for us." Modeste then further offended many by quoting Hines' statement regarding the AFM scandal, "Violence by Alianza is the violence which rises out of intense frustration by virtue of the repression of the society in which we live...it could be interpreted ...as self-defense." Modeste perhaps reached the peak of his offensive remarks by directly associating the opponents of the GCSP with racism.[20] However, Modeste was not the innovator among official church spokesmen in charging the opponents of the GCSP with racism. Hines had criticized the Foundation for Christian Theology (FCT), a conservative and traditionalist group of Episcopalians based in Texas, for their accusation that the church had "sold out" to the black militants at South Bend. Hines called the FCT a "pro-segregation" faction within the church.[21] Although more will be said about the FCT in later chapters, it is enough at this point to note that there is no evidence that they were a racist or pro-segregation organization. Though the 1970 General Convention in Houston had its share of controversial moments, including another episode in which black radicals took control of the podium, it was perhaps the statement by Hines, in which he supported Modeste's call for the church to be willing to die in order to alleviate the suffering of the oppressed, that left a permanent impression among traditionalist churchmen as to how far their church had strayed in so short a time.[22]

Besides the perceived excessive involvement of the church in politics, another issue that became increasingly bothersome to many traditionalist churchmen was that the church was suffering a crisis of authority. The bishops of the church, and the national and diocesan leadership, were increasingly challenging the ability of the average layman to trust their judgment and, by extension, their authority. In an insightful article written in 1970, Fr. L. William Countryman argued that a divide had developed between the leadership and the laity of the church, and that this divide had arisen as a result of a lack of trust between the two groups. The elites of the church increasingly viewed the average layman as a provincial and ignorant hindrance to the "higher calling" of social justice Christianity. The laity increasingly viewed the church's leaders as being out of touch with the common, everyday, often mundane realities of parish life. The bishops, priests, and seminary professors were calling for more social activism, while the laity begged for more assistance in the development of the spiritual life and the attainment of personal salvation.

Fr. Countryman tellingly observed, "Why are the laypeople often unwilling to accept the existing leadership 'at their word?' The problem, certainly, is one of *trust*... But trust must be based on much more than an official title. Even the common name of Christian, alas! In this age in which it can mean so many different things, is not always ground for trust between two people much less so the title of 'bishop' in a church where bishops and people often simply do not speak the same language anymore."[23]

Rev. Countryman was also not alone in pointing out the connections between the erratic and questionable political activism of the church and the condition of theological thinking within the church. He insightfully noted that: "The harbinger of the current crisis was probably the late Bishop James Pike, who brought it [the church] inescapably to everyone's attention that there already existed an immense gap between what the church publicly professed about its doctrine and what many of its clergy actually believe. As laymen and parish clergy struggled with the question of how to deal with Bishop Pike's erratic doctrinal 'development,'" it was the authority of the episcopate as a whole that suffered; for having assured ourselves repeatedly that Jim Pike did not speak for the Episcopal Church, we inevitably began to wonder whether any other bishop *did*. It is no accident, then, that the last couple of years have seen the rise of various *ad-hoc* groups (one is tempted to use the word 'factions') within the church which are attempting to fill the vacuum left by the decline of Episcopal authority with their own leadership." Countryman noted that these "factions" included not only the radicals such the Union of Black Clergy, but also traditionalists groups such as the Foundation for Christian Theology.[24] Thus, while the divisions were growing among Episcopalians along political and social policy lines, a corresponding divide had already developed in the areas of theology, doctrine, and morality.

Beginning in the 1950s, but gathering momentum

in the 1960s, a new spirit of theological investigation began to flourish within PECUSA. A new breed of theologians began to dominate the curriculum of the church's seminaries and, by extension, the theological worldview of scores of priests and bishops who would be inculcated with the new ideas. In 1951 a volume in the Church's Teaching Series appeared titled *The Faith of the Church*. The purpose of the Teaching Series was to present the faith and doctrine of the church in a manner in which it could be understood by the average layman. *The Faith of the Church* was a basically standard presentation of Episcopal theological and doctrinal thought, but its authors were W. Norman Pittenger and James A. Pike, two men who would play a key role in altering the theological thought of many Episcopalians.

Pittenger taught at Union Theological Seminary from the 1930s until the 1960s, and has been described as one of the most influential Episcopal theologians of the last half of the 20th century. Although Pittenger wore the cloak of orthodoxy for his work in the Teaching Series, his serious theological work can best be described as approximating a system that is known as Process Theology.[25] Process theology emphasizes that God is so intimately united to the world that the very being of God is in the process of changing along with the world. The God of process theology evolves along with all matter in the universe. Needless to say, as opposed to the orthodox understanding of God, this kind of God-in-process does not really create the universe, nor does He (read "It" in Process Theology) know the final result of history. Process Theology has been interpreted by its critics as being a representation of pantheism, but tailored for a Christian audience. While Pittenger and other thinkers were wearing their masks of orthodoxy in official works such as those found in the Church's Teaching Series, they were having a more revolutionary impact on the seminarians that were being fed the "higher knowledge" of the new ideas. Pittenger's coauthor on *The Faith of the Church*, Fr. James Pike, would not be as content to remain a revolutionary while working behind the scenes.[26] Fr. Pike would become perhaps the most visible and controversial symbol of what many churchmen considered to be the theological and doctrinal decline of PECUSA.

James Albert Pike was ordained a priest in PECUSA in 1946, became chaplain of Vassar University from 1947 to 1949, received a B.D. from Union Theological Seminary (under the tutelage of Pittenger) in 1951, (the same year in which *The Faith of the Church* appeared), and then became a priest in Poughkeepsie, New York. During the early 1950s, Fr. Pike became chaplain and head of the religion department at Columbia University, and then, from 1952 to 1958, became the dean of the Cathedral of St. John the Divine in New York City. During this time Fr. Pike gained great visibility as the host of an NCC sponsored religious program, *Frontiers of Faith*, which aired on the NBC network for six years.[27] However, Pike also began to express his opinions regarding controversial political matters, such as criticizing Senator Joseph McCarthy's anti-Communist campaigns as "the new tyranny." In 1958 Pike was rewarded for his "cutting-edge" service by being selected as the new bishop of California.

Bishop Pike quickly established himself as one of the leading voices within PECUSA to call for increased church involvement in the eradication of racial and social injustices. However, it was Bishop Pike's personal behavior and publicity-seeking advocacy of reformulating church doctrine that drew the wrath of traditionalist churchmen. Pike began to routinely make public comments that questioned many of the basic tenets of orthodox Christian doctrine, such as the Virgin Birth of Christ, the Trinity, and the Real Presence of Christ in the Eucharist. For instance, in

1964 he referred to the doctrine of the Trinity as "not necessary," "confusing," and "not among the original teachings of the early church." The only response to this heretical statement by the House of Bishops was to issue a warning to all clergy to be careful of how they spoke about doctrinal issues in public.[28] In 1965 Pike raised his controversial profile to another level by ordaining a woman to be a deacon before PECUSA had made it an ecclesiastically legal practice, and by stating in a sermon that "The problem is not the real presence, but the real absence...God is here right now apart from doing anything at that table."[29] Pike also published an intentionally provocative book, *Time For Christian Candor*, which dismissed the Trinity as "excess luggage," along with a host of other heretical statements.[30]

During this time, Pike was also publicly calling for liberalized laws regarding homosexuality and abortion, which, his critics noted, shouldn't have been surprising since Pike's own personal life reflected the acceptance of the moral transgressions he so fervently sought to have legitimized. William Stringfellow and Anthony Towne's biography of Pike document his numerous encounters with the police for public drunkenness, his youthful experimentations with homosexuality, and his three marriages that were peppered with frequent extra-marital affairs.[31] Many of these moral transgressions were well known by churchmen years before they began to be circulated more widely by Pike's detractors. Thomas C. Reeves recalled that Pike's affairs and scandalous personal behavior were well known among those who knew him best.[32] The combination of Pike's increasingly erratic personal behavior, his campaigning for controversial political causes, and his heretical doctrinal positions, eventually led to a grassroots effort among traditionalists to check his influence and standing in the national church.

In 1965 fourteen clergymen from the Diocese of

Arizona petitioned the House of Bishops to formally question Bishop Pike regarding his faithfulness to orthodox doctrine and the office of a bishop. The House of Bishops refused to issue any statement that would question Pike's faithfulness. In early 1966, twelve bishops associated with the American Church Union, a traditionalist High-church organization within PECUSA that will be discussed furthering in chapter 4, appealed to Pike to resign his office. Under the increasing pressure and scrutiny of his critics, Pike eventually agreed to resign as the acting bishop of California, though he would continue to have a voice and seat in the House of Bishops.[33] Pike decided to make one last, grand presentation of his "prophetic" theological understanding by proclaiming in his final sermon at Grace Cathedral in San Francisco, California, that the "all-powerful, all-good, all-knowing God" had never existed.[34] Twenty-eight bishops then wagered that Pike's departure could create a more favorable environment among the more hesitant bishops to make a definitive statement regarding the position of PECUSA on the necessity for bishops to possess and teach an orthodox faith. Lead by Bishop Henry I. Louttit of Florida, the concerned bishops formed the Committee of Bishops to Defend the Faith, and prepared to bring formal charges against Pike before the House of Bishops. The concerned bishops charged Pike with denying an assortment of traditional doctrines: that Christ is God, that Christ was born of a virgin, that Christ was one with the Father and the Holy Spirit, that men could only be saved by Christ, that Christ's atonement is essential to salvation, that Christ's resurrection and ascension were historical realities, and that the Bible is the word of God and authoritative in the realms of doctrine and morals.[35]

Frustrating many traditionalists, the House of Bishops, fearing the negative reaction of many influential members of the ecclesiastical elite, never allowed any formal charges to be brought against Pike, opting instead for a statement of censure against him. The censure, adopted by a vote of 103 to [36], stated that Pike's writings were "too often marred by caricatures of treasured symbols and at the worst, by cheap vulgarizations of great expressions of the faith."36 This action disappointed Pike, not because he was stung by the criticism, but because he had reportedly been hoping for a full-fledged ecclesiastical trial, with the publicity and notoriety that would go along with it. Once the decision of the House of Bishops had been announced, Pike demanded a formal investigation of the charges against him, which would have necessitated a trial, but the bishops remained uninterested in conducting anything that could be construed by the larger church and society as a heresy hunt.[37]

Bishop Pike resigned from PECUSA altogether in 1967, and then began a bizarre, and frankly, sad series of esoteric adventures in the hope of contacting his recently deceased son (who had committed suicide). Pike finished his life advocating psychic research into contacting the dead, searching for words of comfort from countless mediums, and eventually took his third wife on a 1969 honeymoon to the Holy Land to investigate the "unknown life of Jesus." After becoming lost in the desert, James Albert Pike was found dead by a search party. It was noted at his funeral, a Solemn Requiem High Mass, that never before could anyone remember a bishop being mourned by three surviving wives.[38]

The 1960s were, in the estimation of many traditionalists, a time of questionable political activism and lax doctrinal discipline among the leadership of PECUSA. Besides the problems noted above, the PECUSA leadership also became involved in protesting the Vietnam War, in weakening the church's language condemning abortion and homosexuality, in liberalizing canon law regarding the remarriage of divorced persons, and in a host of other "little rebellions" that dominated the landscape of the turbulent period. Most traditionalists were able to weather the ecclesiastical storms of the time by telling themselves that all would be fixed and healed in the end, and that eventually everyone would come back to their senses and return to the faith once delivered to the saints. If nothing else, they contented themselves with the assumption that the chaos infecting their beloved church was a national and regional problem, a problem of the coasts and the larger cities, and that their local parish and priest would remain bastions of traditional faith and worship. However, a small group of churchmen were unable to stomach the changes and events that had occurred "unpunished" during this period. They could not tolerate the "intolerable," and they formed the first modern schismatic, or Continuing, Episcopalian churches.

Chapter 2

THE ANGLICAN ORTHODOX CHURCH

There were many churchmen, particularly in the southern portion of the United States, who were not as able to patiently abide the forays of PECUSA into controversial political activism. For many of these churchmen the most troubling political sin of PECUSA was its support of, and involvement in, the Civil Rights Movement. Most traditionalists were flexible and tolerant enough to wait until the controversies surrounding the GCSP grants materialized before they began to even contemplate leaving the national church over political disagreements. However, because of the especially volatile racial atmosphere in the South, the potential for developing a schismatic movement was a more realistic possibility in the region. Some southern churchmen opposed the Civil Rights Movement due to the lingering allure of racist ideology and traditions, while others opposed it due to their belief that the federal government was expanding its power into realms of control that went beyond those reserved to it in the US Constitution. However, both types of segregationists shared a rhetoric that characterized the Civil Rights Movement as an un-American and radical social force. One churchman who seemed to encompass both types of segregationist thinking was the Rev. James Parker Dees of North Carolina.

Fr. Dees received his B.D. from Virginia Theological Seminary in 1949. He was ordained a priest in 1950, and from 1955 until he left PECUSA in November of 1963,

Dees was rector of Trinity Church in Statesville, North Carolina.39 During the period that Dees was a rector in PECUSA he had become one of the leading organizers of, and spokesmen for, the segregationist White Citizen's Councils that had proliferated across the South in an attempt to organize respectable whites against the movement for black civil rights. The Citizen's Councils were generally careful to distinguish their activities from those of the more terror-inclined Ku Klux Klan, and often included influential business and government leaders as board members. Nonetheless, the racist views held by most of the Citizen's Council activists were just as deep-seated and brazen as those held by the typical working-class Klansman. In 1958, Fr. Dees helped found, and became president of, one such segregationist organization, the North Carolina Defenders of State's Rights (NCDSR), and remained so until the early 1960s.[40]

During this same period Fr. Dees formed a working relationship with the Christian Nationalist Crusade, an organization headed by the Rev. Gerald L.K. Smith, a man often described as America's most notorious anti-Semite and racist. Smith had been a leading anti-Semite since forming the Christian Nationalist Crusade in 1942, and his monthly magazine, *The Cross and the Flag*, regularly warned its readers about an alleged Jewish conspiracy to control the world. Smith was also the largest national distributor of the *Protocols of the Learned Elders of Zion*, a fictitious 19th-century work that purported to be the minutes of a secret meeting of Jews to plot the overthrow of the governments of the world.[41] Fr. Dees used Smith's national distribution network to sell segregationist tracts and promote opposition to the Civil Rights Movement. The question as to whether Dees was himself an anti-Semite is not definitively clear. One could argue that Dees was simply aligning himself with any organization that shared a similar goal, in this case opposition to black civil rights, for reasons of necessity and strategy. However, it is reasonable to assume that Dees must have known of Gerald L.K. Smith's past and activities, for Dees purportedly lionized Smith as "the greatest patriot in this country today."[42] The question of Fr. Dees' possible anti-Semitism is further clouded by his association with the Liberty Lobby, which had been formed in 1957 by Willis Carto.

The Liberty Lobby was the leading anti-Semitic organization during the 1960s and 70s, disseminating numerous books and literature to argue that the Jewish race was the plague of the world, both culturally and politically. Fr. Dees became a member of the Liberty Lobby's national Board of Directors in 1964, at a time when the anti-Semitic character of the organization was obvious to any impartial observer.[43] It is not clear whether or not Dees ever disassociated himself from the Liberty Lobby, but his having any affiliation with Carto[44] casts a pall of reasonable suspicion over any objections to the possibility that Dees was anti-Semitic. Furthermore, in one of his segregationist writings castigating the Supreme Court at that time, Dees referred to the Jewish ancestry of Justice Felix Franfurter, even though Dees does not mention the ethnic backgrounds of the other Justices.[45] Again, a supporter could argue that Dees was simply associating himself with any organization that promulgated political views that were similar to his own. Since anti-Communism and extreme patriotism were both key components of Dees' worldview, and both the Christian Nationalist Crusade and Liberty Lobby emphasized these issues as much as they did the Jewish conspiracy, perhaps Dees was choosing to look the other way in regard to the more negative aspects of these organizations. Either way, his associations with groups that occupied the far right-wing fringe of political ideology made him a controversial figure within many circles of Episcopalians.

Although Fr. Dees's associations with figures such as Gerald L.K. Smith and Willis Carto were an embarrassment to many in PECUSA, and then later, to many in the Continuing Anglican Movement, his real political passion was reserved for the segregationist cause, and it was his confrontations with his own church over racial integration that eventually lead him to re-evaluate the moral and theological character of PECUSA as well.

Dees' presidency of the NCDSR eventually conflicted with his presidency in another organization, the Statesville Area Ministerial Association, an interdenominational group of local clergymen. Many of his fellow clergymen were developing more sympathetic attitudes toward the Civil Rights Movement, and they were troubled by Dees' views on race, especially since they knew that the national church to which he belonged had recently made overtures of support for black civil rights. Dees was censured by the Association early in 1959, which stated that the views of Dees and the NCDSR did not reflect the views of the Association as to "human relationships and the oneness in Christ that should characterize us as ministers of the Gospel."[46] After the censure was passed by a vote of sixteen to two, it was reported by *The Living Church* that Dees had resigned his position in the group. The chairman of publicity for the Diocese of North Carolina reported that the local diocese had done nothing to censure Dees due to the fear that he would become a kind of ecclesiastical martyr, and that a deeper divide could develop between the clergy and some of the laity. However, the diocesan spokesmen also stated that there was a growing feeling that the diocese could soon be forced to take a similar action as that taken by the Ministerial Association.[47]

Dees responded to the news story in *The Living Church* by refuting the assertion that he had resigned his position. According to Dees, he had submitted his resignation, but it had been turned down by the Ministerial Association, and he was thus still its president. He then refuted the magazine's description of him as a white supremacist. He claimed to be a white separatist that believed that the separation of the races would result in benefits for both races, and that he did not support the concept of the white race ruling over the black race. He supported the separation of the races "in the churches and the schools" in order to maintain social order. Coyly, *The Living Church* apologized to Dees for incorrectly reporting that he was no longer the president of the Ministerial Association, but they remained silent regarding any retraction of their description of him as a white supremacist. The implication of his identity as a white supremacist was assumed in the editorial silence, and Dees' reputation as a racist remained securely fixed in the eyes of many within PECUSA.[48]

The question as to whether Dees held racist views is less clouded than the uncertainty regarding his possible anti-Semitism. Dees was an avowed racist. However, his racism was not of the stereotypical variety that one usually associates with a bigot. Dees did not, at least publicly, appear to have hated blacks or other non-white races. He frequently spoke of the need for whites to help blacks, and consistently argued that violent actions against blacks were both un-Christian and harmful to the overall chances of the segregationist movement to succeed. The key social problem, as far as Dees was concerned, was the harmful effects that the nation would suffer under conditions of widespread racial "mixing." Even though Dees shared with the extreme racists the rhetoric that such race mixing would result in a mongrelized society, a careful survey of his writings reveals that he frequently compounded the concepts of race and culture. For Dees, the races were intimately tied to their cultures, and these race-cultures were created by God, and thus inviolable.

In an essay contributed to a collection of writings by church leaders from assorted denominations in support of segregation, Dees stated, "They [the leaders of the desegregation movement] are aiming not simply at de-segregation but rather at the integration and amalgamation of the races...Already we see in many places young people of the white and Negro races going together, dating, a condition that is abhorrent to me, and I believe abhorrent to God, Who, I believe, created the Caucasian race white and the Negro race black, and intended that each should maintain its racial integrity."[49] Dees shared the racial philosophy that was prevalent among some segregationists at the time, in which the races of humanity were seen as being intimately tied to the cultural identity of different groups of people. Each of the world's cultures was seen as being dependent upon and bound up with the racial integrity that was kept within each culture. In many ways such a belief system still exists for many people, but in a different guise, when certain ethnic groups worry that intermarriage with another group threatens to destroy their cultural identity. This is not meant to excuse the beliefs of Dees, but only to offer some insight into the context in which his ideas about race were formed. Although he always expressed his goodwill and best wishes for the black race, and claimed that he had no desire for the oppression of blacks, he still possessed a belief in a hierarchy of racial cultures, with white culture judged to be superior to that of blacks.

The complex, and really contradictory nature of his arguments and thought processes, can be seen in the following quote: "The white race, in turn, would become a hybrid race, and a hybrid race...is an inferior race. I believe that cold, enlightened logic can lead us only to this conclusion...a hybrid race in which the Negro is exterminated and the white race appreciably degenerated. In making this statement I do not mean to argue the superiority of either race;…Races, I believe, were created by God to witness to Him as races, as well as individuals were created to witness as individuals. Every race, I believe, should have something to contribute to the Eternal Plan. The Negro race has developed tremendously and is continuing to develop. I believe that it can continue to develop and in time should make a solid contribution to God's world. What is at stake here is the integrity of the Negro race."[50] Dees states that he is not arguing that one race is superior to the other, but then he quizzically states that the black race still needs to continue to develop in order to eventually make a racial (could be read as cultural) contribution to God's divine plan for humanity. Dees thus betrays a curious theological position on race in which each race-culture is created specially by God, as a race, in order to fulfill a specifically racial role in history. In such a view, the black race is superficially given a divine blessing, but it is assumed that much growth in cultural holiness or perfection must occur. Thus Dees' white supremacist views did not seek to justify or encourage the mistreatment of blacks, but was rather based on a belief that a superior white race-culture should be the model to which the black race should look for guidance and help. If Dees is a relic of an American past in which racist views were common, his views should probably be placed more in the camp of certain black racial theorists who were his contemporaries, such as Marcus Garvey or the early Malcolm X, rather than the simplistic hate mongering of a Klansman.

Although Dees acquired a rather notorious reputation among many within PECUSA and then later, the Continuing Anglican Movement, for his extremist racial views and associations with scandalous far-right organizations, his greatest significance to the Continuum can be found in his early move to break with the national church. Even as he was becoming known as the troublemaking clergyman who lent his support to racist churchmen in the South, he was formulating and solidifying a severe critique of the doctrinal, moral, and theological conditions within PECUSA. Whether or not he developed his criticisms of the national church in order to justify his extremist positions on race and politics, or in order to lay a theoretical framework for the formation of the new ecclesiastical body that he would found, Dees hit upon issues that would both attract the earliest dissident Episcopalians and anticipate the rhetoric of the those in the 1970s who left in much larger numbers. No doubt, there were many close to Dees who were aware of the growing divide between himself and the national church, but churchman around the nation had little idea of the degree to which he had strayed until after his resignation from PECUSA in November of 1963.

Shortly after resigning his position, Dees sent a letter explaining his reasons for leaving the national church to several sources, including *The Living Church*. He made a sharp distinction between his political and theological reasons for departing: "Efforts are being made to tie my resignation to my stand on the racial issue. It is true that I did not go along with the way the Church was handling the race issue, but the basic causes for my dissatisfaction with the Episcopal Church were theological, as my statement indicates."[51] He then expressed what would become one of the most familiar refrains within the later Continuing Anglican Movement, namely, that the national church had left him, rather than that he had left PECUSA. He vented his frustrations at a wide range of alleged deficiencies in the church: "I have had all I can stand of its social, economic, and political program of socialism; of its pseudo-brotherhood; of its appeasement of the Communists; of its so-called civil rights; and of its rejection of much that I consider to be fundamental to the biblical faith."[52] However, although many concerned churchman agreed with Dees' strident opposition to the political and social directions in which the church was heading, it was his consistent focusing on theological issues that seemed to strike the deepest chord with those who would eventually join him in leaving the national church, and those who couldn't quite go the whole way of following Dees, but who nonetheless admired from afar his stance against the national church.

Fr. Dees' basic theological complaint against PECUSA was that it had strayed from its Protestant heritage and moorings. He criticized his church for tolerating clergymen and others who denied the "factuality of the Virgin Birth," and other basic doctrines such as the Trinity. He critiqued those who denied that salvation was attained only through Christ, those who invoked the blessings of Mary, and those who reserved the Blessed Sacrament due to the belief that the elements really become the body and blood of Christ. He characterized such sacerdotal teachings as being "idolatrous" and "of the anti-Christ."[53] He placed the basic blame for the decline of the national church on the House of Bishops for failing to maintain discipline, and he specifically singled out the case of Bishop Pike as an example of the bishops failing to mete out the proper discipline that such a case required.[54] Although many concerned churchmen could agree with Dees' rebuke of the bishops, they could not support his anti-sacerdotalism, for many of them considered themselves to be High-churchmen. Thus, Dees cut himself off from a large pool of potential supporters from the very beginning of his protest. Nonetheless, there were many Episcopalians, especially in the traditionally Low-church South, who agreed with him wholeheartedly when he insisted that the Bible should be the focal point of both Christian morality and doctrine, that the 39 Articles of Religion were the standard statement of this Biblical Episcopalianism, and that the 1928 Book of Common Prayer was the superior liturgical expression of this faith.

When Dees sent his statement outlining his complaints against PECUSA across the nation, he also referred fleetingly to the fact that he was going to establish a nationally-based ecclesiastical body that would offer a home to all Episcopalians who shared his conclusion that the national church had departed from its traditional faith, and that it had left them with no spiritual home. That there were other deeply disaffected churchmen across the country was obvious, and it was thought early on by many that Dees' movement could become a major thorn in the side of the PECUSA establishment. For example, in California, approximately 100 churchmen had separated themselves from St. Mark's Church in Palo Alto in February of 1962, and had formed what they called the Church of the Redeemer of the Anglican Orthodox Church. Although the reasons for the withdrawal were complex, including a dispute over the resignation of St. Mark's priest, Fr. Edwin West, the members of the Church of the Redeemer stressed that they could not in good conscience be in communion with their bishop, James Pike.[55] More than a year later, as Dees was announcing the formation of his new church body (the Anglican Orthodox Church), he had to distinguish his movement from the situation in Palo Alto, since both groups were calling themselves "Anglican Orthodox."[56] In these earliest days of the Continuing Anglican Movement (1962-1964) there was some basic confusion among mainstream Episcopalians, such as the editors of *The Living Church,* as to just how large the groundswell of discontent was, and it is not surprising that there were some who suspected that a potentially large movement was brewing somewhere under the surface. However, the fears were mostly unfounded, and Dees' movement never achieved a numerically significant foundation.

Dees began to take his message to any place where

he could gain a sympathetic audience from concerned churchmen. The first successful missionary outreach occurred in Nashville, Tennessee. A group of traditionalist churchmen had withdrawn from their parishes in 1962 to form what they called All Saints' Anglican Church, lead by Senior Warden Dr. Burnice Hoyle Webster. Dees visited the Nashville group on January 23, 1964, and outlined his plans for the newly formed Anglican Orthodox Church. He stated that his first priority was to establish a strong headquarters for the church in his hometown of Statesville, and that he would then proceed to go wherever else he was needed to form similar parishes. At this early stage, Dees ranged between ambivalence and hostility regarding the question of whether he would seek to retain the episcopate in the Anglican Orthodox Church. During a question and answer period with the parishioners of the fledgling Nashville group, Dees revealed that the laypeople at Statesville were opposed to the maintenance of apostolic succession, and that he didn't see any particular need for retaining bishops, stating, "Confirmation is not necessary to salvation."[57]

The All Saints group decided to become the second parish in the Anglican Orthodox Church, although their affiliation with Dees would be brief. In 1965, partly due to reservations about Dees's strident insistence on Low-church worship standards, All Saints became an independent parish once again. Eventually Dr. Webster, who had disagreements with Dees regarding churchmanship, led All Saints to become the flagship parish of the Southern Episcopal Church, which would eventually grow to encompass about a dozen parishes, most of them located in the Southeastern United States.[58] Webster was consecrated by Bishops Julius Massey, an Old Catholic, and Orlando J. Woodward. Interestingly, the few sources that discuss the Southern Episcopal Church as a religious body do not mention its previous affiliation with Dees and the AOC. Whether or not this is because these investigators relied on the SEC for information about itself, and the SEC was in turn ashamed in some way of the past affiliation, is a question that has to remain in the realm of speculation.[59]

It appears that after his missionary meetings with groups of more liturgically orientated churchmen such as those in Nashville, Dees decided to be consecrated into the episcopacy. He denied that he had changed his mind regarding the necessity maintaining the episcopate in his new church, claiming that other churchmen, who otherwise agreed with his overall position, thought that the episcopate was either necessary or desirable. Dees' action could probably best be attributed to a pragmatic realization that he was going to have to bend a little in order to acquire new parishes. Dees was consecrated on March 14, 1964, in Emmaus, Pennsylvania. His consecrators were Bishops' Wasyl Sawyna, Primate of the Ukrainian Orthodox Autocephalic Church, and Orlando Jaques Woodward of the United Episcopal Church – Anglican/Celtic.[60]

In another instance in which Bishop Dees' career would prefigure later developments within Continuing Anglicanism, the validity of his orders were almost immediately called into question. The best source of traditionalist thought within the PECUSA mainstream at the time, *The Living Church*, included statements in its coverage of Dees' consecration questioning the legitimacy of the episcopal orders held by his consecrators. Besides reminding its readers that PECUSA had no official relations with, nor did it recognize, either of the churches that Bishops Sawyna and Woodward were affiliated with, *The Living Church* also reported that PECUSA officials could not locate a record of Sawyna on any registry of Orthodox bishops. However, the magazine also reminded its readers that this fact alone did not necessarily mean that Sawyna's group did not exist or possess valid orders.⁶¹ As would be the case with so many consecrations of Continuing Anglican bishops, the impression left with many in the PECUSA mainstream was that Bishop Dees' orders were questionable at best. Dees responded to the situation, in quintessential Low-Church fashion, by assuring both his followers and his detractors that the only thing that mattered was that his conscience was clear in regard to the validity of his orders. He then dismissed his PECUSA detractors with a subtle dig: "I am inclined to suspect that even the orders of the Protestant Episcopal Church are not universally accepted."⁶²

Dees' association with Bishop Sawyna appears to have been largely informal and formed only on a temporary basis. His relationship with Bishop Woodward appears to have been more collaborative. Woodward had been the pastor of a Presbyterian church in Fort Orlethorpe, Georgia, but his independent nature eventually lead him to bring his congregation out of the national Presbyterian church. Sometime in the 1950s he led his independent congregation to accept the 1928 Episcopal Prayer Book as their liturgical norm, and the Thirty-Nine Articles of Religion as their doctrinal standard. Woodward was then consecrated by Archbishop William Francis Brothers of the Old Catholic Church in America, thus becoming an independent bishop of an independent congregation. Bishop Brothers had been one of the major transmitters in America of the Arnold Matthew Harris line of Old Catholic apostolic succession, a line traditionally dismissed by most Episcopalians as being either irregular or invalid. Woodward was later approached by a body called the United Episcopal Church Anglican/Celtic (UECAC), and persuaded to join. This tiny group had been formed in 1945 to restore PECUSA to its Anglican and Celtic heritage. Woodward eventually became the Presiding Bishop, serving in this capacity from 1961 until 1965. After having to reduce his activities due to a nearly fatal illness, Woodward recovered (in the 1980s) and again began leading the UECAC.[63] However, it appears that for a short period Woodward worked closely with Bishop Dees, often visiting some of the parishes in the Anglican Orthodox Church. According to one source within the Southern Episcopal Church, during the earliest period of the All Saints parish in Nashville, either Woodward or Dees would visit the parish on a fairly regular basis. However, by 1965 Woodward had assisted in consecrating B.H. Webster to the episcopate, thus making Webster the first Presiding Bishop of the Southern Episcopal Church, and perhaps estranging Woodward from Dees in the process.[64]

Bishop Dees continued to add new parishes to his fledgling Anglican Orthodox Church throughout the remainder of the 1960s. However, at times, the numerical strength of Dees' group was often misunderstood. For example, J. Gordon Melton, the noted scholar of American religious groups, mistakenly reported Dees' claim that there were AOC parishes in most of the fifty states.[65] In fact, there doesn't appear to have ever been more than perhaps a dozen parishes in the United States from the early 1970s onward. Each issue of the *Anglican Orthodox Church News* contained a listing of which church members and parish priests should be prayed for on certain dates. If one safely assumes that every parish would eventually be represented during these prayer cycles, then the existence of AOC parishes in most states would be obvious. However, the same parishes keep reappearing every few months, which could only lead one to assume that these were the only AOC parishes. A more accurate description of the Anglican Orthodox Church is that it contained members in most of the fifty states. Dees had developed an effective system whereby disgruntled Episcopalians across the nation could become members of his St. Peter's parish in Statesville by sending him their tithes. These AOC members were often located in isolated parts of the country where there was no ability for a self-existing parish to develop, and they were encouraged to worship privately in their homes with the 1928 Prayer Book readings, resting in the assurance that they were also worshipping spiritually with the corporate body of faithful Anglicans.

Much more important for Dees was the formation of the Anglican Orthodox Communion in 1969, a worldwide association of like-minded traditionalist Anglicans. Dees had consecrated Fr. Vattappara John Stephen to be bishop of India in May of 1965, and would over the next few years consecrate bishops for Pakistan, Madagascar, Kenya, the Philippines, Nigeria, Liberia, Columbia, and the Fiji Islands. Although it is difficult to obtain reliable numbers, it is clear that the vast bulk of the membership of the Anglican Orthodox Church resides in these foreign bodies. Perhaps one of the most beneficial aspects of the Anglican Orthodox Communion is that it gave Dees the opportunity to demonstrate that he was not a stereotypical racist, and that he had no problem being associated with dark-skinned peoples in carrying out the mission of his new church. Many issues of the *Anglican Orthodox Church News* show Dees visiting these nations, hugging their bishops, confirming their parishioners, and holding their children. These issues also contain frequent reports on the deplorable economic conditions of these nations, and appeals for funds to help alleviate the suffering.

In 1969 Dees further solidified the self-identity of the Anglican Orthodox Church by officially declaring PECUSA to be apostate and no longer a Christian body. Another important development for the AOC was the 1971 foundation of Cranmer Seminary in Statesville.66 Unfortunately for Dees, even as he was establishing a rather stable church with a worldwide missionary outreach and an educational institution to train its own clergy, the AOC began to suffer the fate that future Continuing Anglican groups would come to understand all too well. As was mentioned earlier, the All Saints parish in Nashville had departed from the AOC early on, mostly due to disagreements with Dees over churchmanship. Other parishes would depart as the 1960s reached their end, and continued to depart in the early 1970s. The reasons for this growing discontentment with Dees were complex, but they typically revolved around traditionalist ex-Episcopalians chafing at Dees' insistence on rather rigid Low-Church doctrinal and liturgical standards, as well as frustration with his rather autocratic leadership style. For example, in a 1969 memorandum to his clergy, Dees instructed them not to bring any alcoholic beverages to the national convention (as they had apparently done at the previous convention), nor to consume any that the laity may bring. Dees was also accused of neglecting to send priests to care for mission parishes, and of requiring all tithes collected nationally to be sent directly to the Statesville headquarters. It was often these kinds of personal disagreements with Dees that loomed just as large as any serious doctrinal disagreements. Also, Dees' political views and history as a segregationist continued to bother many who otherwise supported his theological position in defying PECUSA.

In 1968, four representatives of AOC parishes were among the six who met in Mobile, Alabama to form the American Episcopal Church (AEC), and in 1972 an AOC parish in Fountain Valley, lead by Fr. Walter Hollis Adams, formed a new body called the Anglican Episcopal Church of North America (AECNA). Later in the same year, another AOC parish, lead by Fr. Frank Benning in Atlanta, Georgia, joined the Anglican Episcopal Church (AECNA). More will be said about these groups in the next chapter. Further minor schisms and jurisdictional controversies would occur throughout the years.

Bishop Dees continued to exert his power and influence within the small AOC throughout the 1970s and 1980s, achieving his greatest success in forming alliances with foreign groups who had similarly organized themselves in separation from their parent Anglican bodies. He attended the St. Louis Congress in 1977 (covered extensively in chapter 5), but was never impressed with the Continuing Anglican Movement that followed and supplanted his own. He remained mostly aloof from the rest of the traditionalist and Continuing Anglican developments. He criticized other groups such as the Society for the Preservation of the Book of Common Prayer, the Fellowship of Concerned Churchmen, and the Foundation for Christian Theology (all discussed in chapter 4), as well as the Anglican Catholic Church, which was the institutional result of the St. Louis Congress, claiming that the AOC was the only authentic representative of genuine Reformation Anglicanism.[67]

Bishop Dees died on Christmas Day, 1990. His successor, George Schneller, had long been active within the church, having graduated from Cranmer Seminary in 1973, and served as rector of Holy Cross Church in St. Louis, Missouri until his consecration as a bishop in 1991 by Bishop Laione C. Vuki of Polynesia. However, Schneller's term as Presiding Bishop was short lived due to ill health, and the AOC was forced to adopt the provisional leadership of a Standing Committee that was reportedly unable to guide the church as effectively as had Dees. In 1995, Fr. Robert J. Godfrey was consecrated as the new bishop of the United States, as well as being chosen as the new Presiding Bishop of both the AOC and Anglican Orthodox Communion. Bishop Godfrey was said to have reinvigorated the church by allowing for a broader expression of churchmanship and actively campaigning to increase the membership rolls of Cranmer Seminary. However, in 1998, Dees' daughter and son-in-law, along with his longtime personal secretary, reportedly lead a group out of the AOC, forming what came to be known as the Anglican Orthodox Church, International.

The group that remained under Bishop Godfrey appears to have changed its name to the Episcopal Orthodox Christian Archdiocese of America. In May of 1999, Fr. Scott McLaughlin was consecrated to become the Auxiliary Bishop of the Archdiocese by Bishops' Herbert Groce and Larry Lee Shaver of the Anglican Rite Synod of the Americas (covered in later chapters). This was done purposefully to complete an ecumenical alliance between the two small groups, and Articles of Intercommunion were signed between them in October of 1999, making Godfrey's group an official province of the Anglican Rite Synod in the Americas. McLaughlin succeeded Godfrey, whose health had deteriorated, as the head of the Episcopal Orthodox Christian Archdiocese and the Anglican Orthodox Communion in April of 2000.[68] The parish and complex in Statesville, which had served for years as the headquarters of Bp. Dees' AOC, and which many Continuers mockingly referred to as "the shrine," is now the primary church in a much smaller body. As of early 2001, there appears to be only one American bishop and a few clergy, but there are still several bishops and clergy located outside of the United States.

Even though Bishop Dees maintained that his church was different (read: doctrinally sounder) than the later Continuing Movement, the AOC shared many commonalities with the Continuers who followed in its wake. To begin with, the questioning of the validity of Continuing Anglican orders would become a standard tactic for both opponents of the Movement and factious elements within it. Many Continuing bishops would follow Dees' example by accepting consecrations from whatever source they could obtain them from, sometimes with dubious and divisive results. The later Continuing Movement would also suffer from a bewildering array of schisms and jurisdictional conflicts that were sometimes (though not as often as many Continuers insisted) instigated as much by personal disagreements between increasingly ambitious bishops as they were by serious doctrinal or legal disputes. Furthermore, many of the individuals and groups which splintered from Dees' AOC would eventually play important roles within the later Continuing Movement. There was a bewildering cross-pollination between bishops of the various groups, and many leaders of the later Continuing Movement began their clerical careers within the AOC. Thus, even though Dees denied the validity of the later movement, and many within the later movement insisted that they had no link to Dees, his influence was felt throughout the Continuum, both positively and negatively. Finally, his doctrinal emphasis', including the use of the 1928 Prayer Book, the role of the 39 Articles of Religion, the focus on the centrality of the Bible, and the espousal of traditional morality would be echoed by many other groups of disenchanted, Low-church Episcopalians who eventually made their home in the Continuing Movement.

Chapter 3

THE AMERICAN EPISCOPAL CHURCH AND OTHER EARLY CONTINUING GROUPS

As was mentioned in the previous chapter, representatives from four disgruntled parishes of the Anglican Orthodox Church were present in Mobile, Alabama, along with two parishes that had formed independently due to the growing difficulties within PECUSA, to form the American Episcopal Church (AEC) in May of 1968. It was decided at the two-day meeting in Mobile that an organization should be established in order to maintain traditional Anglicanism.[69] A set of canons was drafted, and three bishops were elected. There were reportedly three clergymen in attendance: James Hardin George, William E. Littlewood, and Carlton French. Little is known about Fr. French, and he seems to have disappeared shortly after the Mobile meeting. Although some sources list Fr. Littlewood as an Episcopal priest, he was actually a priest, and later a bishop, of a body known as the Free Protestant Episcopal Church.[70] He too seems to have departed the AEC shortly after the Mobile meeting. Fr.. George had been ordained an Episcopal priest in 1958, and served PECUSA parishes in South Carolina until the time of the Mobile meeting.[71] All three men were elected to become the first bishops of the AEC, but after some purported initial interest from William Moody, a PECUSA bishop from Kentucky, it became apparent that there would be no consecrations forthcoming from anyone with an official position in PECUSA. Perhaps it was because of this delay and frustration in obtaining consecrations to confirm their elections that both French and Littlewood left the AEC.

Another reason for their quick departure may have been due to the initial institutional structure devised for the AEC. Thinking that the problems within PECUSA were to be blamed on its bishops and clergy, the decision was made to develop the AEC canons according to a more congregational model. Primary ecclesiastical authority was given to a National Vestry, which was to be headed by a national Senior Warden and Junior Warden. During General Convention deliberations, the clerical house was to serve only an advisory and pastoral capacity, and the real power was to reside in the lay house, which was to initiate and enact all church legislation.[72] Most probably, the decision to retain the office of bishops was made primarily in order to maintain a connection with Episcopalian tradition and to hold the fragile early coalition of parishes together. The needed apostolic orders were found in the person of Bishop Joseph Chengalvaroyan Pillai (James Charles Ryan), then Metropolitan of the Indian Orthodox Church. Pillai had founded the Indian Orthodox Church in the 1940s, but was living in Ohio by the late 1960s. He had received Old Catholic orders in 1945 from Hugh George deWillmott Newman, one of the primary dispensers of what are generally known as Vagante Episcopal orders.[73]

Though his health was poor, Bishop Pillai agreed to become the first Primus of the AEC, and he in turn consecrated Fr. George to be his suffragan bishop at the end of 1968. Pillai died in February of 1970, and George became the new Primus of the AEC. Unfortunately for George, he soon encountered a difficult situation. Many of the AEC clergy appear to have resented the domination of the church by the National Vestry, or what has also been described as an "oligarchy" of major donors to the national church.[74] George advised the National Vestry that they should immediately elect a suffragan bishop, and they responded by quickly electing Fr. Anthony Forbes Morton Clavier, a former rector within the Anglican Orthodox Church. As was so often the case within the oftentimes strange world of Continuing Anglicanism, what happened next is not clear.

According to one account, during a meeting held around the same time as Clavier's election, a majority of the AEC parishes and clergy came to realize the great divide in outlook and missionary goals between themselves and the National Vestry. After a conflict developed, the National Vestry is said to have then attempted to block the next meeting of the AEC General Convention to be held in June, and the dissenting majority party is said to have responded by holding the General Convention anyway, adopting new canons and a more classically Anglican structure.[75] According to another account, George and Clavier determined that the canonical structure of the AEC, in placing so much power in the National Vestry, effectively hindered the development of a successful church body on the lines of the classic Anglican model. Accordingly, the two bishops reportedly spearheaded a campaign to effectively dissolve the existing AEC by convincing the clergy to resign, and then to reconstitute the church anew by creating a new constitution and canons in March of 1970.[76] If one believes the first account, interestingly written by Clavier's son, Mark F.M. Clavier, then the reformation of the AEC by George and Clavier was forced by the National Vestry, which was trying to stop the majority of the AEC from adopting a more traditional Anglican structure and path for itself. The second account, written by an otherwise unbiased scholar of American religious groups, stresses that George and Clavier organized the reformation of the AEC from the beginning. The second account is probably closer to the truth, since it gives the date (April of 1970) in which a special convention was called in order to precede the regularly scheduled General Convention to be held in June of 1970. The first account doesn't mention that the meeting was held in April, and leaves the impression that the reforming convention developed out of the (June) regularly scheduled General Convention of the AEC in defiance of the National Vestry, which supposedly had called it off. Most probably, the reforming convention was held in April, lead by George and Clavier, precisely in order to outmaneuver the National Vestry with a plan to have all of the AEC clergy resign so as to avoid being disciplined by the canonically empowered National Vestry. This April date for the reconstitution of the AEC is also found in other sources.[77]

The conflicting accounts as to what transpired between February of 1970, when George and Clavier assumed their positions of leadership, and the scheduled meeting of the AEC General Convention that was to be held in June, reflect one of the recurring motifs that plagued the Continuing Movement from the beginning: controversy surrounding the person of Anthony F.M. Clavier. Perhaps no single person within the Continuing Movement's history has evoked as much admiration or opposition as Clavier. During the course of several personal interviews conducted for this study, the mention of Clavier's name either brought forth fawning praise from those who admired his organizational and preaching skills, or scathing criticisms of his personal morality and integrity. Since much of the criticism of Clavier centers upon the alleged questionable nature of his formal theological education, and the validity of the episcopal orders that he claimed to possess prior to entering the Continuum, it would probably be beneficial at this stage to review how he came to the world of Continuing Anglicanism in the first place.

Many Continuers who were troubled by Clavier focused their accusations on his rather eccentric (some would say bizarre) history of receiving several ordinations, as well as his frequent changing of ecclesiastical jurisdictions and allegiances, in a startlingly short period of time during the 1960s. Clavier is said to have been first ordained to the priesthood in 1961 by Bishop Francis E. Glenn of the Catholic Episcopal Church of England. In April of 1963, Fr. Clavier was ordained a presbyter by Bishop Charles Dennis Boltwood, the Primus of the Free Protestant Episcopal Church of England. Then, six weeks later, Clavier was ordained by Bishop Charles Leslie Saul of the Protestant Evangelical Church of England. Clavier then returned to the Catholic Episcopal Church in 1964. He then proceeded to leave that group, and rejoined the Protestant Evangelical Church of England in August of 1965. Four months later he was received into the Old Roman Catholic Church by Bishop George Gerard Shelley. Clavier was then incardinated by Mar Georgius of the Catholicate of the West in July of 1966. In 1967, Clavier then obtained a release from Mar Georgius to go to the United States in order to serve as a rector in Bishop Dees' Anglican Orthodox Church. For reasons that are contested, Clavier was dismissed by Dees in July of 1968, and returned to England and the Catholic Episcopal Church. Reportedly, Dees was unhappy with Clavier's personal morality. The rumors that were spread regarding Clavier included the accusation that he was a hard drinker, unbearably arrogant, that he had coaxed some elderly churchmen into giving him large amounts of money, and that he had engaged in sexual relations with co-eds at Bob Jones University in North Carolina. Dees is also reported to have hired a private investigator to look into Clavier's background, and it was allegedly discovered that all of his claims to formal theological education, and many of his claims regarding the ecclesiastical titles and positions that he had held, were false.[78] Also for reasons that are not clear, Bishop George of the AEC then invited Clavier to return to the United States to become the AEC's new suffragan bishop.[79]

Beyond the fact that his history tended to exhibit a rather casual attitude on Clavier's part regarding the trafficking of holy orders, it was also noted by his critics that all of his ordinations had been obtained from bishops who stood in the Apostolic line of Bishop Hugh George de Willmott Newman, one of the main sources of vagante orders. Thus Clavier was burdened with a double problem from the outset; his recent history as a priest made him appear to be uncommitted and unreliable as a potential church leader, and his orders stemmed from bishops that were regarded as, at best, questionable by many traditionalist churchmen. The situation was not helped when Clavier's last overseer, Bishop Dees of the AOC, issued a series of "reports" which called into question Clavier's personal character and loyalty to ecclesiastical superiors. Particularly damaging was the accusation by Dees that Clavier, while a rector in the AOC, had been secretly corresponding with the Presiding Bishop of the Church of England of South Africa, Stephen Bradley, for advice on forming a breakaway group from the AOC. In his letters, Clavier had allegedly expressed his distaste for the historic episcopate and many of the Catholic elements of the 1928 Prayer Book, such as prayers for the dead and the second part of the Consecration Prayer in the liturgy.[80] Other critical accounts claim that Clavier had been the primary organizing force in the initial secession of the AOC parishes in 1968 that lead to the formation of the AEC.

Bishop George resigned from the AEC in August of 1970, just four months after consecrating Clavier as his suffragan bishop. There can be no certainty that the increasing rumors about Clavier's past had any impact on George's decision to withdraw from the AEC. One account of George's departure interprets his action as a protest of a decision by the AEC not to arrange for individual parishes to assume financial responsibility for the care of the church's clergy. George had reportedly called for this institutional change in order to compensate for the depleted financial situation that beset the AEC once its wealthy lay trustees had withdrawn their support after having been outmaneuvered for control of the church. Under the old system the clergy had been paid out of a centralized account that had been operated by the National Vestry, which in turn had been controlled by the wealthy lay trustees.[81] When the AEC reportedly balked at George's plan to compensate its clergy, he resigned and formed a new church body called the Anglican Church in America. Another account asserts that George, believing that he was gravely ill, had consecrated Clavier in George's bedroom, with no witnesses, in a kind of emergency situation. Accordingly, once George had regained his health, and realized that Clavier was essentially running the AEC, the senior prelate then resigned from the AEC.[82]

Bishop Clavier succeeded George as Primus, and thus, at the incredibly young age of thirty, had rather strangely traversed the journey from archdeacon to bishop to Primus in less than five months. There are many ways in which this kind of rapid rise to ecclesiastical status could be interpreted: as a matter of fortuitous circumstances, as the result of a well-designed plan brought to fruition by an adroit observer of the fledgling Continuing Movement, or as the result of an exceptionally gifted young man having his obvious talents recognized. The truth may include a little of all three explanations. Upon examining Clavier's early history, one is struck by the scattered and eclectic nature of his actions. In moving back and forth so frequently between different ecclesiastical groups, he seems to have been not only restlessly searching for a spiritual home, but also for a place in which his talents could be recognized and bear fruit. He had attended the Bernard Gilpin Society School in Durham, England, which had been established by the Church of England for those young men who could not initially qualify to enter one of their seminaries. However, Clavier had been unable to stay more than one academic year at the school, and was asked to leave due to "immaturity." A symptom of this immaturity during this period could be seen in his listing himself on applications as being two years older than he really was. It appears that, having unsuccessfully tried to become a clergyman in the Church of England, Clavier then moved into the less regulated world of independent ecclesiastical groups claiming to possess Old Catholic orders, in which a young man possessing a skill for eloquently expressing a grand vision for the future of fledgling religious bodies could make great headway. One can imagine the youthful Clavier, golden tongued and full of energy, dazzling the scatterings of predominantly elderly congregants of these quasi-Old Catholic groups with his seeming knowledge of everything ecclesiastical, and his promises of a brighter day. However, the basis of Clavier's learning appears to be almost entirely the result of self-education, for the numerous theological degrees he acquired during this period were apparently obtained from miniscule "paper mill" seminaries with names such as the University of St. John, Madras.[83] Despite the fact that he had no mainstream, academically regulated theological education, he was able to successfully convince many people that he had a firm grasp of Anglican theology, doctrine, and history. Interestingly, as recently as 1964, he allegedly had complained in a letter that the Catholic Episcopal Church to which he belonged was moving too closely toward Anglicanism.[84]

Clavier's two primary skills were his eloquence and

his hyper-activism in matters ecclesiastical. As the AEC's Primus, he could not seem to stop commenting on the controversies developing within PECUSA. For instance, from 1971 to 1975, he had at least ten letters published in *The Living Church*. No matter what the subject being addressed, Clavier usually included some attempted display of his knowledge of Anglican doctrine and history, as well as frequently simplistic answers to a pressing problem. Thus he commented on the attempts to radically change PECUSA: "The stark issue which is appearing is familiar to students of church history. The church, salvation, scripture, sacraments, and ministry are either God's free gift to man, or man's Pelagian steps to God. And if it is permissible to bet on theological issues, I'll wager that when God knocks enough sense into us to get us beyond denominationalism, liturgies, feminism, and the like, it will be justification by faith which confronts us all again. For though it isn't considered very bright to state that history repeats itself, sin always does and the peculiar sin of Anglicans has always been to believe that dear old Pelagius was right!"[85] One of the most striking characteristics of these letters is that they give the impression that they are being written by a man with deep roots in Anglican soil, thus brilliantly concealing the fact that their author seemed to have been a relatively recent convert to the Anglican theological position. The Continuing Church bishop who defends the 1928 Book of Common Prayer as the best available repository of true Anglican faith in 1971 is, in fact, only two years removed from a time in which he was alleged to have been deeply critical of its more catholic elements.[86] Also, the bishop who sounded in the early 1970s nearly as Protestant in his theology as Bishop Dees, was only a few years removed from being an Old Catholic, and even an Old Roman Catholic! However, few within the Continuing Movement or PECUSA seemed to know this at the time, and most no doubt assumed that Clavier was a lifelong Anglican who was simply recalling them to cling to the authentic Anglican position. Upon examining such discontinuities in Clavier's early career, one is forced to conclude that he either received some kind of nearly instant revelation of the truth, somewhat analogous to Paul's on the Damascus Road, or that he had discovered how to entice traditionalist Anglicans by telling them what they wanted to hear.

After the defeat of an attempt by three parishes to use legal action to take control of the AEC away from him, Clavier began the process of building the AEC into a relatively successful operation. Among the important parishes added during Clavier's early tenure were those lead by Fr. Walter Grundorf in Tennessee, and by Fr. Dean Stephens in North Carolina. Both Grundorf and Stephens would later become bishops in the Continuing Movement. Another development was the addition in 1973 of two parishes in New Mexico that had existed independently under the leadership of Bishop Harold Lawrence Trott. Trott had been the Missionary Bishop of New Mexico in the Reformed Episcopal Church, but when the Presiding Bishop of the REC died in 1972, his successor suddenly cut any ties between Trott and the REC. Trott was then assisted for a short time by a retired bishop of the Brazilian National Catholic Church, who conditionally consecrated Trott in 1973. In October of 1974 Trott was elected to be the Missionary Bishop of the Western United States of the AEC.[87]

The most lastingly significant aspect of Clavier's early tenure was his insistence on building ecumenical relationships with other Episcopalians, whether still within PECUSA or in the growing Continuing Movement. Clavier attended the PECUSA General Convention in 1971 in order to forge contacts with traditionalists who had remained in the national church. At the AEC synod held that same year, Bishop William Jerden of the Reformed Episcopal Church (REC) was the guest preacher. Clavier would continue to work informally with members of the REC for many years. His contacts with PECUSA traditionalists resulted in Bishop David B. Reed of Kentucky suggesting that a series of negotiations begin between PECUSA and the AEC in the hopes that the latter could be included within the designation of the "Wider Episcopal Fellowship."[88] Meetings were held in 1975 between representatives of the two bodies, but no lasting result was achieved.[89] The real fruits of these contacts with PECUSA traditionalists would become apparent after 1976, when the larger, second phase of the Continuing Anglican Movement began, and Clavier found himself being feted by traditionalists as an expert and key figure in the world of independent, traditionalist Anglicanism. To Clavier's supporters, his ecumenical contacts with PECUSA constituted a visionary attempt to keep the AEC from becoming a reactionary body that remained isolated outside of the worldwide Anglican Communion. To his detractors, he was said to be attempting to accomplish what he had been unable to in England, namely, to become an influential force within the Anglican mainstream by manipulating the smaller, more malleable Continuing Movement. These conflicting attitudes toward Clavier were only complicated when he stunned many traditionalist observers, in June of 1976, by resigning from the AEC and traveling to Wisconsin to enter Nashotah House, the renowned seminary for traditionalist, High-church Episcopalians.

There seem to be as many explanations as to what transpired when Clavier enrolled in Nashotah House as there were students at the seminary. All that is known for sure is that Clavier left the school in less than two months, and immediately rejoined the AEC as the Bishop of the Eastern Diocese of the United States. An explanation in a scholarly work is insufficient in that it gives the impression that Clavier withdrew from Nashotah House because he had been elected to be the Eastern Bishop of the AEC. However, this explanation seems inadequate since Clavier was already the AEC's Primus, or primary leader, before he entered Nashotah House. A letter to the editor in *The Christian Challenge* of January 1977 explained that Clavier had been promised a parish, but upon making a costly move to Wisconsin, had discovered that the promise would not be honored. However, Clavier himself denied this explanation in a personal correspondence with the scholar Donald S. Armentrout.[90] An explanation in Clavier's own words given at the time also tends to leave one unconvinced. He stated that he had decided to return to his people [in the AEC] in order to share their fate "in this fluid situation." He was referring to the recent decision by the PECUSA General Convention to ordain women to the priesthood. However, he had actually left Nashotah House *before* this change had occurred. He must have entered the seminary with the full knowledge of the very real, and probably imminent, possibility that such a change would likely take place. Problematically, his statement regarding his re-entry into the AEC was made quite a few weeks after he had left Nashotah House, and mistakenly gave the impression that his decision was made in response to the changed situation within PECUSA. In his explanation for returning to the AEC, he also emphasized that the AEC was not interested in picking up dissidents from PECUSA as a result of the women's ordination controversy.[91] It would be interesting to know if Clavier made this statement on his own initiative, or whether it was in response to a question by a journalist. Either way, his insistence on the indifference of the AEC toward Episcopalians disgruntled over the recent decision to ordain women appears to be either misleading or less than frank, for as will be shown in Chapter 5, Clavier was deeply wounded when his input was not sought at the beginning of the second phase of Continuing Anglicanism in St. Louis.

The explanation that seems closer to the truth of the matter, and is emphasized by Clavier's detractors, is that he left Nashotah House once he realized that the school was not going to recognize his previous ordinations and consecrations. In this account, the Rev. Louis Weil, a professor at Nashotah at the time, gave Clavier a book by the Roman Catholic theologian Karl Rahner in order to substantiate the seminary's position, but Clavier chose instead to interpret the work as validating his contested orders.[92] This would help explain why Clavier made such an abrupt turn. In an article announcing Clavier's transference to PECUSA, he eschewed those who warned him to wait until General Convention reached its decision on the question of the ordination of women, emphasizing that it would take much work and understanding between the divided camps within ECUSA to come together again, and that he hoped to be part of that reconciling process in some way.[93] If one takes his statements seriously, then it would appear that Clavier was committed to PECUSA for the long haul, and thus no sudden flash of insight into the deficient nature of PECUSA should have led to such an abrupt departure from Nashotah House. Another account claims that Clavier had initially apologized to his superiors at Nashotah House for having helped start the AEC.[94] The explanation emphasizing that Clavier's orders were not recognized at Nashotah also coalesces with his near-obsessive attention to the question of his and the AEC's episcopal orders. In a booklet written by Clavier in 1975, titled simply *The American Episcopal Church*, only a few paragraphs out of eighteen pages discuss the history or functioning of the AEC, while the rest of the tract is dedicated to justifying, both historically and theologically, the AEC's (read his) orders.

Perhaps the most perplexing aspect of this booklet, when read in the light of what transpired in 1976, is the passage in which Clavier justifies the existence of the AEC: "It is certainly true that the Church must safeguard herself against schism. Yet the American Episcopal Church was founded out of necessity. Its members had nowhere else to go. The Episcopal Church was infected by the novel contagion of strange doctrine. As Anglicans, affiliation with an Orthodox Church was hardly desirable, the only course was to establish parishes and pray that God would bless the new jurisdiction by giving it Orders and Sacraments. The question had to be asked: Which is more important, the jurisdiction of an historic communion, or fidelity to the Doctrine, Discipline, and Worship of the Universal Church?"[95] This statement reveals a spirit that stands in sharp contrast to the reconciling spirit that Clavier displayed while diplomatically announcing his entry into PECUSA less than a year later. Whereas in 1975 Episcopalians had "nowhere else to go," in 1976 the leader of the AEC, and author of a booklet describing PECUSA as a semi-heretical body, could enter one of its seminaries. One is left with the impression that either Clavier was not nearly as grounded in his doctrinal and theological thinking as his supporters had assumed, or that he was cynically playing a game of ecclesiastical cat and mouse, sending out different messages to whichever group of Episcopalians he was trying to win over.

While Bishop Clavier resumed his career in the AEC, Bishop Trott remained in the position of Primus. The AEC, partly as the result of Clavier's vision and activity, had grown between 1970 and 1976 to become a much more important player in the world of Continuing Anglicanism than Bishop Dees' Anglican Orthodox Church. Under Clavier's leadership, the AEC had taken a stand that was very similar to that of the AOC in that both groups emphasized the

Protestant nature of Anglicanism. The fundamental difference between the two groups resided in the differences between Clavier and Dees. Whereas Dees was a rigid Reformation Anglican, Clavier spoke the broader language of moderation and tolerance. Whereas Dees often forced his will within the AOC by way of arbitrary power, Clavier used the more pastoral approach of convincing AEC churchmen to see things his way. In later chapters, the importance of the AEC to the overall Continuing Movement will become even more apparent, especially after Clavier resumed the Primacy of the AEC in 1980.

The AEC was not the only new Continuing body to emerge before 1976. A cluster of small groups formed which would impact the later Movement by providing many leading figures for the later Continuum. As was mentioned earlier, Bishop George of the AEC had departed in 1970 to form the Anglican Church in America. Just as the AEC was primarily formed from parishes in the southeastern United States that had left the AOC and PECUSA, so too another body been formed out of former AOC parishes and disgruntled Episcopalians in the western United States, and at relatively the same time. The Anglican Episcopal Church of North America (AECNA) was organized in Fountain Valley, California on October 10, 1972. The guiding light of the dissidents was Fr. Walter Hollis Adams, a retired thirty-year veteran of the British diplomatic service who had once studied for the ministry under Graham Leonard, the traditionalist High-church Bishop of London. Fr. Adams was elected to be the first bishop of the fledgling group and was consecrated two weeks later by Bishop William Elliot Littlewood in Santa Ana, California. As was mentioned earlier, Littlewood was a bishop of the Free Protestant Episcopal Church, and one of the first three men elected in 1968 to be bishops for the AEC, before he quickly departed. The day after being consecrated by Littlewood,

Bishop Adams was consecrated again in Cambria, California, by Bishop H. Adrian Spruit,[96] the head of an heretical, esoteric sect known as the Antiochean Orthodox Church. Spruit had received his training and consecrations through the Theosophy-tinged wing of the Liberal Catholic Church. Thus Adams provided one of the earliest examples of the practice of Continuing bishops who would accept questionable consecrations at the hands of whomever could be found to pass on Holy Orders, so long as they could be shown to possess some kind of physical Apostolic Succession. Adams managed to mirror the success of Clavier, stressing a Broad to Low-Church traditionalism, and the AECNA began to add parishes. One of the most notable new additions was a former AOC congregation in Atlanta, Georgia, and its priest, Frank Benning (late in 1972), who would be consecrated by Adams as a bishop coadjutor in September of 1973. Adams was assisted in this consecration by Bishop George of the Anglican Church in America, the aforementioned Bishop Orlando J. Woodward, Bishop Larry V. Parker of the Anglican Church of America, and Bishop John Andrew Hollister Perry-Hooker of the Evangelical Catholic Communion. The participation of such an array of bishops in the consecration service gives an indication as to the degree in which Adams rivaled Clavier and the AEC in the attempt to bring the assorted early dissident groups and parishes into greater cooperation.[97]

In the summer of 1975, Adams succeeded in spearheading the creation of the Council of Anglican Episcopal Churches, which brought various groups of dissident Anglicans together to form a plan of action that could lead to possible intercommunion and an eventual merger. The member bodies of the Council were Adams' Anglican Episcopal Church, based in Santa Ana, California; Bishop George's Anglican Church of America, based in

Spartanburg, South Carolina; the Episcopal Church Evangelical, based in Wilmington, North Carolina; the United Episcopal Church, based in Virginia; and the Anglican Church, Providence of New England, based in Vermont.

John Perry-Hooker had formed the Evangelical Catholic Communion along with Bishop Julian E. Ernie of Switzerland. Hooker had been consecrated initially by a bishop of the Holy Apostolic Catholic Church of the East, and then again in February of 1972 by Bishops Armand C. Whitehead of the United Old Catholic Church, and James E. Burns of the United Episcopal Church. Hooker eventually brought his group under the jurisdiction of Bishop George, and changed its name to the Anglican Church, Province of New England. Hooker's relationship with George was such that upon the latter's death in 1977, Hooker became the new head of the Anglican Church of America.

The Episcopal Church Evangelical had been formed sometime before March of 1975, when Fr. Michael Dean Stephens led a parish in Wilmington, North Carolina out of the AEC. Stephens, the former editor of the AEC's journal, *Ecclesia*, had been consecrated by Bishop Russell Grant Fry, who had formerly been a member of the Anglican Orthodox Church. Fry in turn had previously joined with Fr. Thomas J. Kleppinger and Fr. Troy A. Kaichen in leading three parishes out of the AOC in 1973. Fry consecrated Kleppinger and Kaichen as bishops in 1974.[98] As can be seen, there was little rivalry, and much cooperation, between many of these earliest, tiny Continuing bodies. The AEC's Clavier commented on the consecrations of Bishops Kleppinger and Kaichen by noting that, even though he wasn't questioning the validity of their orders, he thought it somewhat scandalous that the UEC had three bishops for its three parishes, and he wondered whether such a "congregationalist" association of parishes could in fact be considered a genuine part of the historic church.[99] However, such observations were largely overwhelmed by the increasingly harmonious relations between these earliest Continuing groups, and the increasingly fragile situation within PECUSA, which caused many to overlook the weaknesses of these groups in order to support the overall direction of the movement to establish alternative, traditionalist Episcopalian possibilities.

The Episcopal Church Evangelical seems to have quickly merged into the United Episcopal Church, which in turn seems to have merged just as quickly with the Anglican Episcopal Church. Bishop Perry-Hooker's group in turn appears to have quickly merged with the Episcopal Church of America. In the summer of 1975, the AECNA and ACA began the process of merging. A "Resolution of Agreement" was drawn up which called for all members of the Council of Anglican Episcopal Churches to agree to accept four points as the basis for union: the Apostle's and Nicene creeds; the continuation of the three-fold ministry of bishops, priests, and deacons; the affirmation that only the sacraments of baptism and holy communion were necessary for salvation; and that no doctrines were to be deemed necessary to salvation unless they were clearly stated in the Bible. When the AECNA held its convention in Bellevue, Washington, Bishop George was allowed to participate in the discussions leading up to the vote regarding the plan for future union. After the convention passed the resolution, it was also decided that Bishops Adams and George would take turns (rotating years served) chairing the committee to oversee the eventual union of the two bodies. Plans were also started to begin fundraising efforts to establish a joint seminary.[100] An enlarged AECNA was effectively in place by October of 1977 when Bishops Kleppinger and Stephens were consecrated by Adams in Spartanburg,

South Carolina, and Bishops Adams, Benning, Parker, and Perry-Hooker jointly laid hands on each other in order to transmit and unify their varying lines of apostolic succession.[101] The AECNA now claimed to have over 30 parishes and missions, located in New England, the Southeast, Illinois, and the Pacific Coast.[102]

Two other small bodies were formed during the early 1970s that deserve some mention. In 1970, an independent parish began meeting in the home of a layman in Columbia, South Carolina. This parish soon decided to affiliate with the AEC and called a former PECUSA priest, Fr. Richard C. Acker, to lead them. Fr. Acker was received into the AEC in 1971 by Bishop Clavier. However, in 1973, the parish withdrew from the AEC, and remained independent for a few years. During this time, Acker became acquainted with Bishop Burns of the United Episcopal Church Anglican/Celtic, and Burns consecrated Acker in 1976, allowing him to form the United Episcopal Church of America.[103] At the other end of the nation, another sprinkling of independent parishes had formed in Arizona and New Mexico between 1970 and 1972, and these eventually came under the leadership of Fr. Jack Capers Adam, a retired PECUSA priest, and director of the renowned St. Jude's ranch for boys in Nevada. Adam was consecrated by Archbishop Walter Propheta of the American Orthodox Catholic Church in 1972, and proceeded to form the Old Episcopal Church, which seems to have never spread beyond Arizona and New Mexico.[104]

By September of 1976, when PECUSA finally voted to legalize the ordination of women, the AEC and AECNA were, relatively speaking, the strongest bodies in the initial phase of the Continuing Anglican Movement. The AOC, largely due to defections and organizational atrophy, had begun a process of slow but steady decline. Bishop Acker's United Episcopal Church of America, the Southern

Episcopal Church, and Bishop Adam's Old Episcopal Church, were smaller, both numerically and geographically. Little noticed at the time by many PECUSA traditionalists who were contemplating their own possible schismatic actions, was the fact that this initial phase of the Continuing Anglican Movement was overwhelmingly dominated by Low and Broad-Church theology and liturgical practice. Each group watched the events that transpired during the early 1970s with anticipation, hopeful that a large influx of new membership would shortly be forthcoming as soon as PECUSA took the fatal step of ordaining women and authorizing a revised Prayer Book. Unfortunately for Bishops Dees, Clavier, and Adams, as well as those representing the smaller bodies, these hopes for a better day would go largely unrealized. The traditionalists who had remained within PECUSA in order to oppose the perceived erosion of the their church had their own ideas about what would constitute an effective and genuine Continuing Anglican ecclesiastical body, and the already existing hodge-podge (in their view) of questionably consecrated bishops with miniscule jurisdictions, were deemed to be an unacceptable alternative. Thus, and also little noticed at the time, the second phase of the Continuing Movement was to be influenced more strongly by a coalition of committed High-churchmen, with the support of traditionalist Broad-Churchmen who were generally more tolerant of ecclesiastical diversity.

Chapter 4

TRADITIONALIST DISSIDENTS IN THE EARLY 1970S

The majority of traditionalist churchmen remained within PECUSA despite its forays into questionable political activism and its lax standards for disciplining theologically unsound bishops. The general attitude of these churchmen was that PECUSA could be reformed from within, by both organizing and educating the laity and the clergy. This process of organization and education was carried out by grassroots pressure groups that were formed throughout the early 1970s as PECUSA continued to move toward what was perceived to be more radical innovations and positions. Many of these traditionalist groups would either become actively involved in the larger Continuing schism that occurred in 1977, or they would play a significant role in convincing many churchmen that PECUSA was beyond the possibility of effective reform, therefore helping to pave the way for large numbers of churchmen abandoning the Episcopal Church altogether.

The oldest, and certainly one of the most important of these pressure groups, was the American Church Union (ACU). The ACU had been formed in 1937 as an American counterpart to the Church Union in England, which had been established to be an organizational witness to the Church of England's Catholic identity. The American organization was likewise committed to maintaining the Catholic identity of the Episcopal Church. The ACU's position was that PECUSA was, and must remain, a part of the worldwide Catholic faith, that is, in basic doctrinal accord with the Roman Catholic and Eastern Orthodox churches. However, the tenuous nature of this Episcopalian Catholicism became more apparent when the High-church members of ACU were confronted with the rapid changes sweeping through the world's religious bodies.

The completion of the Second Vatican Council in 1965 had brought about a mild revolution in both the liturgical and theological explorations of the Roman Catholic Church. Liberal minded Roman Catholics, especially in the United States, purported to have divined a "spirit of Vatican II" which supposedly represented the new, more "modern" direction in which their church would be moving. Many High-church Episcopalians had long sympathized with their liberal counterparts in the Roman Church, and they now anticipated a great opportunity for the two communions to come closer together. However, the leadership of the ACU was largely a conservative and traditionalist lot, and conflicts with liberal High-church Episcopalians were soon to follow. Early in 1971, nine members of the Theological Committee of the ACU resigned, alleging that the ACU's leadership was not "authentically catholic" enough since it didn't support the new atmosphere of theological inquiry that had been inspired by Vatican II.[105] The Executive Director of ACU, Fr. Albert J. DuBois, responded that those who had resigned were not really theologians with doctorates, but priests who were disgruntled over the ACU's refusal to endorse PECUSA's political and theological experimentation.[106] This conflict was but a ripple in the stormy seas that were soon to follow for Catholic-minded Episcopalians.

On the more Protestant or Low-church end of the traditionalist Episcopalian spectrum, the Foundation for Christian Theology (FCT) had been formed in 1966. The FCT had begun in 1962 as a group in Michigan calling itself the Society of Fishermen, publishing a newsletter called *The Christian Challenge*. The Society of Fishermen was primarily concerned with the theological decline of PECUSA, which was blamed as the root cause of the secondary problem of the political radicalization of the church.[107] Upon its founding, the FCT took over the publication of The *Christian Challenge*, and transformed it into the leading journal expressing a stringent, traditionalist Episcopalian commentary on the news and events of the national church. The FCT was also concerned with the theological decline of ECUSA, but it was equally dedicated to critiquing the political transgressions of the national church. Its original founder, Fr. Paul Katzig, wrote a book entitled *The National Council of Churches and the Social Revolution*, which argued that the mission of the NCC was contrary to that of the Christian gospel.[108] The FCT was certainly the most notorious and controversial of the early traditionalist pressure groups. They were slandered as racists by a Presiding Bishop (see Chapter 1), and in 1971 they were rebuked by the Diocese of West Texas for sending unsolicited mailings of *The Christian Challenge* to Episcopalians, which was labeled as "propaganda."[109] In a typically alarmist article that appeared in *The Nation*, Lester Kinsolving, an official in PECUSA's Diocese of California, described the FCT as an extremist organization whose editor, Dorothy Faber, served as the "coordinator" of "Birch-front groups" within the national church.[110]

    Both the ACU and FCT represented early dissident voices within PECUSA, and both also played leading roles in meeting the challenges that would deeply disturb the national church in the early 1970s. Whereas traditionalists had been deeply disturbed by the political and theological scandals within PECUSA in the 1960s, they were more severely traumatized by the twin loci of ecclesiastical activism that seemed to transfix liberal churchmen for the coming years: Prayer Book revision and the ordination of women to the priesthood.

The process of revising the 1928 Book of Common Prayer began in 1961 when PECUSA approved the exploration of creating what were called "trial use" liturgies. Committees were formed throughout the 1960s, including in their deliberations a wide diversity of churchmen, and especially a significant portion of the laity, seeking to update and improve the older Prayer Book. They began devising church rites, to be performed on an experimental basis, with the purpose of testing how the participating parishes responded to them. In 1970, *Services for Trial Use* was published, and over 800,000 copies were sold. Due to the color of its cover, this book was known throughout the church as the Green Book. An editorial published just before the release of the Green Book captured some of the concerns that traditionalists had with the proposed trial liturgy. The editorialist complained that there "cannot be any real 'trial use' of the unrepeatable sacraments of baptism and confirmation." The question was raised as to whether someone baptized and confirmed under the trial rite would have to be re-baptized and re-confirmed if the church later decided that the trial rites were not sufficient. Furthermore, the editorialist worried that the basic slant of the new services placed the emphasis on "man's action rather than God's."[111]

Concern over the proposed liturgical changes found within the Green Book led to the formation in 1973 of the premier organization that opposed the movement for liturgical revision: the Society For the Preservation of the Book of Common Prayer (SPBCP). The SPBCP initially issued reports and tracts outlining their opposition to the new trial services, and they eventually accumulated over 13,000 members just prior to the 1973 General Convention to be held in Louisville, Kentucky. A large part of the Society's earliest work dealt with combating the un-canonical practice of several liberal bishops who had banned the use of the 1928 Prayer Book in their dioceses pending the General Convention vote in Louisville. The official position of the SPBCP was that it was not against liturgical change per se, but only against many of the revisions found within the Green Book.[112]

Just as the issue over Prayer Book revision was intensifying prior to the 1973 General Convention, so too was the debate over the ordination of women to the priesthood. In 1970 the General Convention had approved the entry of women into the deaconate, and it was also the first to vote on whether women should be accepted for ordination to the priesthood. Even though the resolution had been defeated, its proponents were encouraged by the number of votes that had been cast in its favor, and consequently began to organize more forcefully for the Louisville Convention. Part of this movement was fueled by the expectations of a growing number of women who had graduated from church seminaries with the expectation of being ordained. These women formed a large part of the Episcopal Women's Caucus, which was formed in 1971, and which vociferously criticized the more cautious approach being taken by the PECUSA hierarchy. By the 1972 meeting of the House of Bishops, the pressure applied by the advocates of women's ordination resulted in a 74 to 61 vote by the bishops favoring women priests "in principle."[113]

The arguments made against the ordination of women were varied but generally revolved around a few basic points. The first argument was that Jesus had not chosen any women to be among his disciples and apostles. Second, Paul had warned women not to speak in church (1 Corinthians 14:34). Third, there were two thousand years of Christian tradition that spoke against the innovation. Fourth, ecumenical relations with the Roman Catholic and Eastern Orthodox churches would be either greatly harmed or severed altogether. Another argument, less frequently made, was that the very language and symbolism of Christianity was conveyed in male terms, and that to change this would be to change the essence of the faith.[114]

In addition to the activism of the ACU, FCT, and SPBCP, the fight against women's ordination and Prayer Book revision had been taken up by other groups as well. Perry Laukhuff of Connecticut started a small but widely distributed newsletter in 1972, *The Certain Trumpet*, which took up the causes of traditionalist churchmen.[115] Later in the year, and also in Connecticut, the Committee (later changed to "Coalition") for Apostolic Ministry (CAM) was formed by John L. Scott Jr. in order to keep PECUSA from deciding the issue of ordaining women to the priesthood too hastily. A major emphasis of CAM was that PECUSA could not initiate such an important innovation without the consensus of the other churches that maintained the historic episcopate. Thus CAM was not absolutely opposed to the ordination of women, but only to the way in which the national church was undertaking the process.[116] Other smaller groups increased their efforts in the defense of traditionalist faith and values as the women's ordination issue moved closer to becoming a reality. These included the Episcopal Renaissance of Pennsylvania (formed in 1967), the Society for Promoting and Encouraging the Arts and Knowledge of the Church (SPEAK) which was established in 1953 as the Episcopal Book Club, and which began publishing the *Anglican Digest* in 1958, and the Episcopal Guild for the Blind.

The premier organization dedicated to combating the changes being proposed for PECUSA would turn out to be the Fellowship of Concerned Churchmen (FCC). The FCC was an umbrella organization comprised of groups and publications in the United States and Canada that were concerned about the direction of the national church. It began when Canon Albert J. DuBois, head of the ACU, called a meeting to be held in New York, at ACU headquarters, for the purpose of bringing together the various groups that were opposing the distressing trends within PECUSA. Present at the meeting were Canon Francis W. Read of the ACU, leaders of the SPBCP, Dorothy Faber (editor of the FCT's *Christian Challenge*), and Perry Laukhuff (editor of *The Certain Trumpet*).[117] These leaders initially called themselves the Coalition of Concerned Churchmen. They were opposed to the ordination of women to the priesthood, the proposed revision of the Prayer Book, and the loosening of church standards on issues such as divorce, sexuality, and abortion.

The 1973 Louisville General Convention defeated the proposal to ordain women to the priesthood, and recommended that the revision process for the Prayer Book continue in an altered form, which would come to be known as the Zebra Book due to its striped cover. The defeat of the resolution to approve the ordination of women, in retrospect, was perhaps viewed too optimistically by many traditionalists. *The Living Church* described the resolution as being defeated by "a wide margin," and implied that the movement in support of women's ordination was actually losing ground.[118] However, as historian David E. Sumner notes, "it [the motion] was defeated because of parliamentary rules that counted divided votes from diocesan delegations as negative votes. The actual vote was, clerical deputies: yes-50, no-43, divided-20; lay deputies yes-49, no-37, divided-26."[119] These numbers should not lead one to the mistaken conclusion that the proposal had wide support. A poll published at the time showed that nearly 80 percent of churchmen were opposed to the Green Book liturgy, and 90 percent were opposed to the ordination of women.[120] Perhaps due to their having sensed how close PECUSA was to legally ordaining women, the FCC issued its first declaration on October 2, 1973. The declaration listed seven principles on which the FCC would not compromise. The first was the authority of the Bible. Second was the maintenance of the catholic creeds. Third was the maintenance of baptism and confirmation by bishops in the Apostolic line. Fourth was the maintenance of the Eucharist by those possessing orders in the apostolic line. Fifth was the perpetuation of the practice of limiting the episcopate and priesthood to men. Sixth was the "integrity of the Episcopate in its sacramental functions." Seventh was the preservation of the 1928 Book of Common Prayer in order to maintain both faithful worship and doctrine.[121]

During this period the leadership of the FCC and other traditionalist groups stressed that they would remain within PECUSA. The day before the FCC issued its Louisville Declaration, the *Louisville Times* reported that as many as 150,000 Episcopalians would be willing to leave the national church if the controversial proposed changes were passed by the General Convention. Canon DuBois of the ACU and Joseph Witkofshi (president of the FCT) quickly issued statements expressing their intention to remain within PECUSA. DuBois described the traditionalist groups as a "loyal opposition."[122]

While the traditionalists were trying to remain a "loyal opposition," the spurned proponents of women's ordination decided to follow the lead of the radical political activists with whom they had worked so closely. Three retired bishops issued a statement on July 19, 1974, stating their intention to ordain eleven women to the priesthood at Philadelphia's Church of the Advocate. Despite the implorations of Presiding Bishop John Allin and others, the illegal ordinations took place on July 29, 1974. Representatives from both the ACU and CAM were present and were allowed to issue statements of disproval before the ordinations took place, but in a sign of the acrimony that was beginning to dominate the debate, they were jeered repeatedly by the crowd of 1,500. They were also forced to sit in a section of pews being "guarded" by a line of women, dressed in t-shirts and jeans, who stood with their arms interlocked in order to form a barrier.[123] The offending bishops and the priestesses were full of prophetic inspiration, or foolish delusion, depending on one's point of view. The bishops stated, "Hearing his command, we can heed no other. The time for our obedience is now."[124] The officiating bishops also announced that a recently deceased bishop was present "spiritually" to lend his support.[125] A priestess remembered being menaced by a mocking and accusing supernatural voice that sought to intimidate her from being ordained, but then it went away after her defiant ordination.[126] A large number of the spectators raised their fists in revolutionary zeal during the sermon, and one woman went to the altar rail during the communion service carrying a bag of popcorn.[127] Such bizarre statements and actions were quite common among the new priestesses and their supporters.

In response to the changed situation, Presiding Bishop Allin called an emergency meeting of the House of Bishops in Chicago two weeks later, and the bishops voted 129 to 9 to express their disapproval of the non-canonical ordinations of those who came to be known as "the Philadelphia Eleven."[128] However, the bishops only objected to the ordination of the women because it had occurred before it was canonically legal. The bishops would again state their support for women's ordination, "in principle," at their next regularly scheduled meeting. The action of the House of Bishops was largely a symbolic show presented for the purpose of pacifying a greatly agitated segment of the laity. The priestesses, though declared officially to be illegally consecrated, began to be invited to preside at sympathetic parishes across the country. Outcry over the situation led to two ecclesiastical trials of priests who had allowed priestesses to preside as priests in their parishes; Peter Beebe of Ohio and William Wendt of Washington D.C., both of whom were convicted. However, many traditionalists could no doubt see the writing on the wall, since in the case of Fr. Wendt's trial, the three prelates who had voted to convict him still expressed their support of women's ordination, and of the validity of the "Philadelphia 11" ordinations in particular.[129]

The illegal and allegedly heretical ordinations in Philadelphia forced many traditionalists to consider more drastic actions, which included a potential separation from the national church. The ACU demonstrated the seriousness of its stance by removing the retired Bishop of West Missouri, Edward R. Welles, the honorary vice-president of the organization, from its membership rolls due to his participation in the Philadelphia service.[130] Earlier in that same year, 1975, the FCC issued a "Call to Anglican Integrity" that offered a generic listing of principles of faith and worship that PECUSA should uphold. However, the "Call" ended with a subtle warning that, if the upcoming 1976 Minneapolis General Convention approved the ordination of women, faithful Episcopalians would no longer be members in the Apostolic Church.[131] The ACU also tried to draw on the hope that churchmen would respond to the possibility of losing their place in the fellowship of worldwide apostolic churches, and called for an ecumenical council to be comprised of Roman and Old Catholics, Eastern Orthodox, and Anglicans for the purpose of coming to a decision on the controversy over the ordination of women.[132] That this appeal was most probably made for the purposes of traditionalist propaganda is obvious, since no right thinking churchmen, even the most Catholic of churchmen, would expect the Pope or the Patriarch of Constantinople to recognize the status of the Anglican

Communion as being equal with their own. In September of 1975 the ACU took a more concrete step toward opposing the coming innovations within PECUSA by forming a steering committee called Episcopalians United (EU) in order to initiate an emergency program that would prepare an effective witness to the essential principles of Anglicanism.[133] EU adopted as its philosophy the slogan, "No Surrender, No Desertion," which meant no surrender from the Apostolic heritage of PECUSA, and no desertion of the church body as it was "presently constituted."

The "no surrender, no desertion" slogan eventually exposed the fragile nature of the coalition of traditionalists that were working to save PECUSA. At its meeting in late January of 1976, a division developed within ACU over what the slogan obliged ACU members to do if the upcoming General Convention voted in favor of legalizing women priests. The Executive Director, Fr. Charles H. Osborn, resigned after he was accused by Fr. Jack Baker, Fr. George Clendenin, and Fr. Francis Read of incorrectly interpreting the "no surrender" pledge as meaning that the ACU would remain within PECUSA, no matter the decision reached in Minneapolis.[134] Fr. William C. Wantland, who was present at the meeting, reported that Osborn had also been accused of circulating a Canadian news story that purported to quote Canon DuBois as having already begun planning for an exodus from the national church. It should be noted that Fr. Robert S. Morse, the newly elected Executive Director of the ACU, denied that the debate over the "no desertion" pledge had even occurred.[135] However, this seems unlikely since within the ACU there was clearly a growing sentiment for a possible ecclesiastical separation from PECUSA, and this became apparent within a short time as many members of the organization played leading roles in the schism that was formalized in 1977. If anything, the traditionalists appear to have been holding back their cards in their contest with the PECUSA establishment. In February of 1976 the FCC issued an "Open Letter to the Bishops of the Episcopal Church" which stated that they would not accept the validity of women priests or the authority of any bishop who participated in such invalid ordinations.[136] This is clearly a rebellious position, but it is a muted rebellion, and there is no direct statement of intent to leave PECUSA. A few months later the ACU issued a statement to the bishops of the church that denied that the organization planned on leaving the national church.[137] At nearly the same time, CAM also repudiated any accusations that they espoused separating from the national church.[138]

As the 1976 General Convention grew nearer, and the prospects for blocking the canonical legalization of women priests seemed to grow dimmer, traditionalists began to state their position more forcefully, and with greater clarity. Meeting in Cleveland in July, the FCC issued a document titled "A Call to Episcopalians to Pray and Be Steadfast." This statement offered the first acknowledgement that a meeting could be called in order to organize a "new" ecclesiastical body. However, the authors viewed themselves as being abandoned by PECUSA, rather than vice versa: "It is our conviction that any action altering the Apostolic ministry…would result in the creation of a new body outside of the Holy Catholic and Orthodox Church." It ended with the promise that: "We are determined that the Church as presently constituted in Doctrine, Discipline, and Worship, will continue, God being our helper."[139]

Another important development during this period was the publication in July of 1976 of Fr. Robert C. Harvey's *A House Divided*. Harvey had first come to the attention of many traditionalists with his founding of the Company of the Paraclete in 1971. The Company of the Paraclete had been designed to be a monastic settlement house manned by idealistic Episcopalians in order to help minorities find employment in inner-city areas such as Philadelphia. Harvey hoped that his experiment would prove that orthodox churchmen could provide the social service that the more liberal and radical churchmen were espousing in programs such as the GCSP. The Company of the Paraclete failed within a few years due to a lack of financial support, as well as some health problems with Harvey's wife. Despite this disappointment, Harvey organized the Canterbury Guild in order to distribute his booklet, *A House Divided*, to as many churchmen as could be reached before General Convention.

    Fr. Harvey's booklet was largely a collection of vignettes detailing the moral and theological decline within PECUSA, which was said to have occurred due to a takeover of the church by liberal and left-leaning church leaders. He began by postulating that the divisions within the church were no longer between High and Low-churchmen, but between "left" and "right" churchmen, which had caused an uncomfortable alliance between High and Low-churchmen under the designation of "traditionalist."[140] He then chronicled, refusing to use real names, the abuses and indignities that traditionalists had suffered and/or witnessed under the liberal domination of the church. Among the shocking accounts were stories of jazz masses, of a priest who brought a dying woman her last Communion while wearing sneakers and jeans, of divorced priests, of priests "living with" women, of seminarians who had never been allowed to see the 1928 Prayer Book, and the political activism and theological heresy that were seemingly beginning to become dominant behaviors among the church's elite.[141] Harvey concluded by offering traditionalists the choice between a supernaturally orientated orthodoxy, or a naturalistic humanism,[142] and then suggesting what traditionalists should do if General Convention voted on the side of secular humanism. He advised that those who were considering schism should realign their parish properties so that all of them would be owned by the local parish rather than by the diocese or national church. A final piece of advise, which would turn out to be somewhat prophetic, was that, due to the fact that no bishops were likely to forego their position within the establishment to join a Continuing Movement, and because a deeper understanding of the nature of the episcopate was necessary, a new church body would do well to wait a few years before electing any bishops for itself.[143]

Although Fr. Harvey's words had a strong impact on many traditionalists, they failed to convince very many who were on the other side, or unsure of which side they were on. As many traditionalists had feared, the Minneapolis Convention approved both the ordination of woman priests and the *Draft Proposed Book of Common Prayer*. The FCC quickly issued a statement titled, "Hold Fast!" They described PECUSA as no longer being a part of the Apostolic faith, of becoming "just another Protestant denomination," and of formally becoming a heretical body. They advised traditionalists to only receive the sacraments from orthodox bishops or priests, and concluded by promising to hold a "Church-wide convention as soon as possible in early 1977."[144] At this point the official ACU and EU were still working in unity with the broader coalition that comprised the FCC. The full membership list of the FCC at this time was as follows: EU, The Congregation of St. Augustine, Episcopal Renaissance of Pennsylvania, the FCT, the Society of the Holy Cross, the ACU, the Canterbury Guild, Episcopal Guild for the Blind, SPEAK, the SPBCP, *The Living Church*, *The Christian Challenge*, *The Anglican Digest*, *The Certain* Trumpet, and *The American Church News*. The ACU held a meeting in Nashville on November 3, 1976, one day before the FCC would hold its own meeting in the same city. The ACU rejected the decisions of the

Minneapolis Convention, and stated that it would only work with orthodox bishops and priests. It also endorsed an immediate calling of a council of faithful and orthodox churchmen to address the new situation. The FCC meeting on November 4th announced that such a council would be held in September of 1977, in St. Louis, Missouri "for the purpose of presenting the spiritual principles and ecclesial structure of the continuing Episcopal Church." This meeting also endorsed the drafting of a statement that would be the basis for a Continuing church, as well as a committee to organize the financial and other structural factors involved in forming a new ecclesiastical body.[145] Although the ACU and FCC obviously held their meetings jointly in order to coordinate their efforts, a division soon became apparent among different leaders as to how quickly to proceed with the formation of a Continuing body, and as to what the nature of that body would or should be.

By the end of 1976 the ACU had disbanded the EU committee due to its lack of support for the FCC and the upcoming St. Louis Congress. Canon DuBois, the primary opponent of the proposal to form a Continuing church body, then formed Anglicans United (AU). AU and DuBois's position was that the FCC was not moving swiftly enough to form a new structure, and that a Continuing church should seek to work toward becoming an independent province that could eventually be taken into an Apostolic church (either the Roman Catholic, Eastern Orthodox, or Old Catholic).[146] The ACU officially dissociated itself from AU, and continued its participation with the FCC. The FCC held another meeting in Philadelphia, in January of 1977, and also voted to formally dissociate itself from AU.[147] In December of 1976, CAM held a meeting in Chicago in which it honored its pledge to remain within PECUSA, but stated that it was re-organizing itself as the Evangelical and Catholic Mission (ECM). The ECM was distinguished from the FCC in that it included some active PECUSA bishops in its leadership, such as Stanley Atkins of Eau Claire, and in its strategy of working for the formation of a separate entity or structure within PECUSA, in which traditionalists could retain their existence within the national church.[148]

In early 1977 there were three primary groups of traditionalists within PECUSA, and each had formulated different approaches to the problem created by the Minneapolis Convention's actions. The FCC was planning to form a Continuing Episcopal Church, the ECM was planning to work toward establishing an independent status within PECUSA, and AU was planning on becoming an "Anglican rite" jurisdiction within another Apostolic church body. The seeds of disagreement and schism within the larger (as opposed to those groups discussed in earlier chapters) traditionalist and Continuing church Movement were thus present from the very beginning, and would pose a serious stumbling block to its effective establishment.

Chapter 5

THE ST. LOUIS CONGRESS

The FCC had initially intended the upcoming church congress in St. Louis to be the starting point for the formation of a Continuing Anglican church. The designation "Anglican" in replacement of "Episcopalian" became an easy transition for the departing traditionalists since PECUSA had committed so many grave errors, and more importantly, because many catholic or High-church traditionalists had long preferred the term as a way of signifying that they were a distinct branch within the worldwide catholic faith, rather than members of the *Protestant* Episcopal Church. Despite the intentions of the FCC's leadership, who seemed to desire a smoother transition into a new ecclesiastical body, work toward the creation of a Continuing church would be initiated by forces, largely independent of the FCC, almost as soon as the decisions at the now notorious Minneapolis Convention had been reached.

A significant move was initiated within the Diocese of Colorado on November 28, 1976, when the members of St. Mary's in Denver held a special parish meeting to make amendments to their articles of incorporation, which included the deletion of their acceptance of the Constitutions and Canons of both PECUSA and their diocese. Specifically, St. Mary's claimed that they would adhere to PECUSA's Constitution and Canons as they existed on January 1, 1970. The Bishop of Colorado, William C. Frey, was barred from attending the decisive parish meeting, and soon after, inhibited St. Mary's priest, Fr. James Mote. At the time, Fr. Mote claimed that at least a dozen Colorado parishes, and perhaps 50 to 60 nationally, were prepared to depart the national church. He claimed to have been told by Bishop Clarence R. Haden of Northern California that some bishops in Canada and the Caribbean would assist any parishes that withdrew from PECUSA. Haden had addressed the parishioners of St. Mary's two weeks prior to the special meeting, but denied to reporters that he had made any commitments to parishes or churchmen wishing to form a new church body. However, the parishioners of St. Mary's were under the impression that he would guide any seceding parishes, including their own. Although Frey initially expressed no desire to seize the St. Mary's property, he eventually began a process of legal harassment that would take several years to conclude, and which would be the model for the legal impediments that many Continuing parishes had to endure in order to be free of PECUSA.[149]

In early February of 1978, four parishes seceded from the Diocese of Los Angelus and its bishop, Robert C. Rusack. Fr. George H. Clendenin, rector of Holy Apostles in Glendale, though deposed from service and taken to court by Rusack, led the other parishes in forming the Alliance of Anglican Parishes.[150] A set of "Agreed Anglican Principles" was drafted in order to define what the group would stand for. The document stressed the Catholic faith as found in the Bible, Creeds, and Church Fathers; the Apostolic and male ministry; the worship and discipline of the Prayer Book; and the centrality of the Eucharist in worship.[151] On May 1, at a meeting held at St. Mary of the Angels in Hollywood, the Alliance reorganized itself as the non-geographical diocese of the Holy Trinity. During the gathering, the retired Bishop of Springfield, and past president of the ACU, Albert A. Chambers, heard nine priests vow their loyalty to him as a leader who would offer episcopal oversight to seceding parishes.[152] Chambers was perhaps the greatest unifying factor in the earliest stages of the Continuing Movement. In the same month he had confirmed twelve people at St. Peter's in Oakland, California, even though the rector of the parish, Fr. Robert S. Morse, had been inhibited by his bishop, C. Kilmer Myers.[153] Morse was the Executive Director of the ACU and Editor of the *New Oxford Review*, which had recently replaced the ACU's *American Church Union News*. Fr. Jerome F. Politzer, Press Officer for the ACU and Contributing Editor of the *New Oxford Review*, had earlier joined Fr. Morse and Fr. Graham Lesser in leading three Bay Area parishes out of PECUSA. The group of traditionalist separatists led by Morse had the advantage of not having their parish property rights challenged by their bishop.[154] The initial unity between the Diocese of the Holy Trinity and the Morse group was evidenced by Fr. Clendenin's accompaniment of Morse while traveling around the country to speak to disgruntled traditionalists who were considering leaving PECUSA, and to promote the upcoming St. Louis Congress.[155]

The FCC met with the ECM in June and agreed to work toward the same goals, but with different strategies. By this time a significant difference between the two groups had become apparent; the ECM favored the proposed new Prayer Book. A generic statement was prepared calling for more fidelity to the doctrinal and moral standards of historic Christianity. Several ECM representatives expressed their desire to attend the St. Louis Congress.[156] Fr. Robert C. Harvey of the FCC critiqued the ECM's strategy of working within the system, and predicted that they would unfortunately discover that their plans would result in their being collaborationists rather than loyalists.[157] During its August meeting, the SPBCP issued a statement of "goodwill" to the FCC and the St. Louis Congress, and urged its membership to attend.[158] Disgruntled traditionalists waited impatiently for the St. Louis event to arrive, and many of the most committed of them made plans to attend in person, while the FCC continued to work to develop a plan that would satisfy everyone involved in the burgeoning movement.

The St. Louis Congress was held at the Chase-Park Plaza Hotel from September 14 to 16, 1977. There were several estimates as to the number of churchmen that attended the meeting, ranging from as low as 1,500 to 2,000, and the FCC's President, Perry Laukhuff, estimated the attendance at approximately 1,800.[159] Historian Donald S. Armentrout recorded that there were 1,746 registered for the Congress at the hotel for the event.[160] Several PECUSA bishops attended as observers, including Presiding Bishop Allin, who attended in order to show his sympathy and concern. Other Continuing Anglican figures, such as Bishop Dees of the AOC and Bishop Clavier of the AEC, were also in attendance. Clavier complained that he and some of the others had sought to play a role in the Congress, but were instead dismissed as being invalidly consecrated bishops.[161] The leaders of the campaign to exclude the pre-St. Louis Continuers were key leaders within the FCC, which passed a resolution declaring that these groups were not to be recognized by the St. Louis Congress, purportedly due to the invalid consecrations of their bishops.[162] Three PECUSA bishops actively took part in the proceedings: Bishops Chambers, Charles F. Boynton (retired suffragan of New York), and Haden of Northern California. Haden was thus the only active bishop to participate in the activities of the Congress.[163]

The Congress opened with evening prayer and a sermon by Fr. Wayne Williamson of Glendale, California. The meeting was then convened by an opening address delivered by Perry Laukhuff. In his presidential address, Laukhuff explained the purpose of the gathering, which was to express the faith of the participants, and to offer a provisional plan and platform for a new ecclesiastical body. In an attempt to present the overall stance of the Congress, Laukhuff stated that it was neither "high church," nor "low church," but "a united Catholic witness and action for the Faith as we all received it."[164] Three keynote addresses were then given which reflected the difficult task that Laukhuff and the FCC had undertaken in trying to define what type of Anglicans the Continuers would be.

Fr. George W. Rutler, a member of the ACU's Executive Committee, defined the problem afflicting PECUSA as being not one of a crisis of authority, churchmanship, or politics, but rather that of a spiritual war, stating, "We are waging here nothing less than the battle between Christianity and secular humanism." Though this was clear enough to most of the churchmen present in St. Louis, he then strained to delineate the ills of PECUSA. On the one hand, the crisis was due to four centuries of compromises and ambiguity within Anglicanism. He then went on to commend the example of both the nineteenth-century Evangelicals and the Tractarians, and the modern day Charismatic movement. One wonders if Rutler really thought that such diverse elements could be held together in the unambiguous model that he seemed to be calling for. His espousal of the rather slippery concept of "classical Anglican Catholicism" simply continued the long suffering tradition of trying to merge the fundamentally opposed theologies of, say, a Tractarian who believed in baptismal regeneration and the real presence of Christ in the "mass," and an evangelical who considered both of these beliefs to be either errant or blasphemous. That Rutler was a rather High-churchman cannot be doubted, for he would convert to Rome within a few short years, eventually becoming an influential speaker on the Roman Catholic EWTN (Eternal Word Television Network). However, his address appears to have been intended to offer both Catholic and

Protestant churchmen a place within the new Continuing Movement. That this was a well-intentioned attempt should not be doubted, but whether it was an effective strategy is questionable at best. Rutler's address ended with the equally ambiguous (as it would turn out) suggestion that the Continuers should consider themselves to be Catholics who happen to be Episcopalians, rather than vice versa.[165]

The next two speakers exemplified even more sharply the theological and doctrinal ambiguity that would be exhibited in St. Louis. Fr. Carroll E. Simcox, the recently retired editor of *The Living Church* and Vice-President of the FCC, addressed the moral weakness infecting PECUSA. His message was that the new body should base its morality on that of the Bible. Describing himself as "an old-fashioned Bible Christian," Simcox stated clearly that, "Anglicanism when true to itself is biblical Catholicism. Whatever is received, believed, taught, and enjoined …as essential doctrine or as Christian morality must be rooted and grounded in Holy Scripture."[166] Professor Thomas G. Barnes then delivered an address that stressed the essentially un-catholic view that the laity should play a strong role in church leadership and administration. He also envisioned a very tolerant form of Anglicanism in which only a few basic and easy to establish doctrines would be required of its members, and in which the only material bond of unity would be a common Prayer Book liturgy.[167] Although both Simcox and Barnes, along with many other members of the FCC, described themselves as Catholics, the Catholicism that they were espousing was quite different from that of many of the High-churchmen present at the St. Louis Congress. The Simcox-Barnes type of Anglican Catholicism was either that which is usually termed *Reformed Catholicism*, in which Catholicism is defined simply as the maintenance of the apostolic episcopate and belief in the Bible and creeds, or that known as *Anglo-Catholicism*, which defines Catholicism in terms of worship and ritualism. The way in which the term "catholic" was casually used by many in St. Louis belied the essentially Broad to Low-Church nature of many of the statements made during the Congress, and would contribute to the long term confusion of many Continuers, as well as having negative repercussions in the history of the Continuing Movement.

The second day of the Congress began with Morning Prayer and a sung Eucharist, which had been preceded by a procession of priests, and then the entry of Bishops Chambers, Boynton, and Haden. Chambers was the chief celebrant of the service, and Fr. Jerome Politzer delivered the sermon.[168] Although only ministers in sympathy with the event were allowed to participate in the service, all people in attendance were allowed to receive communion, and many of those present considered Presiding Bishop Allin's receiving of Communion at the hand of Chambers to be a sign of his empathy with the Continuers, even though Allin had had his request to address the gathering rejected.[169] The afternoon of the second day was taken up with workshops dealing with assorted topics; the legal problems involved in securing the property of seceding parishes, clergy pensions, clergy placement, forming new parishes, ministering to those churchmen who were isolated from a Continuing parish, and the status of the Canadians who had separated from their national church. A series of short speeches followed during which assorted traditionalist churchmen expressed their frustrations with PECUSA. Among those speaking were some of the major players in both the past and future of the Continuing Movement, including Fr. Carmino de Catanzaro, Fr. George H. Clendenin, and Dorothy Faber.[170] Their grievances included the manner in which the Bishop Pike affair had been handled by the PECUSA bishops, the GCSP controversy, Prayer Book revision, and the opening of the priesthood to women. Later in the day, representatives from the Diocese of the Holy Trinity elected Fr. James O. Mote as the first bishop of the new Movement, perhaps the most fitting choice since he had been the first priest to withdraw from PECUSA after the 1976 General Convention.

The final day was devoted to the presentation of a statement, titled *The Affirmation of St. Louis*, which proposed the principles upon which the new ecclesiastical body was to be organized. The participants were told that their local parishes would have to return home, pray, discuss the document, and then decide whether or not to affirm their membership in the new body. The proposed name of the new body was also unveiled; the Anglican Church in North America (Episcopal), often referred to as the ACNA. It was also made known that the new body would not officially come into being until a number of yet-to-be-formed dioceses had drawn-up and ratified a church constitution at some point in the near future. Just prior to this, Bishop Chambers had explained his intended role as the Episcopal visitor to the Diocese of the Holy Trinity, and then introduced Bishop-elect Mote to the Congress amid loud applause. Mote stated that he had "prayed fervently the good Lord wouldn't lay this on me."[171] Perry Laukhuff announced that three bishops would eventually be sought out to consecrate Mote. The St. Louis Congress was then drawn to a close with a Eucharist celebrated by Bishop Haden, which included a sermon by Fr. Robert Morse in which he implored those present to, "join us, march with us into the desertfor God calls us to himself!"[172]

The press coverage of the St. Louis Congress was quite extensive, included the television networks, and resulted in the PECUSA schism being voted by the Religion Newswriters Association as the top religion story of 1977. The Episcopal schism bested the Evangelical "born again" movement, the concern over cults such as the Moonies, and Archbishop Mercel Lefebvre's dispute with the Roman Catholic Church.[173] The coverage was accurate for the most part, but often exhibited more sympathy among the press for the PECUSA liberals, with whom they shared a similar worldview, than the Continuers. The *Christian Century*, the standard bearer for liberal Protestantism, described the Congress as "the Old Schism Trail," and mentioned that armed guards were present outside the Congress due to the hotel's policy regarding "controversial" meetings.[174] Bishop David B. Reed attended the Congress and stated plainly what many of more liberal temperament clearly thought of the proceedings, "It was too negative, lacked appropriate leadership, and was obviously attended by people with too great a diversity of interest to have great inner strength. There seemed to be a notable lack of Gospelrepentance, redemption, grace, hope and above all charity."[175] However, for most of those involved, the St. Louis Congress was, to a great extent, the peak of the Continuing Movement, and one of the fondest memories of their lives within the Continuum. The attendees left St. Louis full of confidence and convinced that they were embarking on a prophetic adventure.

Little attention was paid at the time to the fact that the *Affirmation of St. Louis* was a compromise document that contained the hidden seeds of future disagreements and ecclesiastical splits. The document had been created by a committee formed by the FCC, which had engaged in a long process of study and review that resulted in several drafts and revisions.[176] It was not only the seriousness of the document's intended purpose that made its drafting so difficult, but also the emergence of the age-old tension between Catholic and Protestant interpretations of Anglicanism. The FCC had been organized at the behest of the Catholic-minded ACU and Canon Albert J. duBois, but many among the FCC's leadership, coming largely from the South, were more orientated toward a Protestant or Broad to Low-church understanding of Anglicanism.

This tension is evident in the ambiguous standards set forth in the *Affirmation*. The document was clearly intended to placate a largely High-church, Catholic-minded ecclesiastical body. The *Affirmation* accepted as a standard for doctrine the "Tradition of the Church and its teachings as set forth by the ancient catholic bishops and doctors, and especially as defined by the Seven Ecumenical Councils of the undivided Church, to the exclusion of all errors, ancient and modern." The concluding words to this section on Church Tradition ("to the exclusion of all errors, ancient and modern") could have only been meant to be confusing and ambiguous, to keep all sides at the table. Was this a reference to the teachings of ancient heretics, as the Catholic-minded could interpret the words, or was it instead a reference to those parts of the Ecumenical Council dogmas and decisions that the Protestant-minded dismiss as being non-Biblical or heretical (such as the ever-virginity of Mary or the real presence in the Eucharist)? Likewise, the sacraments were numbered at seven, thus pleasing the Catholic-minded, but then the "necessity" of Baptism and the Eucharist was emphasized, mimicking the old Protestant practice, enshrined in the Prayer Book Catechism, of referring to these sacraments as those "necessary for salvation." The wizardry of Cranmer's double-speak liturgy was echoed in the *Affirmation's* catholic description of the Eucharist as both "His Body and Blood" and a sacrifice, while simultaneously maintaining the old Protestant insistence on the "all-sufficient Sacrifice of Christ on the Cross,"[177] which is normally used to dismiss the Catholic understanding of the Eucharist as being a sacrifice. The *Affirmation of St. Louis* ended up being a manifesto for those who wished to "continue" the Episcopal Church as it had been constituted at some difficult-to-determine time prior to the Minneapolis

Convention. Its authors sought to continue the tradition of co-existence between High and Low-church parties, and, probably naively, assumed that it was possible to have a church both reformed (in a Protestant sense) and Catholic. The difficulty arose when it became apparent that those who eventually joined the ACNA were not only some of the most dedicated activists for traditionalism, but often also those who were most staunchly committed to a precisely defined dogmatic and theological position. Especially committed were those who held to an extreme form of Anglican Catholicism that seeks to reconstruct Anglicanism on the model of the pre-Great Schism period of the eleventh-century, undivided Church. It seems that, in retrospect, a clash of strong wills was inevitable from the very conclusion of the St. Louis Congress.

The dust had hardly settled from the traditionalist triumph in St. Louis when Bishop Haden, whom the ACNA was counting on to be one of the consecrators of Bishop-elect Mote, withdrew his endorsement, and was soon followed in this backpedaling by Fr. Richard W. Ingalls, who had resigned from his presidency of the FCT.[178] As the Congress attendees returned home to begin planning and organizing for the formation of ACNA, the PECUSA House of Bishops held its annual meeting in Port St. Lucie, Florida, from September 30 to October 7. Presiding Bishop Allin opened the meeting by addressing himself to the recent Congress he had attended in St. Louis. He criticized those bishops who had initiated legal actions against seceding parishes in civil courts. He also suggested that the House of Bishops should give pastoral help to the dissidents by offering to consecrate a bishop for them.[179] He then stunned the gathering by announcing that he had not yet been able to accept the ordination of women, and that, if the bishops felt that his objection to women priests would harm the national church, he would be willing to resign. Perhaps sensing that the resignation of Allin might alarm and disturb those who, though still uncomfortable with the recent major changes, had remained within PECUSA, the bishops quickly worked out a compromise that came to be known as the "conscience clause." This clause allowed for bishops who remained opposed to the ordination of women to go unpunished for refusing to ordain priestesses or employ them in their diocese. The other issue at hand, and of interest to the Continuers, was the repudiation of Bishop Chambers by the House of Bishops. The bishops refused to censure Chambers, but they decried his actions, which primarily consisted of his having transgressed the diocesan boundaries of other bishops while ministering to the separated parishes. Interestingly, Chambers refused to promise that he would cease his activities with the separatists, and he generally chastised his fellow bishops for their long history of failing to discipline doctrinally unsound bishops such as Bishop Pike.[180] The bishops ended their discussions of the dissidents by directing Presiding Bishop Allin to appoint a committee that would seek possible avenues for reconciliation.[181] Among the repercussions from the Port St. Lucie meeting was a renewed sense among the Continuers that they perhaps had powerful forces within PECUSA that were very sympathetic to their position, and that they had succeeded in forcing the retrenchment of liberal Episcopalians, many of whom thought that Allin's actions were disgraceful and that the conscience clause was a copout by the bishops.[182]

The fledgling, provisional ACNA began to gather momentum in the weeks following the St. Louis Congress. Groups of individual churchmen and entire parishes began meeting together for the purpose of forming provisional dioceses within which they could come to a decision regarding the *Affirmation*. A gathering of 75 clergy and laymen, from Michigan, Indiana, Ohio, and Kentucky met on October 22 in Columbus, Ohio, to begin the formation of the Diocese of the Midwest. The *Affirmation of St. Louis* was adopted by a unanimous vote, and plans were made to start the process of creating Canons for the new diocese.[183] A group representing parishes from Alabama, North and South Carolina, Georgia, and Florida met two days later to begin a similar process for forming the Diocese of the Southeast.[184] A group of nearly 200 Continuers met in Salem, Massachusetts in November to discuss the possibility of forming a Diocese of the East, and another group met in Charlottesville, Virginia to form the Virginia Conference of the Church, which was meant to become another ACNA diocese.[185]

The second diocese to form itself officially (Diocese of the Holy Trinity being first) was the Diocese of Christ the King in Glendale, California on December 10. Fr. Robert S. Morse was elected to be the first bishop.[186] The Diocese of Christ the King (DCK) was organized along the same non-geographical basis as was the Diocese of the Holy Trinity (DHT), meaning that any parish in the United States could ostensibly place itself under the oversight of one of these dioceses. The formation of the DCK provides another example of the basic problem that plagued the formation of the ACNA: the continued disagreement between Catholic and Protestant-minded traditionalists. This must be stressed because much of the commentary from within the Continuing Movement has maintained that the problems stemmed mostly from petty personality clashes among prominent Continuing churchmen, or the thirst for power by egomaniacal Continuing bishops. However, the DCK appears to have been formed precisely because the issue of churchmanship had already begun to alter the initial course of the post-St. Louis organizing. As was mentioned earlier, Canon duBois had organized Anglicans United in order to form a traditionalist Anglican province that could eventually be absorbed into one of the established Apostolic churches. The leadership of the newly formed DHT was, unfortunately for the organizers of the St. Louis Congress (the FCC), largely led by priests who were committed to the AU program. An account of the situation by Dorothy Faber, who worked closely with the FCC inner circle and the Southern Phalanx, reveals (despite herself) the true nature of what probably occurred. When the FCC discovered that the AU priests "virtually controlled" the DHT, the FCC leadership held a "synod" of the DHT the night before the St. Louis Congress, and established the "new DHT." Fr. Mote was also selected to be the bishop of this "new" diocese. The ease with which Faber could gloss over the fact that a synod had been held for a diocese in which some of its leadership was not present, and the apparent lack of suspicion by most Continuing churchmen regarding such an action, exhibits the degree to which the Southern Phalanx had come to dominate the post-1976 Continuing Movement.[187] Further collaboration of the possibility that the Southern Phalanx essentially orchestrated a restructuring of the DHT by way of veiled manipulations of the diocese is found in a news item from *The Living Church* that refers to Mote being chosen as the bishop for DHT during a September "meeting of the Fellowship of Concerned Churchmen."[188] In fairness to those who formed the second DHT, it is possible that Canon duBois' group could have been acting less than honorably, and perhaps even misleading churchmen within the first DHT about the nature of their plans for their flock. Unfortunately, the Southern Phalanx's actions regarding the DHT would turn out to be just one of many instances in which Continuing churchmen stretched the truth and bent the rules in order to bring about their own particular vision as to what constituted an authentic Continuing Anglican church.

    Complicating matters further was the fact that Fr. Morse was the Executive Director of the ACU at the time that Canon duBois had formed AU, and there was strong disagreement between them as to what constituted a genuinely reformed Episcopal Church. Fr. Morse was also a strongly High-church Anglican, but he didn't think that it was necessary to join the Roman, Orthodox, or Old Catholic Communions while maintaining an Anglican rite, as Canon duBois seemed to favor. Morse was also the Executive Director of the ACU when it had approached Perry Laukhuff and less Catholic groups of churchmen to form the FCC in the hope of defeating the legalization of women priests. However, the FCC, due to the very makeup of its constituency, was destined to push for a less Catholic body than many members of the ACU would probably have preferred. Morse had continued to participate in the formation of the ACNA, but he couldn't have helped but notice that the Low-church wing of the FCC (the Southern Phalanx) was beginning to take over the effective leadership of the Movement, and that, consequently, the ACNA might turn out to be too Low-church for his taste. Consequently, the DCK seems to have been formed in part with the intention of hindering the likelihood of a Low-church rump developing after the ACNA had become an ecclesiastical reality. In addition, Morse may have wished to provide a structure into which Catholic-minded churchmen could enter if they felt left out by an overly Protestant-minded ACNA, and therefore only left with the alternative offered by Canon duBois.

    The third diocese to be established was the Diocese of the Southeast (DOS) on December 16. The DOS elected Fr. Peter F. Watterson of Tampa, Florida to be its first bishop. Around the same time, the Diocese of the Midwest (DMW) was officially constituted, but they did not initially elect a bishop. On January 7, 1978, the Virginia Conference of the Church organized itself as the Diocese of the Mid-Atlantic States (DMAS) in Charlottesville, Virginia. Although the DMAT did not elect a bishop at that time, the

DMW finally elected Fr. Charles Dale Doren of Pennsylvania to be its first bishop. Thus, by the end of the first week of 1978, the dissidents had created five (or six?) dioceses, all of which had voted to accept the Affirmation of St. Louis, and they had elected four bishops. All of this had been accomplished within a dizzying period of three and one half months.[189] Even more taxing than all of these accomplishments, however, was the process of finding two more bishops who would be willing to perform the consecrations of the bishops elected by the new Movement (Bishop Chambers had already agreed to do so).

The reality in the immediate aftermath of the St. Louis Congress was that only one more bishop would have to be found to perform the consecrations for the Continuing bishops since Bishop Haden was assumed to be willing to join with Chambers in the service. The initial process was complicated even before the St. Louis Congress had met because PECUSA officials had already begun contacting their own bishops, as well as those in the Polish National Catholic Church, imploring them to have nothing to do with the new movement. Nonetheless, Bishop Boynton had expressed to the FCC during the St. Louis Congress his willingness to join in the future consecrations. Unfortunately, and for reasons that remain unknown, Bishop Haden withdrew his support of the new movement during the House of Bishops meeting in Port St. Lucie. After receiving many rejections, by mid-November of 1977 the ACNA had finally gained the consent of Bishop Mark Pae of Korea to participate as a consecrator. Bishop Pae's identity had been withheld to all but a few insiders in order to avoid any obstructionist machinations on the part of PECUSA. The date for the consecrations was set for January, which pushed the newly formed dioceses to work even harder and faster. The PECUSA establishment was no doubt relieved when the identity of the third consecrator was leaked to *The Episcopalian*. They began, with the help of the Archbishop of Canterbury, to threaten Bishop Pae that he would be removed from the Anglican Communion if he participated in the consecrations for the schismatic group. Almost simultaneously, another difficulty arose when Bishop Boynton's health deteriorated to the point that he was not allowed by his doctor to attend the service. It was felt by many Continuers that the pressure applied on him by PECUSA officials had played a significant role in bringing about his debility. However, unknown to all but a few insiders, another man, Bishop Francisco J. Pagtakhan of the Philippine Independent Church, had agreed to participate in the consecrations, which had now been officially set for January 28, 1978, in Denver, Colorado.[190]

Meanwhile, the faction of the DHT that had been maneuvered out of their leadership of the diocese continued to maintain a fragile relationship with the wider movement, largely by way of its continual reference to itself as the Executive Committee of the DHT.[191] There was some thought within this Executive Committee that it would seek to have Canon duBois consecrated as one of the ACNA bishops. However, as they watched the formation of the other dioceses and the election of the other bishops, this Executive Committee began to protest that it did not approve of the whole process. Their specific complaint against the direction in which the ACNA was heading seems to have been that the new group would not be officially recognized by any church that possessed the apostolic succession.[192] The *Affirmation of St. Louis* had stated that the ACNA would consider itself in communion with the other churches in the Anglican Communion, but the events of the preceding months had made the likelihood of that occurrence seem implausible. On January 7, 1978, the Executive Committee led by duBois then held a meeting at St. Mary of the Angels in Los Angeles, California, during which they re-designated themselves as the Convocation of the West Coast of the Diocese of the Holy Trinity (CWC), and then elected Canon duBois to be their bishop. The purpose of this action was to press their case as a legitimate diocese within the ACNA, and to have duBois consecrated in Denver.

At this point the matter became somewhat confusing. Reportedly, Bishop Chambers refused to consecrate duBois because he was too old according to the canons of the Episcopal Church, which require a bishop to retire at the age of 72. However, duBois claimed that he was refused consecration for purely personal reasons on the part of Chambers.[193] The *Christian Century* seemed to confirm that the question of age was somehow involved when it quoted the newly consecrated Bishop Mote as predicting that Canon duBois would never be consecrated because of his advanced age.[194] However, according to another account, the CWC had "demanded" that duBois be consecrated along with the other four bishops, and Chambers had simply ignored both the threat and the CWC. This would seem to be a rather strange explanation since some of the CWC people were included in the program as major participants in the consecration service. For instance, duBois was listed as the crozier bearer. The question remains as to why duBois would even be invited to Denver since his group had already been positioned outside of the "official" DHT for quite some time, and especially after the formation of the CWC only a few weeks earlier. One source stated that duBois chose not to attend the Denver event, but the question remains as to why he would even be invited to take part in the service if he and his group had engaged in the unseemly practices that had supposedly made it necessary to form the "new DHT" at St. Louis?[195] It is quite possible that duBois and his group's status within the ACNA had actually been an unresolved matter for many churchmen due to doubts as to the validity of the FCC's actions in St.

Louis, and that Bishop Chambers helped the Southern Phalanx clean up the potential messy situation by simply denying him consecration on Canonical grounds, rather than risking a confrontation over the legitimate constituency of the DHT. This must remain speculation, but the CWC responded to the snub of duBois by issuing several statements questioning the legitimacy of both the newly formed dioceses and their elected bishops, as well as withholding their support for the Denver consecrations.

Complicating matters even further was a report that Bishop-elect Mote had received a telegram from the CWC offering their blessing to the consecration service, perhaps because they were purported to have claimed that they were assured that "there would be adherence to some catholic or orthodox body."[196] If this actually occurred as it was reported, than either Bishop Mote and the Southern Phalanx were fabricating something, or the whole affair is nearly too confusing to be recounted with certainty.[197] On February 2, 1978, in Sun Valley, California, the CWC announced that it would re-constitute itself as the Diocese of Saint Augustine of Canterbury, and would seek to retain its Anglican liturgy and forms after having joined another apostolic jurisdiction.[198] Though it would take a few years, duBois and five parishes were eventually received into the Roman Catholic Church as "Anglican-Rite" parishes.[199]

By the time the Denver consecrations took place, Chambers and Pagtakhan were the only two bishops physically present, but Bishop-elect Doren had returned from Korea with a letter from Bishop Pae expressing Pae's consent to the consecration of Doren. The service was held on January 28, 1978, at the Augustana Lutheran Church, which was the second choice for a facility, since the Roman Catholic Church had denied the use of its local cathedral due to their ecumenical relationship with PECUSA's Diocese of Colorado.[200] Approximately 1,400 people attended the ceremony, which was recorded by network and local television crews, all of whom witnessed a grand and colorful Missal Service. Doren displayed a bishop's mitre that had been presented to him by Pae, and three items that were gifts from the clergy of Pae's diocese; two bishop's rings and a pectoral cross inscribed with the words, "Bishop Dale David Doren." Pae's letter was then read aloud, and Chambers accepted it as expressing the will of Pae. Doren was then consecrated by Chambers, with Pagtakhan acting as co-consecrator, and then Doren, acting as the third bishop, assisted in the consecrations of Bishops-elect Morse, Mote, and Watterson. When the four new bishops were presented to the crowd, a loud and lengthy mixture of cheers and applause filled the church. Pagtakhan then surprised everyone by reading a message sent with him from the Supreme Council of Bishops of the Philippine Independent Catholic Church (PICC), awarding Chambers and "his group" the Bishop Aglipay Cross for their courage in maintaining the Catholic Faith. The Cross had been named for the first Supreme Bishop of the PICC, and had only been awarded once before, to a former Archbishop of Canterbury, Arthur Michael Ramsay.[201] During a press conference after the ceremony, the new bishops answered questions and reiterated their reasons for leaving PECUSA, and even engaged in some colorful prognostication. Morse predicted that, within fifty years, theirs would be the only Episcopal Church in existence, since PECUSA would most probably dissolve into the grand unification scheme of COCU.[202] Mote stated that the group would have 100,000 members by mid-year, and eventually one million.[203]

Although the membership of the provisional ACNA was ecstatic since it now considered itself to be under the guidance of validly consecrated bishops, the reactions from outside the Movement were uniformly cynical and, in the case of those in PECUSA, designed to undermine confidence in the new group. Within a few hours of the consecrations, the Archbishop of Canterbury, Donald Coggan, announced that he would not recognize the validity of the consecrations or any group formed out of them.[204] Immediately, PECUSA bishops also dismissed the consecrations as being invalid, mostly on the grounds that the service lacked the three consecrators required in the Canons,[205] but also with the accusation that two of the consecrators acted fraudulently. The ACNA supporters responded to the first charge by appealing to instances in Church history in which only one bishop had performed a consecration, or in which Ecumenical Councils had decided that it was permissible for one bishop to consecrate a new bishop when difficult or grave situations had left no other choice.[206] However, discounting the more serious accusations would prove to be a more involved and complicated task.

The accusations against Doren stemmed from the decision of Pae, most assuredly under even greater pressure from Anglican authorities, to deny to a *Time* magazine reporter that he had given the letter of consent to Doren. Chambers dismissed the charges, pointing out that the message was written in the same handwriting as that found in three other letters that had come from Pae's own hand.[207] Doren was essentially accused of manufacturing a letter of consent, and of obtaining his episcopal gifts by way of either deceit or forgery. Making matters worse for the ACNA, nearly simultaneous with the controversy surrounding Doren's consecration, Pagtakhan was accused of misrepresenting his role as a representative of the PICC and, therefore, of not having the jurisdictional backing that is required in order for a consecration to be valid. Pagtakhan claimed that he had asked the Supreme Bishop of the PICC, Bishop Ga, if it would be a good idea if Pagtakhan participated in the Denver consecration service, and according to

Pagtakhan, Ga had expressed his approval of the proposition. However, Ga and the Supreme Council of the PICC issued a statement on February 9, 1978, denying that they had given their consent to Pagtakhan's participation in the Denver ceremony.[208] Most of those within the St. Louis Continuing Movement believed that both Pae and Ga had been pressured into reversing themselves out of fear of ecclesiastical sanctions from the other churches in the Anglican Communion. In the case of Pae, this was quite probably true, but few at the time knew that Ga's actions reflected a deep divide within the PICC that would eventually result in a schism. The bishop who authorized the bestowing of the "Bishop Aglipay Cross" to Chambers, Manuel L. LaGasca, was in the second highest position in the PICC, and apparently represented a significant faction of PICC bishops who were opposed to Ga's leadership. The fact that LaGasca telegrammed Pagtakhan to inform him that the Supreme Council had not taken any action against him, and thus denied that the Supreme Council itself had sent the message refuting the PICC's affiliation with the Denver consecrations, meant that there was clearly disagreement among the Philippine bishops as to who was really in charge.[209] Unfortunately, no mention of the PICC's bestowal of the special cross to the St. Louis Continuers appeared in sources other than those who were in sympathy with the Continuing Movement, and the general impression left with many, both inside and outside of PECUSA, was that the consecrations were surrounded by scandal and serious questions as to their validity.

The secretary-general of the Anglican Consultative Council,[210] Bishop John Howe, expressed his doubt that any consecrations had actually taken place, claiming that neither Chambers nor Pagtakhan had been authorized by their parent bodies to perform the consecrations.[211] The St. Louis Continuers seem to have paid little attention to such critiques of their episcopal orders. The most common criticism was that the Canonical and traditional requirement for three consecrators was not met in the Denver event. Probably the best argument made against this claim was that there existed examples throughout the history of the Church in which single-bishop consecrations had been performed, but only when necessitated by a grave or unusual circumstance that called for such an exemption. The St. Louis Continuers claimed that their situation met the criteria for such an exemption from the norm. As Thomas G. Barnes noted, "If any situation in the history of the Church constituted extreme necessity this one did. The band that came together at St. Louis...was forced to turn to the few bishops who had the courage of the Faith to continue the Apostolic Succession for the new branch. Without the continuity of the Apostolic Succession, the new branch could not remain Catholic." Barnes also noted that Chambers was in his seventies and in bad health at the time, and being the only bishop firmly committed to the consecrations for the new branch of the Catholic Church, the St. Louis Continuers did not have the luxury of taking a longer amount of time to find the normal three consecrators.[212] In retrospect, it is somewhat surprising that the St. Louis Continuers did not seem to be especially concerned over the questions regarding the validity of their orders. However, most of the sources left by these churchmen derive from what one critic labeled "the FCC-FCT propaganda apparatus,"[213] (referred to in this work as the Southern Phalanx), and there seems to have been little concern among their largely Low-church ranks over the delicate theological definitions of Apostolic Succession.

In many ways the Denver consecrations can be seen as the conclusion of the St. Louis Congress, since they represent the last point at which most of the St. Louis Continuers were still jurisdictionally united. In the view of those who remained within PECUSA, the Denver consecrations had placed the St. Louis Continuers in the same position as those separatists who had gone before them (Dees, Clavier, et al), namely, beyond the pale. There would be little interaction between the St. Louis Continuers and PECUSA from that point onward. Bishop Chambers was asked by Presiding Bishop Allin and the other PECUSA bishops to resign, and when Chambers refused, he was tried by the House of Bishops, ultimately being censured rather than convicted, and reached an agreement with the bishops in which he promised not to participate in any more schismatic actions.[214] Ironically, the circle had been closed, and the church (PECUSA) that lacked the sense of orthodoxy required to depose a heretical bishop (Pike) now proved that their liberal, guiding spirit of comprehensiveness also lacked the spine to depose a bishop who openly admitted to creating a schismatic body. In the ecclesiastical fellowship that was the PECUSA church, you could be against the orthodox definition of God, and against the Church itself, and still remain an Episcopalian. The St. Louis Continuers considered themselves blessed to have found the courage to leave an ecclesiastical body with such porous boundaries, and they seemed confident that theirs was a bright future.

Chapter 6

THE DALLAS SYNOD

Having drafted a document containing principles around which the St. Louis Continuers could ostensibly unite, and having formed four dioceses for the purpose of electing bishops, and then having these Bishops-elect consecrated in January of 1978, the next step in the process of officially establishing the Anglican Church in North America was to draft and vote on a church Constitution and Canons. The first Synod of the provisional church was scheduled for October of 1978 in Dallas, Texas, and it was agreed that the Constitution and Canons for the new body would be finalized during this meeting. In April of 1978, the four bishops (Doren, Mote, Morse, and Watterson) met in West Palm Beach, Florida, purportedly to discuss the ways in which they would work together so that order could be maintained within the new body. Of particular importance, an accord was reportedly reached in which each bishop agreed that no new dioceses could be formed, and no new bishops elected, until the council of bishops (the four bishops present in West Palm Beach) had agreed to such changes or additions.[215] Importantly, only the supporters of Bishops Morse and Watterson would later emphasize this meeting, and the supporters of the other bishops (especially the Southern Phalanx) strangely seem to be unaware of or uncommitted to it. According to *The Christian Challenge,* the only development from the Florida meeting was an announcement by the bishops that they were uniformly opposed to abortion, fornication, and the ordination of women and homosexuals to the priesthood."²¹⁶

It appears that shortly after the Florida meeting of the bishops, Doren and Mote decided to move in a direction that contradicted the status quo that Morse and Watterson seem to have assumed had been established. The trouble arose when Mote's Deanery in the lower Northeast, only a few weeks after the Florida Bishop's meeting, and with no announcement to the rest of the church, or to Morse and Watterson, organized a diocesan meeting for the stated purpose of fostering unity and inspiration within the Diocese of the Holy Trinity. For some reason it was decided by Mote and the Deanery that it should organize itself as a separate body to be called the Diocese of the Resurrection, which would be comprised of parishes in New York, New Jersey, and Eastern Pennsylvania. Fr. William Francis Burns of New Jersey was then elected to be the proposed diocese's first bishop. However, a challenge was brought from within the boundaries of the new diocese, charging that a diocese could not be formed without an announcement and invitation being given to all who may be interested in attending. Mote responded by calling an official Synod of the new diocese, and Fr. Burns was once again elected, or "reaffirmed," as a new bishop. Even though Morse and Watterson were displeased at the violation of the Florida accords, they reportedly agreed to overlook the matter for the sake of peace within the church.

At nearly the same time, Bishop Doren began requesting that his Midwest Diocese be allowed to elect a Suffragan bishop. The Council of Bishops had already denied permission to Doren regarding the matter on three separate occasions, and Doren had been appointed, along with Morse, to consult the Canadian Continuers as to whether or not they wished to join the Anglican Church in North America. Morse reported back to the other bishops that the Canadians indeed wished to organize their own

Canadian diocese. Doren apparently issued no report, and instead proceeded to gain the support of his diocese for the election of a Suffragan bishop, Fr. Carmine J. deCatanzaro of Ottowa, Canada.[217] Thus the promises made in Florida had apparently been broken by two of the bishops, and the prospects of retaining a united St. Louis Continuing Movement began to dim.

An obvious divide between Morse and Watterson (who were more concerned with a Catholic understanding of theology and churchmanship), and Doren and Mote (who were more concerned with a Broad and Low-Church Episcopalian understanding of orthodoxy), was now apparent. There is no difficulty in understanding the concern of Morse and Watterson over the actions of their fellow bishops, which could be interpreted as trying to stack the Episcopal deck against them, so to speak. Obviously, if there were more dioceses headed by bishops who were either Broad or Low-church at the upcoming Dallas Synod, the chance of a more Catholic structure being enacted would be more remote. How else could Morse and Watterson have interpreted Doren's actions, in which he proceeded to have another bishop elected after having been previously denied this course of action by the Council of Bishops? It would be interesting to know the "other" side of the story, but the primary sources that generally interpreted Doren and Mote's actions (mainly publications that gave voice to the Phalanx) failed to mention anything about the issues that most concerned Morse and Watterson. There is a possibility that the assertions made by Morse and Watterson regarding the period between their Florida meeting and the Dallas Synod were simply untrue, but the charges do not seem to have been answered by the other side, and instead seem to have been ignored.[218]

Another difficulty developed over the issue of the organization of the Diocese of the Southwest in July of

1978. While Bishops' Mote, Morse, and Watterson were in England trying unsuccessfully to attend the Lambeth Conference, a group of churchmen, reportedly led by the FCC's Dorothy Faber, held a meeting in Plano, Texas, for the purpose of organizing a new diocese. Without informing the bishops of their meeting, or of their intent to form a diocese, the Texas group attempted to elect a bishop the same day that they had officially created the new diocese.[219] After the fourth unsuccessful ballot to choose between Fr. Mark Holliday of Texas and Fr. Ralph Pressley of Oklahoma, a decision was reached to search the local neighborhood for a child who would be asked, with no knowledge of its purpose, to draw from two lots that had been placed in a chalice. The child drew Fr. Holliday's name, thus making him the Bishop-elect of the new Diocese of the Southwest (DSW).[220] The Texas meeting involved a small number of parishes,[221] and three priests, including one who reportedly had been divorced and remarried. However, perhaps because of the loss of the election for the office of bishop, the two parishes and one priest from Oklahoma withdrew from the new diocese soon after the meeting was adjourned. Thus the DSW was constituted with, at the most, seven parishes.

The new diocese proceeded to put forward the proposition that it should be seated on an equal basis with the original four dioceses during the upcoming Constitutional Synod in October. A committee, comprised mostly of members of the Fellowship of Concerned Churchmen, had been appointed by the bishops to create the plans for the upcoming Synod, and especially to draft a provisional version of the Constitution to be presented for review by the delegates in Dallas. During its last scheduled meeting before the Dallas Synod, the committee met in Des Plaines, Illinois. During the first session of the meeting, the committee was forced to come to a decision as to the standing of the DSW. The four bishops consulted with each other during the lunch break, and reached an agreement that placed restrictions on the new diocese if it were to be seated as a voting diocese at the forthcoming Synod. The DSW was required to have as many parishes and clergy in its jurisdiction by the time of the Synod as had the smallest of the original dioceses at the time of their founding. If this condition was met, the DSW was then to be limited to a reasonable geographic area for its boundaries. The debate over the DSW that occurred in the morning session seemed to carry over into the afternoon session as the Constitution drafted by Fr. Francis Read and Richard E. Clark, both of whom were sympathetic to the position of Morse and Watterson, was rejected in favor of one drafted by Canon F. Andrew Stahl of Canada. Unfortunately, the committee did not have the time to properly review the new draft, which still had not been completed. On the meeting's final day, Doren read a statement in which he criticized the other bishops (calling their actions unChristian and uncharitable) for placing restrictions and conditions on the admittance of the DSW. Consequently, Watterson began to doubt that the draft Constitution could be properly reviewed by the time of the Dallas Synod, let alone by the end of the Des Plaines meeting. He made a motion to postpone the Dallas Synod until such time as the draft Constitution could be given a proper review. The motion was defeated by force of the argument that a postponement would be too costly, in terms of both the financial issues involved and the spiritual and psychic damage that would be done to anxious churchmen if the ACNA were perceived as not having its act together. The Des Plaines committee had to appoint a subcommittee to meet ten days later in order to complete further review of the draft Constitution. This second meeting was also unable to complete its review of the document. Andrew Stahl and E.J. LaRoque were given the task of completing it on their own and making it available to the Dallas delegates in time for everyone to have made a complete review and evaluation of the document.

The DSW spent the last two months before the Dallas Synod franticly trying to meet the requirements that had been placed on them by the bishops in order to be given standing as an official diocese. Bishop Mote, who it will be remembered was alleged to have assumed the bishopric of the Diocese of the Holy Trinity by means of the Phalanx's effective reconstitution of that diocese, proceeded to "transfer" some of his parishes to the jurisdiction of the DSW. Two Continuing priests further came forward to issue letters stating their willingness and intention to transfer to the DSW.[222] The basic motive of those involved with the DSW seems to have been the desire to ensure that the theological and structural composition of the church to be established in Dallas would not be according to the model that Morse and Watterson seemed intent on seeing implemented, i.e., a more Catholic structure.

The message coming out of the Phalanx from Continuum media outlets tried to sow seeds of suspicion among laymen towards a potential power-grab by the bishops. In an "Open Letter" that had to have been composed at nearly the same time that she was playing a leading role in the formation of the DSW, Dorothy Faber counseled the bishops and priests not to construct the church on the lines of a powerful Episcopate. She reminded them that the laymen of the St. Louis movement had suffered under the arbitrary actions of their "ruthless" leaders in the Episcopal Church. With the painful experience of the laity in mind, Mrs. Faber warned, "It would…be a mistake to expect these people to accept an authoritarian church structure that is not based on spiritual leadership." She further explained, "They look to Christ as the authority in their lives, and to their bishops and priests as they preach and teach His

Gospel and offer their lives to His service."[223] In the issue of *The Christian Challenge* that appeared just in time to be read by delegates to the Dallas Synod, an address to the FCC by Perry Laukhuff, which had been delivered in May, was given a wider audience. In many ways Laukhuff echoed the thoughts of Dorothy Faber, speaking of the pesky problem of giving too much power to the bishops, "Let them [bishops] lead us by grace, not command us by arbitrary decree. We have had enough of that." In an admirable but theologically simplistic attempt to lay the groundwork for unity at the Synod, Laukhuff identified the other major problem that could derail the church: the continuance of the old debate over churchmanship. He dismissed the old divisions by reciting the "essentials" of Anglicanism: "What is it that unites us? It is common faith, common belief, common acceptance of the Creeds, the sacraments, the apostolic doctrine, the teachings of the Fathers and the undivided Church, the centrality of the Eucharist in our worship."[224] Thus, the Phalanx had presented its final message to the delegates who were heading for Dallas: they should beware of power-mad bishops trying to bully them into accepting a church structure in which the bishops are the ultimate authority, and to also be careful not to put too much significance on any of their differences of worship style or personal theological beliefs, for they should recognize how essentially united they really were. Unfortunately, few Continuing churchmen were aware at the time that the bishops who would be lionized at Dallas as the supporters of giving a greater amount of authority to the laity (Doren and Mote) had actually been the ones engaging in arbitrary ecclesiastical actions to increase their power prior to the Synod, which is what the caricature of Morse and Watterson would become.

  In late September, Watterson apparently had decided that the actions of Doren and Mote could no longer be tolerated, probably because the election of Bishop-elect deCatanzaro by the DMW had just occurred earlier in the month.[225] The problem facing the formation of the new body, according to Watterson, was "a fundamental crisis of order in the emerging Church." He decided that he could no longer agree to participate in the consecration of Fr. Burns as Bishop of the questionably constituted (in Watterson's view) Diocese of the Resurrection (DOR). Watterson sent his notification to all interested parties approximately six weeks before the consecration was to occur, but only a few weeks before the Dallas Synod.[226] That a grave crisis now threatened the ACNA should have been obvious to everyone involved in the St. Louis movement, however, the plans for the Synod were not postponed.

The Constitutional Synod met at the Sheraton Hotel in Dallas, October 18-20. According to Dorothy Faber's report on the event, the "Spirit of St. Louis" was not initially present in Dallas. Faber referred to the "troublesome rumors" that had been circulating widely during the weeks leading up to the Synod that had "confused" and "spooked" many of the delegates. The first order of business concerned the credentials committee, which was to decide if the DSW had qualified to be seated as a voting diocese. According to Faber, a debate developed between those who were concerned about the possible establishment of "prince bishops," and those who feared for the establishment of "congregational" Anglicanism. The latter group (though not identified as such by Faber) had been misled by a rumor that there had been a conspiracy "on the part of the Fellowship to 'hatch bogus dioceses' in order to be able to out-vote the Anglo-Catholic delegations." Faber dismissed the concerns about the nature of the Catholicism presented in the draft Constitution and Canons as the result of the "unfortunate" delay of the delivery of the documents into the hands of delegates until a few days before the Synod. Since the delegates had not had the proper amount of time to read and reflect on the draft documents, many of the delegates were not "aware" that the Constitution and Canons presented to them were "aimed at the establishment of a Catholic, not a congregational, church structure." There were serious and emotionally charged accusations made during the long debate that eventually concluded with the Assembly voting by a narrow margin to seat the DSW.[227] During these debates, the shaky foundations of the new dioceses and bishop elections became apparent when Fr. de Catanzaro of Canada, who had been elected by the DMW to be Doren's Suffragan, stated, "I am a Catholic first and an Anglican second. I shall live and die Catholic, and I am not going to be a Protestant under any circumstances. If this thing goes up in smoke here, I will have to make immediate contact with the Polish National Catholic Church." Clearly, Fr. de Catanzaro and Bishop Doren were not as familiar with each other's theological outlook as they probably should have been, and the responsibility for the situation resided primarily with Doren. Catanzaro would eventually turn down his election as Doren's Suggragan.[228]

The "other" version as to the facts surrounding the debate in Dallas asserted that Fr. Simcox had supposedly taken it upon himself (without consulting the bishops) to arbitrarily accept the report of the Credentials Committee, ruling that the DSW had met the proposed conditions for entry, and would therefore be seated with both voice and voting power in the Synod, and furthermore, that it possessed the right to vote on challenges to its own validity. If this version is correct, it suggests that the DSW was given voting status *before* the angry debates began, and also that, incredibly, the DSW delegates were allowed to vote on the question of their own status in an election that supposedly was intended to establish their right to vote. If this were true, it would be analogous to illegal aliens being permitted to vote in a ballot proposition to determine whether illegal aliens can vote in elections.

Despite the differing accounts as to how the DSW actually won voice and seat as an official diocese, both sides agreed that the real issue behind the conflict was the question over what kind of authority structure was to be established in the new church.[229] The Southern Phalanx and Broad-Church coalition of churchmen had pushed for a classic Episcopalian structure, to be comprised of episcopal, clerical, and lay bodies, each having voting power on all essential issues within the church. The Catholic-wing pushed for the structure that had been established in the "undivided Church of the Councils," namely, that bishops have the ultimate power of decision in the church.

The first day ended with Bishops Watterson, Morse, and Pagtakhan (who was present as an observer) going to the microphone, and Watterson announcing that he was convinced that the new Church was on the verge of being organized to function under a congregational system. He warned, "We will have nothing to do with a Church that is not Catholic and Apostolic." Then he announced that Morse and Pagtakhan would be joining him in leading the delegations of the Catholic party out of the Assembly in order to meet separately for the purpose of drafting their own Constitution and Canons. The three bishops and their delegates then walked out of the stunned room. The breaking point for the bishops had come when the Assembly had finally officially voted to seat the DSW.[230] The following morning Bishop Mote, either on his own initiative (implied by Faber) or reluctantly upon the urging of his delegation (Stenhouse's version), called for a recess in order to allow him to hold a meeting with the protesting dioceses. Eventually, a fourfold program of conditions were agreed to by both factions, which upon their reception by the Assembly, would result in a return of the departed dioceses. The first demand was that the two men who had chaired the event, and who happened to be the Chancellors for the dioceses of Doren and Mote, step down in order that the four bishops could chair the rest of the proceedings. The second demand was that the bishops be allowed to dissolve the Assembly so that their third condition (a Constitutional Synod) could take place. According to Faber, the significance of this was that in an Assembly there are no votes by Orders, and thus a bishop can not veto a proposal that he disagrees with, while in a Synod format, the bishops have this power along with the clergy and laity. The fourth request was that the DSW be denied a vote in the Synod, though they could be seated and heard.

Bishops Morse and Watterson led their delegations back to the Assembly in the early afternoon and, according to Faber, were seated after a "slight delay."[231] According to Stenhouse, various procedural maneuvers and ploys were allowed by the Chair in order to delay the Assembly from deciding on the matter of reconciliation. After his delegates had stood in the aisles for two hours, Watterson began to lead them out of the Assembly once again, but was stopped from leaving by a layman from North Carolina, who convinced the bishop that he should at least stay until a decision had been reached on the terms of reconciliation.[232] Another long period of intense debate occurred after the terms of the agreement had been read to the delegates. A delegate from the Diocese of the Mid-Atlantic States (DMAS) offered perhaps the best protestation from the Broad-church wing, stating that the St. Louis Congress had encouraged traditionalist Anglicans to proceed to form their own dioceses, but now the Assembly was being asked to reject a group of churchmen who had done just that. The only problem with the complaint is that the Catholic party agreed that the formation of dioceses was an ongoing process, but, once bishops had been consecrated for the church, the formation and structure of new dioceses were supposed to have been controlled by the bishops from that time forward. The Assembly finally voted to agree to the conditions for reconciliation that had been set before it, thus voting to dissolve itself, and recessed in order to prepare for what would now officially be called a Constitutional Synod.[233]

The third day began with Mote, acting as Chair, and flanked by the other bishops, opening the Constitutional Synod. The Synod decided to examine the Majority Document (22 pages long) that had been prepared by members of the Phalanx, rather than the Minority Document (6 pages long) that had been prepared by Fr. Francis Read and Richard E. Clark, the co-chairs of the Special Committee. This action repeated the decision reached at the Des Plaines meeting of the Special Committee. The Synod next examined and debated the proposed Constitution and Canons for the remainder of the day. Significantly, an amendment proposed by a delegate representing the DCK, which would have allowed a bishop to veto something without having to state his reasons, was defeated, as were all amendments that would, in Faber's words, "give undue power to the episcopate." After several votes, the name of the new body was changed to the Anglican Catholic Church, rather than the provisionally adapted Anglican Church in North America moniker.[234]

By 11:00 a.m. on the final day, the Solemn Declaration, The Preamble, eight of the twenty-two Articles of the Constitution, and four of the Canons had been approved by the Synod. With everyone realizing that the entire document could not be properly reviewed by the conclusion of the Synod, a motion was made to provisionally accept the rest of the Constitution and Canons until they could be adopted at the next Synod.²³⁵ A number of amendments were then proposed, mostly from the DCK and the Diocese of the Southeast (DSEUS), which were defeated. Faber described these events as taking on the "appearance of a filibuster" by those who wished to see no Constitution or Canons come from the Dallas Synod.²³⁶ Before the vote was to be taken, the delegates asked the bishops for guidance.

    Wattererson stated, "Before I came here, I thought we were not ready for Dallas, I am convinced now I was right. We were not ready to do what we are doing. But we need to go away from here with something in our hands and as united as God will allow." Mote said, "We are never really ready to adopt a constitution and canons, and politics don't bother me if it ends up good. Besides, there isn't anything in this document that isn't Catholic." Morse's only statement was rather cryptic, "God writes straight with crooked lines." Doren inexplicably declined to make a statement. The Synod voted in favor of the resolution, with Watterson joining Doren and Mote in their affirmation, and Morse tellingly abstaining.²³⁷ The task of preparing and distributing an official text of the Constitution and Canons was then given to the DHT, which by mandate of the Synod, was to have the documents prepared and distributed to the other dioceses for review within sixty days of the Synod.²³⁸ The documents would become the law of the church when four of the seven dioceses had ratified them. The weary delegates then left Dallas with what Faber described as a "fragile reunion."²³⁹ The description of the Synod given by *The Living Church* was perhaps the most fitting, "It was fascinating for most spectators, frustrating for most participants, and puzzling for most of the general public."²⁴⁰ However, by creating three new dioceses against the wishes of Morse and Watterson, and then having the Synod accept those dioceses on an equal basis with the four original dioceses that possessed consecrated bishops, the Phalanx had quite shrewdly guaranteed that the Church would be formed under terms more acceptable to their Broad to Low-Church preferences. The ratifications of the DCK and DSEUS would not even be needed, and these Catholic-minded former Episcopalians would be forced to either join with the other dioceses or go it alone. The Phalanx may have been counting on the obstructionist dioceses losing their will to obstruct the growth of the Anglican Catholic Church after being faced with the possibility of an isolated existence from the rest of the Continuing Movement. If this was their reasoning, they miscalculated.

Chapter 7

THE FORMATION OF THE ANGLICAN CATHOLIC CHURCH

For the average churchman who supported the St. Louis movement, the interpretation given to the events that occurred during the Dallas Synod depended largely on which group they were affiliated with. Watterson had strong support, but it was largely limited to the Southeastern United States. His sphere of influence was limited due to his lack of a means by which he could generate propaganda on a national level, being helped only by a diocesan paper and parish newsletters. Doren was better known nationally due to his prior missionary work in the Far East and for his strongly held Low-church convictions, and more importantly, he was affiliated with the Southern Phalanx's inner circle. In contrast to Watterson, whose influence was largely limited to his own diocese, the message of the Phalanx was promulgated widely across the nation. They had the benefit of producing, or having great influence within, several nationally distributed and widely read publications, including the *FCC Newsletter*, and especially *The Christian Challenge*, through which they could present their views and opinions concerning the new Movement to the largest number of churchmen. The vast majority of St. Louis Continuers received their only news about the Movement, outside of their small diocesan and parish newsletters, from these nationally distributed sources.

Morse had a large national following due to his presidency of the American Church Union and his development of its *American Church Union News* into *The New Oxford Review*, which was designed to reach a mostly Catholic, traditionalist audience that extended beyond the realm of Episcopalians. Thus Morse had some ability to influence the wider Movement due to the influence of his publication, but it did not reach as many Continuers as those of the Phalanx. Due to his being the first priest to lead his parish out of the post-Minneapolis Convention Episcopal Church, and his generally amiable pastoral style,[241] Mote had taken on an image in the eyes of many St. Louis Continuers across the nation that approached that of a martyr or a saint. The Phalanx had shrewdly chosen him to replace the overly Catholic Canon duBois in order to be the figurehead of the Movement. Thus it probably should not have been a surprise that both of the non-geographic dioceses (Christ the King and Holy Trinity) were led by the two bishops with the largest national exposure and following.

The Phalanx, by virtue of its status as the primary organizer (or manipulator) *and* interpreter of the St. Louis Continuing Movement, was able to create the widely accepted, semi-official version of what occurred at Dallas. The basic party line was that the dispute had been caused by renegade bishops trying to assume too much power for themselves at the expense of the laity. The theological and ecclesiastic dimensions of the conflict were largely ignored or simply dismissed as pointless squabbles over churchmanship. A churchman from Virginia wrote, "it is clear to me that we have two quite different views of the Church now operating…One is what I would call a Roman Catholic view…an authoritarian view, with the power resting in the Bishops; sort of a 'Father Knows Best' …way of looking at things. The other I would call an Anglican or perhaps *American view* [emphasis mine], which sees the Bishops as defenders of the faith, holding authority in spiritual matters, but sharing the authority with the Synod in other matters."[242] A parish newsletter claimed "the chief issue was the question of whether bishops in the Church will have the monarchical and almost absolute power they had in much of the earlier history of the Church, or whether they must, like everyone else, be subject to Constitutional definition of authority and limitation of power."[243] These letters are but a few examples of the essentially Protestant assumptions that underlie most of the criticisms of Morse and Watterson, revealing as they do an egalitarian outlook in which the church should be run like a government, since the only real authority in the temporal Church is Christ, and Christ works His will through each individual believer in the system of "checks and balances" found in the Synod form of church government.

The most thoughtful analysis of the dispute given by the Phalanx did not surface until March of 1979. Fraser Baron insightfully wrote that the real struggle was not between Catholics and Protestants, or Low and High-churchmen, but between Anglican "Loyalists" and Catholic "Revivalists." The former group was proud of their Anglican heritage, all of it, and they assumed that classic Anglicanism was genuine Catholicism, as opposed to the recent foray into heretical non-Catholicism by ECUSA.[244] In contrast, the Revivalists were never really comfortable with their Anglican heritage, and gave "the appearance of being rather impatiently headed in another direction." Thus Baron, who considered himself to be a High-churchman, and felt that most of those in the ACC were likewise High-churchmen, claimed that the other side was fundamentally anti-Anglican.[245] In this conclusion he was partially correct. The Revivalists such as Morse[246] and Watterson were indeed opposed to the classic Anglican position because they thought that it wasn't fully Catholic, but they were not so much opposed to Anglicanism as they were to Protestant,

Broad-church Anglicanism. If they were trying to revive Catholicism, it was the Catholicism of the early church that the Anglican Church had always claimed to represent. If Anglicanism's claim to be a branch of the Catholic Church was either an error or a misrepresentation, and it had not fulfilled its promise, then the Revivalists felt it was their duty to correct the mistakes that had been made. The problem, once again, was that both sides were talking past each other. For while churchmen such as Baron had no doubts that their position was Catholic, they also had a limited knowledge of what Catholicism really is, and could not see that their opponents were also correct. Everyone in the provisional Anglican Catholic Church considered their position to be the Catholic one, and everyone was indeed Catholic, but only according to how they understood the term. One side assumed that their ritualized, less dogmatic Protestantism, so long as it maintained the Apostolic Episcopate, was authentic Catholicism. The other side recognized the Protestant nature of much classic Anglicanism, argued that it was at best a deformed version of authentic Catholicism, and hoped to build the new church on a more solidly Catholic foundation.

The "fragile reunion" that had been achieved at Dallas turned out to be more of a strategic truce. Within a week of the Synod's completion, Philip C. Davis, Chancellor of the DSEUS, sent Doren a letter claiming that the Dallas Constitution was really a "work product" of the Synod that should be sent to the bishops for analysis and final action. The bishops would then prepare and issue a short constitution that would be the basis upon which the church could then draft its canons. Doren replied, in true Low-Church fashion, "The government of the Church is not, as you believe it to be, in the hands of the bishops alone. With Jesus Christ as the Head of the Church, the entire body must be concerned with the rules and laws by which it shall be governed."²⁴⁷

Only a week after this exchange, Doren and Mote consecrated Fr. William Francis Burns as the first Bishop of the DOR, against the wishes not only of Morse and Watterson, but also those of the Standing Committee of the DHT. The Committee's reservations about the consecration centered on the fact that the recently adopted provisional Constitution stated that a three-fourths consent of the bishops, meeting in council, was required to legalize the consecration of a new bishop, and that the situation was not urgent enough to justify a two-bishop consecration. Mote's reply, given on November 3, 1978, also exhibited a deeply Protestant mindset, dismissing his critics, "I disagree with you. If I am willing once more to go against a strong conscience, even if not a certain one, and to bow before the pressure of Bishops Morse and Watterson in an entirely illegal, unreasonable position, I do not see how I can expect anybody to honor my word. I think it would be far more damaging than the gleeful reaction of our enemies [critics within ECUSA] to a two-Bishop consecration."²⁴⁸ A majority of the Standing Committee then asked Mote to resign, intending, according to Faber, to withdraw it soon after the consecration date had passed. It is also possible that they may have been genuinely worried about what seemed to be a rash and unnecessary course of action being undertaken by their bishop. After all, unbeknownst to them, Mote had already made up his mind that he was going to perform the consecration no matter what his Standing Committee decided. Although this fact is offered by Faber as an example of a kind of heroic act of individual conscience, it also unknowingly reveals the often hypocritical position of the Phalanx. For Mote had allegedly deceived his Standing Committee, telling them that he would resign if they thought he should, "rather than go ahead with a two-Bishop Consecration."²⁴⁹ In other words, in light of his conviction to consecrate no matter what they did, Mote not only deceived them, he essentially tried to pressure them into accepting his unilateral actions. Furthermore, he was acting much like the monarchial bishops that the Phalanx spent so much time fretting over.

Morse and Watterson tried to persuade Continuers that the consecration of Bishop Burns was invalid, basing their claim on the three-fourths requirement in the provisional Constitution, and also on the current ECUSA Canon Law that required a majority decision by both the diocesan bishops and the Standing Committees. When Burns was consecrated, only two of the four bishops had given consent, and only one of the Standing Committees possessing bishops had given consent. An argument put forth in support of the consecration's validity was made by E.J.M. LaRoque. He claimed that single-bishop consecrations were not only allowed by extreme necessity, but also as a general practice in some Apostolic churches, thus making the demand for three superfluous. He also claimed that a letter of consent from Bishop Chambers (who was too ill to attend) proved that the requirement for majority consent had been met, since Bishops Chambers, Doren, and Mote outnumbered the other two.[250] This claim was challenged, countering that Chambers had only written a letter of congratulations, and furthermore, that he had later denied that the letter was meant for the purposes of consenting to the consecration.[251] More quizzically, LaRoque quoted some ancient Canons that supposedly validated a principle by which it was charged that Morse and Watterson were guilty of withholding their consent for the consecration, against the wishes of the people. This bizarre claim was made even though a careful reading of the text reveals that what is meant is that individual bishops who do not respond in any way to repeated requests by their fellow bishops shall be found in violation of their ministry. Morse and Watterson had repeatedly made their opposition to the consecration known, thereby leaving them outside of LaRoque's definition. Unfortunately, most Continuing churchmen were too unfamiliar with the history of the early Church, and especially of its early Canon Law, thus leaving them susceptible to the flimsy arguments of purported experts such as LaRoque.

On January 6, 1979, the Phalanx initiated another questionable move during the Synod for the DMAS. After several ballots to elect a bishop, during which a priest had won election in the clerical order, but not the lay order, Fraser Baron, acting openly as a lay delegate and silently as a member of the Phalanx, put Bishop Doren's name forward as a candidate. Barron explained that Doren had been told by his doctor that he would have to resign his duties as bishop due to the physical strain required to administer to such a large geographical area. Barron suggested that it would be a shame to lose such a valuable bishop, and suggested that Doren could be transferred to their diocese since it included only a few states. Perry Laukhuff, also a lay delegate and leader within the Phalanx, "immediately rose" to nominate Doren, and the Synod responded by unanimously electing Doren to be their first bishop. Both Barron and Laukhuff worked closely with the Phalanx's inner circle and its orbit of influential supporters. Interestingly, Doren claimed to have been totally surprised by the election since, "I had not had time to notify the Standing Committee of the Midwest of my doctor's orders," yet he had been close enough to Fraser Barron to inform *him* of his medical condition just in time for the DMAS Synod. The Phalanx's explanation was that these turn of events were "a sudden and unexpected move."[252] It seems more likely that Doren and his supporters, realizing that he could not physically handle the duties of being the bishop of the DMW, initiated the process of having himself transferred to another diocese that would be more suitable to his physical condition. Most importantly, Doren's Low-Church position fit well with the Phalanx's Low-Church elite, many of whom lived within the boundaries of the DMAS. The DMAS Synod also became the first to ratify the Dallas Constitution.

The Catholic-wing challenged the canonical legality of translating Doren to the DMAS. The Canons of ECUSA had forbidden the translation of a bishop without the consent of the other bishops. The provisional ACC Canons required a letter of resignation be given to his episcopal superior or the bishop next in line in terms of seniority. Morse and Watterson claimed that they were not notified of the election or the transfer until after it had been announced. They also claimed that the proper consents had not been obtained from the bishops or the standing committees of the other dioceses.[253] However, by the time these complaints were being made, they were largely being preached to the choir. The Phalanx and the Catholic-wing had essentially stopped communicating with each other.

A parish newsletter in Alabama revealed the chasm that was developing between the two groups: "Despite Dallas, the FCC[254] still claims to be our ecclesiastical guide, completely ignoring the fact that at Dallas we bid them thank you and good-bye. Its version of the Dallas Synod carries all of the distortions which might not have appeared evident to those who were not allowed to sit in closed caucuses, and thus did not know most of the inner workings of the meeting. The Diocese of the Midwest and the FCC have worked hand-in-glove together, its bishop ever being a protégé of the FCC. The impression given is that the Southeast and the Diocese of Christ the King were naughty children who didn't want to play with the others. The truth is that the delegations were partially rigged by the FCC and the Midwest, and we were not willing, after all we had been through, to accept a constitution that would make us just another PECUSA."[255]

The institutional FCC continued to maintain that it was a neutral participant in the development of the ACC, even though Fr. Carroll Simcox, in his January (1979) presidential address to the FCC, admitted, "if historians do their jobs adequately they will record that the Fellowship of Concerned Churchmen, and it virtually alone, brought these momentous events to pass." Simcox claimed that the FCC had completed its job as midwife of the Movement, and that it would now concentrate on an educational program to inform churchmen, both inside and outside of the Episcopal Church, as to the damages that had occurred in the national church. He concluded with a reference to the conflicts surrounding the Dallas Synod, stating, "The problem posed by this division is one which cannot be solved by the Fellowship as such; it can only be solved by the bishops and people of the continuing Church. However strongly we may feel individually about that issue, it is clearly not the duty or the calling of the Fellowship as such to take sides in that conflict."[256] In retrospect, it was quite convenient for influential members (the Phalanx) within the FCC to claim that the matter was now in the hands of the clergy and laity of the ACC, for this Phalanx had already manipulated the events in such a way as to form the ACC into a body in which Episcopalian "loyalists" could feel more comfortable, thus there was apparently no longer as strong of a need to take sides anymore, at least not as blatantly.

The Synod of the DCK met in late January, 1979, and took no action on the Dallas Constitution, claiming that they still had not received a corrected copy of it. The Standing Committee of the DEUS then met on February 10, 1979, to discuss the recent strife within the ACC. Claiming to have not received accurate[257] copies of the Dallas Constitution and Canons (which were supposed to have been received within sixty days, but weren't), they concluded that the provisional Constitution was not eligible to be ratified by any diocese. They concluded that the Canons of the Episcopal Church as of 1967 were thus the only legal Canons in the ACC, and therefore condemned both the consecration of Bishop Burns and the translation of Bishop Doren as "illegal and disorderly." The minutes of the meeting reveal the degree of distrust that now permeated the leadership of the DSEUS, "The episcopate has become dominated by intense political manipulation, deviousness, dishonesty, and scandal."[258] The DOR Synod met in late February and voted to ratify the Dallas Constitution, as well as to recognize the resignation and translation of Bishop Doren. On February 29, the Standing Committee of the DCK issued a resolution taking the same position as that of the Standing Committee of the DSEUS, but placing more emphasis on the issue of timely transmission of the letters requesting consent for Doren's translation. Doren's proponents admitted that a mistake had been made, and apologized for the fact that "secular lawyers" had been given the task of handling the translation, and thus were unaware of the canonical requirement for timely notifications and consents. In what would become a typical response whenever they were confronted with accusations of non-canonical or irregular actions, the Phalanx and its supporters within the ACC leadership chastised their antagonists for lacking Christian charity in dealing with the "blunders" of their fellow believers.[259] By mid-March, the Standing Committee's of the DHT, DSEUS, and DMW had also officially consented to Doren's translation. The translation became official on March 17, 1979. Meanwhile, during the Synod of the DMW on March 9, yet another bishop was elected without the consent of Morse and Watterson, Fr. William Oliver Lewis of Michigan.

    In a portent of events that would transpire years later, the April *Christian Challenge* gave Bishop Clavier of the American Episcopal Church the opportunity to comment on the problems within the fledgling ACC. Clavier's analysis of the situation essentially mirrored that of Fraser Barron: the conflict was the result of a small group of Catholics, who were Catholic in a non-Anglican way, trying to force the majority of traditionalist Anglicans to conform to a narrow view of the church. However, another purpose in inviting Bishop Clavier's comments seems to have been to allow someone from outside of the St. Louis Movement to hurl a little mud at the Catholic party. For example, Clavier pointed out that the real breakdown in Anglicanism had been precipitated by the acceptance of liberalism in theology by the Anglo-Catholic party within the Church. The basic message of the piece was that the ACC would succeed only if it avoided the divisions between High and Low-churchmen, and accepted the fact that Anglicanism was both Reformed Evangelical and Catholic.[260]

The campaign to convince as many High-churchmen as possible that the classic Anglican position was truly Catholic (or Catholic enough) spread widely, and many Continuing churchmen adopted the argument in the hopes of keeping as much of the St. Louis Movement together as possible. The argument even had its influence among rather staunchly Catholic churchmen, such as Fr. Sterling Rayburn of Florida. Rayburn pleaded with the disaffected Catholic party to realize that the *Affirmation of St. Louis* and Dallas Constitution were thoroughly Catholic documents. He stated confidently, "No official Anglican document has ever been so uncompromisingly Catholic." Ironically, he also stated that there was nothing in the ACC's doctrinal position that an Eastern Orthodox Christian could not also agree with.[261] However, within three months of composing this letter, Rayburn seemed to have discovered that there was something about the ACC that was not Catholic enough, for he resigned from the ACC to join the

Orthodox Church in America.[262]

In late April the Synod of the DSEUS convened to officially decide whether they would ratify the Dallas Constitution, even though they had only received official copies of the document a week before the event.[263] By a unanimous vote in the clerical order, and a nearly unanimous vote in the lay order, the DSEUS voted to refuse ratification. A resolution was then passed that called for the creation of a committee to explore "reunion with other Catholic bodies." However, two serious charges were made against Bishop Watterson, reported by Dorothy Faber, which may call into question his ultimate motives. The first claimed that he had actually been the one member of the committee that had prepared the draft Constitution to request that the Solemn Declaration and the Preamble be protected from possible amendment, even though one of his major public complaints against the document was that these portions could not be amended. If this is true, it means that Watterson was either contradicting himself in a desperate quest to form another church body, or that he had planted one of the seeds with which he could cynically corrupt the formation of the ACC. The second accusation was that the DSEUS Synod had passed a resolution to allow Watterson to accept parishes that lay within the boundaries of other ACC dioceses if they preferred to be under his jurisdiction.[264] The second accusation was true, and serves to somewhat undermine a complaint of the DSEUS that would later surface.

Within a week of the DSEUS Synod's actions, the Synods of the DMW and DSW voted overwhelmingly to ratify the proposed Constitution, bringing the number of diocesan ratifications to four, and thus satisfying the Dallas Constitutional Synod's requirement that the ACC would become official upon four ratifications. Nonetheless, the refusal of the DSEUS to ratify the proposed Constitution, although no doubt expected by the Phalanx, disturbed many other churchmen within the provisional ACC, especially in the DHT, which, perhaps not coincidentally, had been the first diocese to be interfered with (or reformed) by the Phalanx. Two priests within the DHT appealed to Bishop Chambers to try and bring all of the bishops together in order to iron out their differences and avoid starting the ACC without two of its original dioceses. After first declining, Chambers contacted the other bishops in order to organize the meeting. Unfortunately in the estimation of many, the meeting did not occur, though the reasons for this differ. One version is that Chambers had cancelled the meeting after concluding that Bishops Doren, Mote, et al, would use the occasion of the meeting to claim that Chambers agreed with their actions. The other version claimed that the meeting had been organized, but then abruptly cancelled after Watterson had sabotaged it.[265]

When the DHT held its Synod on May 10-11, in Los Angeles, there was clearly a significant faction of delegates who thought that ratification without the two dissenting dioceses would be a mistake. Bishop Mote brought "expert" consultants with him from outside the diocese in order to present the case for ratification, including Andrew Stahl, the principle author of the document, and Bishop-elect Lewis. Purportedly, the key moment came when Mote informed the delegates that a meeting had been called by Bishop Chambers for the purpose of bringing unity back to the Church, which no doubt delighted those who opposed ratification. However, Mote then told them that, unfortunately, Bishop Watterson had pulled out at the last minute in order to derail the meeting. Mote then informed the delegates that a movement within Watterson's own parish, as well the DSEUS, had been initiated in order to seek admission into the ACC.[266] With this troubling (but disputable) information before them, the DHT voted to adopt the

Constitution by the slimmest margin of any of the dioceses, with an eleven to five margin in the clerical order, and a thirty-five to twenty-three margin in the lay order.

The facts as to the second of Mote's revelations to the delegates of the DHT Synod were another point of contention between the Phalanx and the Catholic party. The version that gained the widest circulation claimed that there was a growing movement of churchmen within the DSEUS who were disheartened by Bishop Watterson's actions, and therefore wished to become members of the ACC. The other version asserted that the "FCC-FCT propaganda apparatus" had engaged in a surreptitious campaign to subvert the DSEUS from within. Accordingly, small minorities of churchmen, who were said to be in cahoots with Mote, had begun trying to take over their parishes in order to guide them into the ACC.[267]

The consecration of Bishop Lewis took place on May 26, 1979, and, once again, Bishops Morse and Watterson did not participate. Immediately after the consecration, the first meeting of the College of Bishops was held in order to declare that the ACC was now a legal reality. Ironically, they claimed that they would take no actions unless there was unanimous agreement among them. Few seem to have noticed that the viewpoint expressed in this promulgation sounds strangely familiar to the position taken by Morse and Watterson, namely, that each bishop has an inherent independence. The College of Bishops concluded their first meeting by scheduling the next ACC Synod, which was to be held in Indianapolis, Indiana, once again in the month of October.[268] The Standing Committee of the DSEUS then met on May 29 and reaffirmed the decision made by their recent Synod to reject the proposed Constitution and Canons. After discussing various options as to the future direction of the diocese, it was decided both to work with Bishop Morse toward establishing another body, and to start the process of making ecumenical contacts with other Catholic bodies in the hope of establishing intercommunion while retaining their Anglican forms of worship.[269] A member of the Standing Committee who resigned during the meeting sent a letter to the ACC bishops that claimed to reveal the issues that were discussed, such as replacing the 1928 Prayer Book service with Missal services, and this "report" was in turn published by *The Christian Challenge*.[270]

Bishop Watterson's parish held a meeting on June 10, while he was away dedicating another parish,[271] to discuss a resolution drafted by nine of the twelve members of the vestry that proposed disassociating themselves from their bishop and joining with the ACC. Among the charges brought against Watterson were that he had caused divisions within the wider ACC, that he had kept information from his parish and diocese, and that he had issued a pastoral letter praising the Dallas Constitution as a Catholic document, only to contradict himself a short time later. According to the Phalanx, no discussion or secret balloting were allowed during the meeting, and forty-three proxy votes were accepted. There were 74 votes cast against leaving the diocese, and 32 in favor, while 32 parishioners abstained. Within a week of the parish meeting, those who had voted to leave had formed their own parish and called a retired Episcopal priest, Fr. Frank R. Knutti, to be their rector. The new parish apparently joined perhaps as many as a dozen other parishes from the two dissenting dioceses (though most were in the DSEUS) in petitioning the ACC College of Bishops for pastoral oversight.[272] According to Watterson's supporters, this new parish had been formed with the assistance of Bishop Mote and his family,[273] and the other breakaway parishes were also attributed to Mote's secret contacts with vestrymen who wished to join the ACC.[274]

The ACC College of Bishops held their second meeting on June 20, 1979, and, claiming to be besieged with requests by parishes within the dioceses of Bishops Morse and Watterson to join the ACC, voted to form a special non-geographic diocese called the Patrimony, which would exist specifically to accept disaffected parishes. The Patrimony was to be under the jurisdiction of the College of Bishops, but Bishop Burns was given the title of Vicar General of the Patrimony, as well as full authority to assist parishes in joining the Anglican Catholic Church. Burns was also given the authority to call a Synod in which the newly accepted parishes could meet and ratify the Constitution. The College of Bishops also issued a letter to Morse in order to determine if he was going to remain in the ACC or not, requesting his response by July 8. Morse must have considered this a hollow gesture since the College of Bishops had now held two meetings without him, although they were supposed to be acting only after reaching a unanimous consent, which supposedly still included Morse. Unsurprisingly, before the letter had reached Morse, he and Watterson had issued a joint statement on June 22 calling for a Church Congress to be held in Hot Springs, Arkansas, for the purpose of drafting a new Constitution and Canons for a body to be provisionally known as the Anglican Church in America. A statement by Morse, which claimed that the mandate of the St. Louis Congress would be fulfilled in Hot Springs, was challenged by the FCC's president, Fr. Carroll Simcox: "That Congress was entirely a project of the Fellowship of Concerned Churchmen, and I believe I speak for all members of the Fellowship in saying that this proposed new body of Anglican separatists violates the spirit and the intent which led to the great meeting in St. Louis."[275] This statement is revealing in that it reveals the extent to which the Phalanx within the FCC considered the ACC to be *their* creation, as well as the fact that the FCC's recent pronouncement of neutrality regarding the disagreement between the original four bishops was issued more for strategic effect than out of genuine conviction.

With the announcement of the Hot Springs Congress, several clergy and laymen scurried to organize a movement in order to issue one final appeal to all of the bishops for unity. A meeting was held in Nashville, Tennessee, on August 7 and 8, for the purpose of discussing a course of action. Lead by Fr. Frederick E. Preuss, a priest in the DSEUS, the Nashville gathering was attended by Continuing churchmen from across the nation, and only one bishop (Mote). The Nashville group issued a resolution calling for a 6-month postponement of both the Indianapolis Synod and the Hot Springs Congress. They also called for two meetings between the bishops, one including all six bishops, and the other only the original four.[276] Similar proposals for salvaging the original unity of the St. Louis Movement were proposed, including one by the vestry of the Anglican Church of the Good Shepherd in Woodbury, New York, issued on August 10, which called for the establishment of two provinces within the same body, each of which could have a Constitution and Canons tailored to its needs. The parish, which was a member of the DCK, also announced that it would remain in communion with all of the bishops, irregardless of the their ecclesiastical unity.[277] Several parishes across the United States issued similar appeals

Shortly after the Nashville meeting, Bishop Morse issued a letter to Fr. Preuss in which he agreed to participate in a unilateral postponement of the Indianapolis Synod and the Hot Springs Congress, so long as two problematic conditions were met. The first was that the newly established Patrimony of the ACC be terminated, and those churchmen who had joined it be instructed to return to their original bishop. The second was that the first meeting to be held among the bishops could only include the original four bishops and their assistants.[278] Morse must have known that these conditions would never be met by the ACC bishops, who had most probably planned on going forward without Morse and Watterson for some time, thus his letter was likely issued for strategic effect in order to make himself appear open to the cause of unity. Needless to say, no such meeting between all of the bishops would occur.

The Anglicans that had separated in Canada held their first synod on September 21-22 in Winnipeg, Ontario. The Synod elected Fr. Carmine J. deCatanzaro as its first bishop, and adopted a Constitution and Canons for their new body. However, there was some confusion as to their relationship to the ACC. A report on the synod in *The Christian Challenge* referred to the Canadian gathering as the "Anglican Catholic Diocese of Canada."[279] However, a letter from Fr. Roland F. Palmer of Victoria, British Columbia, stated that the Canadian group was essentially independent. He claimed that Bishop Mote had attended the synod as an observer, and that Bishop Morse had sent a letter expressing his congratulations and regret that he could not attend. The synod had issued a resolution declaring the Anglican Church of Canada to be in communion with all of the Continuing bishops consecrated out of the St. Louis meeting. The Canadian separatists had not adopted the Constitution and Canons of the ACC, but had instead voted to use the 1965 canons of the Church of Canada. They had also passed a resolution to seek communion with the Old Catholic Churches. Palmer noted that any Anglican who accepted the *Affirmation of St. Louis* would be welcome at the altar of the Anglican Church of Canada.[280] This initial misunderstanding regarding the nature of the Continuing Movement in Canada would eventually turn out be the cause of further friction within the American Movement.

If any Continuing churchmen had retained some hope for a last-minute miracle that could bring all of the bishops together, the holding of a synod for the ACC's Patrimony on September 28 and 29, 1979, put the final nail in the coffin. The Synod of the Patrimony, held in Atlanta, Georgia, voted to ratify the ACC Constitution and proposed Canons, and elected delegates to the upcoming Indianapolis Synod.[281] Bishops Morse and Watterson considered the Patrimony to be nothing more than an attempt by the ACC to sow divisions within the two dissenting dioceses. Since the DCK was a non-geographic diocese, and as was mentioned earlier, the DSEUS had moved to allow for parishes outside of its jurisdiction to join with Bishop Watterson, the ACC considered the accusations of the dissenting bishops to be groundless. The two opposing camps were now committed to separate courses, and the meetings in Indianapolis and Hot Springs were set in stone.

Chapter 8

INDIANAPOLIS AND HOT SPRINGS

The DCK and DSEUS met in Hot Springs, Arkansas, from October 16 to 18, 1979. Apparently, no outside reporters were permitted to cover the Hot Springs Congress. Fr. George D. Stenhouse sent a letter to *The Christian Challenge* stating the position of the Congress organizers in regard to issuing press credentials: "I feel sure credentials for any who might be invited would be established on the basis of their ability and disposition to report fully, objectively and accurately on the proceedings. It seems to me personally that you would hardly qualify under these criteria, the editorial bias (of *The Christian Challenge*)... having been so consistently and so strongly negative for so long."[282] Despite this suspicion of outsiders, some information about the Hot Springs Congress did emerge. The proposed Canons for the Anglican Church in America were reportedly adopted with little debate,[283] but the vote of the Congress was also reportedly to be only an advisory action, with Bishops Morse and Watterson having the ultimate power to accept or reject the documents. Foreshadowing problems for the ACC, Bishop-elect de Catanzaro of Canada and Bishop Pagtakhan both spoke to the Hot Springs delegates, appealing for unity within the entire St. Louis Continuing Movement. However, the biggest development during the gathering was the reported breakdown in unity precipitated by Watterson. According to a report from a parish newsletter within the DSEUS, the new body was to be established as an "Anglican Communion," and not a new church body." The newsletter then reported that Watterson had quizzically demanded that the new body be called the Anglican Catholic Church, which could only have resulted in a legal battle with the "other" ACC. He is also said to have made four additional demands. The first was that strict geographical boundaries be set between the two dioceses, with Watterson to be designated all territory east of the Mississippi River. The second would have forbidden any bishop to publicly speak badly of another bishop. The third required that all dissidents be disciplined promptly. The final demand was that the priests serving under a bishop were to be subject to him, rather than their parishes. The report concluded by claiming that the clergy and Standing Committee of his diocese had asked for Watterson's resignation.[284]

The second Synod of the Anglican Catholic Church met in Indianapolis, Indiana, from October 18 to 20, 1979. The delegates finished reviewing and adopting those portions of the Constitution and Canons that had been adopted provisionally in Dallas. However, they were also presented with 70 pages of new Canons that had been prepared by a special committee appointed by the College of Bishops. Once again, the Synod had to adopt many Canons on a provisional basis, in the hope of being able to finish reviewing and adopting them at the next synod. In an attempt to placate the differing parties of churchmen, the Synod adopted a provision that allowed for parishes to refer to themselves as members of the Anglican Catholic Church, the Anglican Church in North America, the Anglican Church, the Continuing Episcopal Church of the United States, or the Continuing Anglican Church of Canada. The delegates also passed a resolution stating that the ACC accepted several historical documents and concordats that had been agreed to by the Episcopal Church. Finally, the delegates also approved a proposal from the College of Bishops to allow the Diocese of the Mid-Atlantic States to elect a Bishop Coadjutor.

As far as the ACC was concerned, the Indianapolis Synod was, for the most part, a welcome relief from the internal strife that had plagued the Dallas gathering. Unfortunately, an address given to the Synod by Bishop Pagtakhan would lead to further fracturing of the St. Louis Continuing Movement. As he had done at the Hot Springs Congress, Pagtakhan again echoed de Catanzaro's call for unity among all of the bishops. However, unlike his address in Arkansas, he claimed that if the ACC re-united with Bishops Morse and Watterson, he would recommend the ACC for intercommunion with the Philippine Independent Catholic Church, promising that if this came to pass, the ACC would also be in communion with the Old Catholic Churches. In contradiction of Pagtakhan's claim, the Old Catholic Church had reportedly decided a few months earlier that Anglican dissidents could attain intercommunion with the See of Utrecht through the only recognized Old Catholic body in America, the Polish National Catholic Church.[285] Pagtakhan then dropped his ecclesiastical bombshell, stating that he was considering forming an "umbrella jurisdiction" of the PICC in the United States, specifically for the purpose of providing a home for Continuing Anglicans who were frustrated with both the ACC and the newly formed (so everyone thought at the time) Anglican Church in America.[286]

During the Indianapolis Synod, Fr. Robert Q. Kennaugh is claimed to have resigned from the Diocese of the Holy Trinity, and then to have requested Pagtakhan to accept him into the PICC.[287] On December 5, 1979, Pagtakhan informed Bishop Mote via letter that a missionary jurisdiction of the PICC was being established in the United States. He also reported that Kennaugh had been appointed as Archdeacon, and that Fr. F. Ogden Miller and Fr. Herman Nelson had been appointed to be canons. This was claimed to have been the first time that Mote knew that these three priests had withdrawn from his diocese, and that the Philippine province was to be established.[288] However, the Standing Committee of the DHT had issued a letter to Pagtakhan on November 14, 1979, which included Mote's signature, expressing their best wishes for the new province, and that they would welcome ecumenical contacts in the future.[289] This communication to Pagtakhan most probably resulted from the make-up of the DHT's Standing Committee, which included several members of the Deanery of Southern California.

The Deanery of Southern California had been the primary group that opposed Bishop Mote's call for the ratification of the Dallas Constitution when the DHT had held its Diocesan Synod in May of 1979. The Deanery was a rather unusual association of priests and laymen who had been among the first in the Los Angeles area to withdraw from PECUSA after the Minneapolis Convention. What made the Deanery unusual was that its membership included 5 parishes affiliated with the DHT, 2 parishes that belonged to the DCK, and 1 each from the American Episcopal Church and the Anglican Episcopal Church of North America.[290] The guiding philosophy of the Deanery called for unity within the whole Continuing Movement, and especially in the St. Louis Movement. Because a deanery had often been the organization from which new dioceses may develop, Bishop Mote had to be especially careful in his dealings with the Southern California Deanery. The ties between Mote and the Deanery were not strong. For example, during its final meeting before the Indianapolis Synod, the Deanery had discussed the possibility of withholding funds from the DHT, had endorsed the Nashville resolution calling for a postponement of the Indianapolis and Hot Springs gatherings, and had criticized the establishment of the ACC's Patrimony as a divisive hindrance to unity.[291] Complicating matters further was the fact that the Deanery had been in contact with Bishop Pagtakhan, as well as priests of the PICC who had parishes in the Los Angeles area, and had often been allowed to speak during Deanery meetings, as was Bishop Morse.[292]

The December newsletter of St. Luke's in Covina, California, a parish in the DHT, then published an article arguing that the ACC, as well as Bishops Morse and Watterson, were really under the jurisdiction of Pagtakhan. The article, probably penned by the parish's rector, Fr. Odgen Miller (mentioned above), argued that Pagtakhan was an active bishop who had been given permission by his Church to perform the consecrations, and was thus the only bishop among the Denver consecrators to meet the canonical requirement of jurisdiction. Bishop Chambers, conversely, had been a retired bishop acting against the wishes of his church, and thus did not have jurisdiction. According to this argument, all of the bishops derived from the St. Louis Movement were ultimately required to answer to Pagtakhan and the PICC.[293] The counter to this argument was that the ACC was under its own jurisdiction, which it had been received from Chambers. The fact that Chambers acted in contradiction of his fellow bishops was excused as a necessary action due to the descent of PECUSA into heresy.[294] The question of jurisdiction would continue to trouble many Continuers, and especially those who were unhappy with the divisions among the original bishops.

Fr. Miller, and Pagtakhan's new jurisdiction, would somehow manage to co-exist for a few months within the ACC orbit, as many parishes in the ACC considered the pros and cons of joining with Pagtakhan's newly forming group. For example, Fr. Miller was allowed to maintain membership in both the ACC and Philippine mission until

September of 1981. During the early months of 1980, Archdeacon Kennaugh began contacting parishes and individual churchmen (mostly priests) in the ACC about the possibility of joining with Pagtakhan's American province. In March, Pagtakhan and Kennaugh are said to have begun traveling across the nation, especially in Bishop Watterson's diocese, in an attempt to convince parishes to join the new province.[295] However, much of the potential for this missionary journey had been limited by a rumor that had begun circulating in February of 1980. Supposedly, a layman had visited the Philippines and contacted Bishop Ga, who in turn had denied that Pagtakhan had been given permission by the Philippine bishops to organize an American mission.[296]

It was during this time that a date of April 12, 1980, was set for the consecration of Fr. de Catanzaro to the episcopate. The ACC College of Bishops decided on March 8 that they would adopt a position of neutrality toward the event. However, within a few days the Canadian Continuers had issued an invitation to the ACC bishops to participate in the consecration service, which would include Bishop Morse as well as Bishop Pagtakhan and two other Philippine bishops. The news of the invitation spread throughout the ACC, and its members divided into two camps, one angry that the bishops were considering the offer, and the other hopeful that greater unity could be achieved by way of their bishops' participation. The ACC bishops agreed to participate as co-consecrators, but only under the condition that Bishop Burns be one of the principle consecrators, and that Warrants for the consecration be submitted to the ACC bishops sufficiently in advance of April 12. Reportedly, the ACC representative in the negotiations had been promised by de Catanzaro that Pagtakhan would not be the chief consecrator, nor would he make any claim to jurisdiction of the PICC over the Canadian Church. These agreements were then transcribed and returned to de Catanzaro for his signature as to the facts of the telephone conversation and the conditions required by the ACC bishops. Fr. Catanzaro is said to have failed to return the document with his signature by April 7, thus precipitating a personal visit from Bishop Lewis to get the needed signature. Bishops Mote, Burns, and Rutherford then joined Lewis in Ottawa, even though there was vocal resistance within their own dioceses for taking part in the consecration.

Upon their arrival, the ACC bishops discovered that Pagtakhan and Kennaugh had contacted Watterson, who was also in Ottawa, and also expecting to participate in the consecrations. Furthermore, the ACC bishops are said to have discovered that the Warrants they had requested would not be made available to them until one hour before the service. As the service began to draw nearer, the ACC bishops are said to have demanded to see the Warrant taking Order for the consecration, and were told that no Warrant had been issued. The ACC bishops, on the advice of canonist Andrew Stahl, decided to balk at participating in the consecration. Pagtakhan then produced two Warrants, both of which claimed that the jurisdiction for the Continuing Canadian body would be through his new group, the Anglican Rite Jurisdiction of the Americas (ARJA). The ACC bishops are said to have been shocked, and to have refused to accept either Warrant. Pagtakhan then prepared and signed a new Warrant claiming that the PICC would take Order for the consecrations. The ACC bishops then proceeded to participate in the consecration service. Bishops Burns and Morse were the co-consecrators, as was Bishop Lope Rosete of the PICC. Unexpectedly, during the portion of the service in which the laying-on-of-hands occurs, Pagtakhan rose from his seat and proceeded to consecrate Fr. de Catanzaro. Kennaugh revealed later that this was done so that Bishop de Catanzaro would have proper jurisdiction through the PICC, since the other bishops present were all without jurisdiction due to their schism. Of course the Canadian Church did not consider themselves to be a part of the Philippine Church, and had only invited Pagtakhan and the Philippine bishops for the same reason they had invited the other bishops; to show that the Canadians considered themselves to be in communion with all of the Continuing groups that had come out of the St. Louis Movement.[297]

Within two weeks of the Ottawa consecration controversy, Burns is said to have received a message from Bishop Ga and the Supreme Council of Bishops of the PICC, stating that no permission had been given to Pagtakhan allowing for the organization of a Continuing Anglican jurisdiction of the PIIC in the United States. The situation was complicated by the reports from the Philippines that the Supreme Council was divided between followers of Bishop Ga and Bishop Pagtakhan, and that each of them had been tainted with a Presentment. Further muddying the waters was the report that Pagtakhan and Kennaugh had visited the leaders of the Polish National Catholic Church, and that the PNCC had issued a statement in May of 1980 declaring that no intercommunion agreement had been reached with parishes represented by Pagtakhan.[298]

Despite the contention over his jurisdictional authority and status, Pagtakhan's ARJA continued to gain strength. The month of April witnessed the withdrawal of nine parishes from the DSEUS, under the leadership of Fr. John Bruce Medaris of Florida, into the ARJA. Medaris was soon named the Archdeacon of the Province of St. John the Evangelist (or Southeastern region) of the ARJA. Pagtakhan proceeded to quickly ordain a priest and three deacons to assist the new province. Also during this time, Fr. G. Wayne Craig was also affiliating his parish in Ohio, which had left the ACC in 1979, with the ARJA. Pagtakhan and his followers had high hopes that many more parishes from the ACC would be joining the ARJA in the coming months.[299]

At the April 28, 1980 meeting of the Southern California Deanery, Fr. Ogden Miller informed the group that four priests of the ARJA were traveling to the Philippines to be consecrated on May 8. According to Miller, the intent of this mission was to insure that the PICC endorsed the formation of the Anglican jurisdiction in the United States.[300] It seems probable that neither of these goals was attained. Instead, the ARJA was officially "incorporated" in Cavite City, Philippines, on May 8, 1980, and an organizational meeting was held on May 11. Medaris and Fr. Herman F. Nelson were named Archdeacons at this time. Pagtakhan's group may have received the blessing of a faction of the Philippine bishops, although how sizable of a faction is not known, but they did not receive the consecrations to the episcopate that they had sought.[301]

While the ARJA was concentrating a large portion of its early efforts on drawing parishes from the DSEUS, it also appears that Bishop Morse likewise had his eyes on the same region. At its Synod in February of 1980, the DCK elected Fr. Frederick E. Preuss (mentioned earlier as the organizer of the Nashville unity meeting), and formerly a member of the DSEUS, as Assistant Bishop. Preuss had been suspended from the DSEUS for defying the authority of Bishop Watterson. After the entry of Preuss into the DCK, Watterson issued a pastoral letter in which he intimated that Bishop Morse "may have been involved...for some time in covert and surreptitious activities" against the DSEUS. The letter contained an assumption that there was still organizational unity between the two bishops, but also revealed the strains that were developing within Watterson's diocese, as he had to admit that several parishes had seceded from his authority to join other groups.[302] It was also reported that a few parishes and their priests had seceded and converted to Eastern Orthodoxy.[303]

In June of 1980, the ARJA organized itself into four jurisdictions or Archdeaconries. The Western Jurisdiction of St. Matthew, Evangelist, which included most of the western states, was under the care of Bishop Ordinary Pagtakhan and Auxiliary Bishop Ogden Miller. The West Central Jurisdiction of St. Luke, Physician and Evangelist, including states in the Southwest, Midwest, and parts of the South, was to be headed by Bishop Ordinary Designate Bartolome Remigio of the Philippines, and Archdeacon Thomas Gore. The East Central Jurisdiction of St. Mark, Evangelist, including states in the Great Lakes area and the Northeast, was to be led by Bishop Ordinary Designate, G. Wayne Craig. The Eastern Jurisdiction of St. John, Evangelist, including states in the upper and lower South, was to be led by Bishop Ordinary Designate, Herman F. Nelson and Auxiliary Bishop Designate, John Bruce Medaris. Archdeacon Robert Q. Kennaugh was named Archbishop Designate for the ARJA.[304]

As Pagtakhan's new jurisdiction was being established, the bishops of the ACC came under increasing fire from within their own dioceses. The first issue to be confronted was the dismay expressed by many of the laity that the bishops had participated in the Ottawa consecrations with Bishops Morse and Pagtakhan, both of whom were seen as the primary agents responsible for bringing disunity to the ACC. In May of 1980, the ACC's College of Bishops issued a pastoral letter explaining their motivations for participating in the consecration service, arguing that they considered it their pastoral duty to be present at Bishop de Catanzaro's consecration since the Canadian Church had been originally created by the ACC. However, within a few months, the criticism of their actions had increased due to the claims made by many of Pagtakhan's followers that his jurisdiction was the only legitimate continuation of the St. Louis Congress. The ACC College of Bishops responded in August with another pastoral letter in which they again stated their reasons for attending the Ottawa service, and claimed to have had no knowledge of the fact that the Canadian officials would later use documents from the ARJA as part of the official promulgation of Bishop de Catanzaro's consecration. More importantly, they rejected any claim that Pagtakhan had any authority over the ACC, and they refused to recognize the ARJA's canonical legitimacy.[305]

The Southern California Deanery responded to the pastoral letter with a letter of their own, stating that they considered themselves to be in full communion with all of the bishops consecrated since the St. Louis Congress. They rebuked the bishops for stating that Bishops Morse and Watterson had separated themselves from the ACC, countering that neither of them had ever publicly declared their desire to be independent or schismatic. Furthermore, they rejected the ACC bishops' condemnation of Pagtakhan, and intimated that he was a necessary component of the overall Continuing Movement since the other bishops had not been able to work out their differences.[306] The outlook of the Deanery was no doubt aggravated by their indignation over a cartoon that appeared in the August, 1980 issue of *The Phoenix*, the newsletter of the ACC's Diocese of the Resurrection, which depicted Pagtakhan with stereotypically large teeth, imitative of the anti-Japanese propaganda used during the Second World War.[307] In addition, the Deanery was probably unsure as to the future status of the ACC. During the September meeting in which the Open Letter was adopted, a member of the Deanery with close ties to the DCK reported that Bishop Morse considered himself to still be in communion with the Deanery. More confusingly, it was reported that Bishop Lewis had sent Morse a message stating that Lewis had refused to sign the pastoral letter, and that he considered himself to still be in communion with Morse.[308]

While most churchmen within the ACC were concerned primarily with the establishment of Pagtakhan's jurisdiction, the actions of their bishops in Ottawa, and perhaps the continued separation from Morse and Watterson, few at the time noticed that a far more significant and divisive issue was smoldering in the minds of the Southern Phalanx. Before the ACC College of Bishops pastoral letter had dealt with Bishops Morse, Watterson, de Catanzaro, and Pagtakhan, they felt it necessary to assure Continuing churchmen that "we are thankful for those various modes and traditions, and especially of liturgical expression in worship, which are part of our unique Anglican character and heritage. And, lest anyone be concerned, we are all of one mind on this matter, and absolutely determined that none shall be put to the test in this regard."[309] The reason that the College of Bishops had to include this assurance in their message was due to the fact that the Phalanx, which had always backed them in any ecclesiastical dispute, was now beginning to express some dissatisfaction. The Phalanx, in their own view, after successfully standing against the Catholic encroachments of Morse and Watterson, had somehow lost control of the overall direction of the ACC.

The dissent of the Phalanx began to openly appear at the beginning of 1980. Fr. Robert C. Harvey, the president of the Foundation for Christian Theology, editorialized on the newly adopted, as well as the proposed, Canons from the Indianapolis Synod. In December of 1979, he praised the new Canons for their statements upholding traditional morality and values.[310] However, a month later he offered his objections to the proposed Canons. His overall complaint was that the ACC had been organized to cleanse the Episcopal Church from theological and political radicals, and not other traditionalist churchmen. He was particularly troubled that ordinands were required to submit to the Canons of the Church, which "have been, or shall be, passed from time to time." He interpreted this as a totalitarian Canon that would in effect be asking new clergy to "sign a blank check." He also criticized the vocabulary of the proposed Canons, which contained ancient terms like Primate, Metropolitan, and Prolocutor. He was also disturbed with the practice by some within the Church of addressing the bishops as "Your Grace," or "Your Lordship," and concluded that "in the United States it is preposterous."[311] Shortly after this editorial appeared, Harvey was elected to be the Bishop of the Diocese of the Southwest. His last editorial appeared in April of 1980 (since he would be resigning from his position as president of the Foundation for Christian Theology), and was even more frank about the difficulties he perceived in the ACC. He claimed that most of the laity were moderate to Low-churchmen, and that most of the clergy appeared to be High- churchmen. He counseled both sides in the ACC, "The upshot is that these laypeople must now accept the clergy they have got, and those clergy must lead them, gently and honestly, to a fuller knowledge of the Holy Catholic Church." After this rather moderate and conciliatory suggestion, he then scolded, "At the same time the clergy have got to get rid of the idea that there is no room for Protestants in the Church."[312]

In expressing his concerns, Harvey was echoing the complaints being made across the spectrum of the Phalanx. Perry Laukhuff wondered, "Why do so many of our Bishops don garb which makes them look Roman instead of like the Anglican Bishops they are? Why the towering mitres and the cardinal cassocks and zucchettos (skull caps) of Rome...? Our Bishops are not princes...why then do they dress like princes? And why are our consecrations...not simplified more along the lines of the Rite of Consecration found in the Book of Common Prayer…? Why must interminable time be spent in consecrations in reading consents and other documents *ad-nauseam*?" Assuming the royal "We," he spoke for all concerned traditionalists (more probably the Phalanx and its sympathizers), "We strongly believe that the canons (and perhaps the Constitution) of the Anglican Church need rather sweeping overhaul. Simplicity and the essentials have died under the knife of antiquarianism. The present canons read in places like the dreary do's and don'ts of Leviticus instead of the bugle call to evangelism."[313] One of the more interesting aspects of Harvey and Laukhuff's complaints about the cumbersome details and language of the Canons is that this was precisely one of the major complaints about the Canons made by Bishops Morse and Watterson.

The divide between these traditional Anglicans and the newly defined "hyper-Catholics" was even more apparent in the commentary by Dorothy Faber on Harvey's consecration to the episcopate on April of 1980. She described the consecration as, "a sign of hope to those who have expressed concern that the Anglican Catholic Church might be straining too hard to cast aside its Episcopal Church heritage and, in the process, is becoming something other than a traditional Anglican body." She then described the "other side" as viewing the consecration with "foreboding," since Harvey was an advocate for "a more flexible attitude toward churchmanship in the ACC." More telling was Faber's comment on a statement made by the "other" bishops after the consecration, in which they said Harvey would be "a strong addition to the College of Bishops." Faber relayed this statement, and then cynically added, "if one can take at face value their public comments to various individuals."[314] The Phalanx was apparently becoming increasingly critical of the ACC bishops, and was no longer going to be a propaganda apparatus for the ACC. This new stance probably developed as a result of the Phalanx being unable to create the ACC as clearly in its own image as it had hoped. Having played their part in maneuvering Morse and Watterson, and arguably du Bois, out of the ACC, and having co-operated with Bishop Mote to achieve these ends, the Phalanx probably assumed that the Anglican Catholic Church would have a Broad to Low-church structure and Canons, and would tolerate High-church ceremonial for those parishes that so desired. What appears to have happened instead is that, as had happened in the Episcopal Church, the clergy, probably out of deference and respect accorded to them by the laity, came to dominate the ACC. These clergy were mostly of the High-church persuasion, and consequently sought to establish a church with a more Catholic structure and Canons. The irony is that the Phalanx's complaints were greatly overblown, since both sides were seeking what were essentially very similar goals. The Phalanx wanted a traditional Anglican Church that tolerated Catholic ceremonial in the local parish, while the Catholic Party wanted a Catholic Church that tolerated what was traditionally associated with Low-church Anglican ceremonial, such as Morning and Evening Prayer services, at the local parish level. The real issue appears to have been one of control, and the Phalanx began to realize that they were losing it rather quickly.

Bishop Doren, who was a board member of the Foundation for Christian Theology, also protested the growing levels of Catholicism within the ACC by refusing to preach the sermon at Fr. William Dejarnette Rutherford's consecration as the Bishop Coadjutor of the Diocese of the Mid-Atlantic States. Doren explained that he had increasingly become the lone representative of the "low church" view among the College of Bishops. He held the straightforward position that the ACC was supposed to have been the "Continuing" Episcopal Church, and that the other bishops seemed to be establishing another kind of Continuing church, one that was not really faithful to traditional Episcopalian doctrine and worship.[315] Likewise, Dorothy Faber editorialized against those churchmen ("mostly clergy") who were "infected with near-fanatic zeal to gain recognition by some ancient See." In consistently Protestant fashion, she argued that the only "recognition" that mattered was that given by Jesus Christ through grace.[316] More importantly as to later developments within the ACC, Bishop Clavier of the American Episcopal Church began writing a near-monthly column for *The Christian Challenge,* under the pseudonym of "Bishop Hobeau," (a dismissive inside joke referring to what many High- churchmen considered to be his questionable or vagante orders).

The third provincial Synod of the ACC was held in Mobile, Alabama, in October of 1980. The Mobile Synod was even more peaceful than that held in Indianapolis the previous year. The only event that approached being controversial was the reading of a letter by Bishop Doren, who was not present, addressed to the delegates. Doren chastised many of the doctrines and practices of the High-churchmen, such as referring to the Eucharist as a "Mass" and a sacrifice, and the use of Missal services in conjunction with the Prayer Book service. Bishop Harvey gave a gentle rebuttal to the letter, and the issue seemed to have died the death of disinterest among the delegates. Another interesting development was the attempt to unseat Andrew Stahl as Senior Canonist because of his Canadian residence, but this failed because he was an active member of a parish in Michigan. The real motivation behind this attempt was undoubtedly the desire among the Phalanx to be rid of the man who was largely responsible for crafting the Canons that so irked them. An attempt by the Phalanx to make it easier to amend the Constitution and Canons was nonetheless defeated. This proposal would have reduced the percentage of votes required in each order of the Synod, from a three-fourths vote to a two-thirds vote, in order to amend the Church documents. Another defeat for the Phalanx came when Fr. Carroll Simcox, the then president of the Foundation for Christian Theology, and past president of the Fellowship of Concerned Churchmen, failed to be elected into a pool of priests from which a diocese may elect a bishop.[317] The priest elected into the pool of potential bishops was Fr. Louis W. Falk, a man so seemingly High-church that he had once written an article extolling the virtues of Marian devotion, including keeping the Feast of the Assumption (though he tellingly called it a "pious opinion" and tried to justify the practice with Biblical evidence).[318]

The Mobile Synod also formalized the boundaries of the dioceses. In the process, the Patrimony had met the canonical requirements for diocesan status, and thus became the Diocese of the South (DOS). If any act finalized the fact that there were no plans for the ACC to bring Bishop Watterson back into the fold, this was it. The Assistant Bishop of the Patrimony, Frank R. Knutti, was given episcopal oversight of the new diocese until they could elect their own bishop. The bishops then created the Missionary Diocese of the Missouri Valley, and appointed Fr. Falk as its Ordinary. The Diocese of the Missouri Valley, which encompassed mostly the upper Northwest, was created in order to shrink the Diocese of the Holy Trinity, which had been a non-geographical diocese, into a more manageable size for Bishop Mote. Few realized at the time just how much power Bishop Mote (as the leader of a growing High-church party within the ACC) had gained in Mobile. His diocese had been downsized with the creation of a new diocese, which was then placed under the head of his former Diocesan Dean, Fr. Falk, who could be counted on for sympathetic votes in the College of Bishops. Furthermore, the attempts by the Phalanx to ease the requirements for amending the Constitution and Canons, and to unseat Canon Andrew Stahl, had failed. Perhaps this is why, that during his caucus with the delegates of his diocese in Mobile, Mote backtracked on a promise he had made to members of the Southern California Deanery that he would continue to honor their stand of ecumenical neutrality among traditionalist Anglicans in the Los Angeles area. However, shortly after the Synod, Mote informed Fr. Clendenin (a member of the DCK) of the Deanery that they were no longer in communion with each other. This severance was apparently initiated after a request made by Fr. Clendenin that priests from the DCK and the DHT be allowed to minister in each other's parishes should an urgent need arise.[319] Mote, no doubt feeling more secure in his position as leader of the Church, had finally put his foot down in regard to the ecumenically inclined Deanery of Southern California.

Also during this time, Archdeacon Medaris decided to lead his parishes out of the ARJA. He stated, "Little by little our investigations brought out facts and conditions that tended to eliminate the options from truly serious consideration. Finally, it became increasingly apparent that the only real hope for a strong Continuing Church as originally envisaged at the St. Louis Congress lay with what is now titled the Anglican Catholic Church." Shortly after this message was released on November 20 of 1980, most of the ARJA's Eastern Jurisdiction joined the Diocese of the South in the ACC.[320] Thus the year 1980 had ended well for the Catholic party in the ACC. The ARJA had suffered a considerable setback at the ACC's expense, and the Phalanx had been stalled in Mobile. This situation should probably be attributed to the shrewdness of Mote, who, although he was a rather staunch High-churchman in matters liturgical, had apparently aligned himself with the

Phalanx in order to us its extensive propaganda apparatus to initially increase his effective control of, and influence within, the ACC. Once this control had been achieved, Mote seems to have asserted his independence from the Low-church forces that had initially backed him. Conversely, the Phalanx, which had similarly aligned itself with Mote for strategic reasons, discovered that Mote's personality and charisma carried more weight within the ACC than did their near-monopoly on the information apparatus among Continuing churchmen.

Chapter 9

THE PHALANX STRIKES BACK

The Catholic Party had gained effective control of the ACC by the conclusion of the Mobile Synod. Bishop Doren's clarion call for a return by the Church to its traditional Anglican heritage had hardly caused a ripple. Perhaps sensing that he had become a powerless minority of one within the College of Bishops, Doren did not attend the Synod to read his letter to the delegates, claiming instead to have been too ill to attend. Shortly after the Synod, Doren issued another letter in which he invited disgruntled members of the ACC to join him in forming a new, more authentically Low-church body. Among his complaints was the accusation that the ACC was soon going to replace the 1928 Prayer Book with Missal services, and that the 39 Articles of Religion were not being accepted as authoritative in doctrine.[321] Only two parishes (one his own) initially responded to Doren's call for a return to a more traditional (read Protestant) Episcopal Church. Meeting on December 7, 1980, in Coshocton, Ohio, representatives from the two parishes established the United Episcopal Church. The new body voted to establish itself under the Constitution and Canons in effect in the Episcopal Church as of 1958.[322]

The ACC's College of Bishops, apparently in response to many letters received from troubled churchmen who sympathized partially with Doren's complaints, issued a statement on December 17, 1980, in order to quiet fears and rumors. They specifically addressed the issues of churchmanship, episcopal authoritarianism, and the position of the Prayer Book, assuring Continuing churchmen that no one would be excluded from the ACC over these issues, nor forced to conform to a certain level of churchmanship.[323] At this time the College of Bishops appears to have begun a process of trying to convince the laity that there would not be a kind of High-church inquisition against those who held to a Broad or Low-church position. As if to confirm this assertion of their own moderation, in January of 1981, formal discussions were initiated with the American Episcopal Church. The meeting was held in Deerfield Beach, Florida, and bishops from the two bodies discussed the issues of episcopal orders, doctrine, discipline, and worship. It was agreed that further discussions would continue until the Synod's of both bodies had either approved or disapproved of a formal move toward intercommunion.[324]

One may wonder how it could be that a supposedly hyper-Catholic College of Bishops, who were accused of being authoritarians by Broad- churchmen, could then enter into ecumenical discussions with the AEC? After all, Bishop Clavier and the AEC were committed to the Broad-church interpretation and practice of Anglicanism. One possible answer is that the ACC bishops feared mass defections from their fold over the churchmanship issue, and saw the AEC as the most likely haven for such disaffected churchmen, since the AEC had a more sizable membership than any of the other Continuing bodies (excluding the Catholic DCK), and relative stability (having been in existence for 12 years). Another possibility is that the College of Bishops were not necessarily the High-church tyrants that the Southern Phalanx were increasingly accusing them to be.

Meanwhile, on January 23-24, 1981, the new Diocese of the South had elected Bishop Knutti to be its first bishop. Knutti had been the Assistant Bishop of the Patrimony of the Metropolitan, and the Episcopal Administrator of the DOS since its formation, and thus seemed like a natural choice for the position. However, there were reportedly complaints among some of the diocesan delegates that Bishop Burns, the Vicar General of the Patrimony, had been present at the Diocesan Synod, and had somehow coerced the delegates into electing Knutti. Although these complaints seem to have not appeared in any of the Phalanx's publications until August, Bishop Harvey issued a pastoral letter to these disaffected members of the DOS on March 4, urging them to stay in the ACC. Harvey stated, "It was not their [the College of Bishops] expectation that your former officialis [a title of Senior Canonist Andrew Stahl] would be there to lend assistance. It was not their will that your former Vicar General should push you into electing a bishop before you had drafted a Constitution and Canons." Harvey then suggested that a possible solution to the problem these churchmen were encountering with their new bishop could be the formation of a new diocese. Harvey defended his unusual action by claiming that he had been unable to reach Knutti by telephone, and that the situation had grown urgent due to reports that several parishes were meeting to decide whether or not to remain in the DOS.[325] One obvious question (which was never asked or discussed in any of the Phalanx-tinged publications) is how did it come to pass that Harvey was contacted about these disaffected churchmen, but none of the other bishops were? The answer can most likely be found in the fact that Harvey was a member and former president of the Foundation for Christian Theology, and one of the leaders of the disaffected churchmen in the DOS was Fr. Simcox, the then president of the FCT, which had been accused of being the primary guiding force in the formation of the Diocese of the Southwest. When taking this "coincidence" into consideration, and then adding the fact that the months of April, May, and June passed without the Phalanx managing to report on Harvey's letter, or the disaffected churchmen in the DOS, it seems quite possible that a schismatic movement of some kind was in the works.³²⁶

The rest of the ACC bishops met in early April of 1981 to consider what action should be taken in regard to Harvey's letter. The bishops reviewed a report issued by Andrew Stahl in which Harvey's actions were labeled "divisive" and rebellious. The report also recommended possible courses of action that the bishops could take in regard to Harvey; the first being that he be given the opportunity to apologize to the entire ACC, and the others being either a request for his resignation or an ecclesiastical trial. On April 7, the bishops issued a letter to Harvey (who had been "unable to attend" the bishop's meeting) requesting that he retract all erroneous statements made in his letter, and that he "abstain and desist from invasion of any bishop's diocese." Furthermore, they warned him that, if he did not issue a retraction by April 27, the College of Bishops would rebuke him, and if he continued such actions, he would be brought to trial. What followed the College of Bishops' ultimatum is another example of the divide between the Protestant and Catholic wings within the ACC.

The only reply that Harvey made to the ultimatum was a short note stating that he had been advised not to respond to the College of Bishops. On April 11, the first of many memos to be distributed throughout the Church, lasting well into May, were issued by the ACC's Provincial Chancellor, Lewis E. Berry Jr. of Texas, to the College of Bishops. Chancellor Berry claimed that the Canonical requirement for proper notice of a meeting of the College of Bishops had not been met, since he had not been notified of their meeting. Berry had thus declared that the College of Bishops meeting was held illegally. In a comment revealing the Protestant nature of Berry's interpretation of the College of Bishops' ultimatum, he stated, "[The] judgments which the said letter proclaim upon and against the said Bishop Harvey were unlawfully arrived at and are *outside the competence* [emphasis mine] of those signing said letter and would be *outside the competence of the College of Bishops itself* [emphasis mine]. No authority in this Church can impose prior censorship on anyone or restrict anyone's right to engage in lawful communication with any person or group of persons." It is clear that Berry did not think bishops had the right to discipline a fellow bishop for advising churchmen outside of his own diocese that they could form another diocese in protest against their bishop, or that they could meet in emergency session to deal with a serious internal problem without having to first notify a laymen with the title of Provincial Chancellor. It could be argued that Harvey's interference with another bishop's diocese was no different than that diocesan interference into PECUSA affairs upon which the ACC was established. However, the ACC's violation of episcopal authority within a diocese was based on the alleged descent of said bishops into heresy. In contrast, Bishop Harvey may have been acting according to urgent need, but the appropriate action on his part would have been to consult with all of the ACC bishops, who could have then issued a corporate pastoral. Unless of course, Harvey thought that his fellow bishops had fallen into heresy. However, such a corporate pastoral letter would not have included any advice or suggestions about forming a new diocese, and thus would have defeated the probable purpose of Harvey's plan all along. Further cementing the Protestant nature of his stance, and thus perpetuating another link in the symbolic chain stretching all the way back to Luther, Berry opined that the bishops were demanding that Harvey act against his conscience.

Another of Berry's complaints, which also echoed criticisms made by the Phalanx, was that the new Holyrood Seminary had been mismanaged by those persons, appointed by the bishops, to oversee the project. However, his most troublesome charge was that the College of Bishops were required to only take action when they had voted unanimously on an issue, and that since Harvey had not participated, the decision was of no effect. The ACC College of Bishops met again on June 5-6 in Des Moines, Iowa, and reaffirmed their position. More importantly, they adopted a resolution declaring that, due to a procedural flaw, Chancellor Berry had never actually been legally elected to his office. Though this was obviously an arbitrary and self-serving move on the part of the bishops, it seemed to be the complementary action to Berry's declaration that the College of Bishops had not legally met in April. In regard to the fact that they had not acted in unanimity in April, as they had once promised to do, the College of Bishops passed another resolution that changed the system so as to require only a majority vote by the bishops in order for the College to take action.[327]

While the Phalanx was ignoring the story of Bishop Harvey and Chancellor Berry as it was actually occurring, they did manage to continue their critiques of the ACC as it was constituted at that time, especially in regard to its Canons. Perry Laukhuff warned in the February *Certain Trumpet*, "Either the next Provincial Synod must select a new *and independent* [emphasis mine] Committee of Revision, or we shall have to endure a long, slow process of amendment and change, point by point, synod by synod, for years to come. One way or the other the incubus of the present Canons must be shaken off."[328] In April, the anonymous Bishop Hobeau (Bishop Clavier) was also given the forum to criticize the ACC's Canons. Bishop Hobeau spoke of the Canons as being oppressive, "Just as the citizen today seems at the mercy…of legal experts in a growing part of their lives, so the laity of the [Continuing] Movement seem to be at the mercy of *our [emphasis mine]* ecclesiastical lawyers, and in a manner quite new to them." It should be noted that the anonymous Clavier here refers to *our* lawyers, and thus represents himself as being part of the ACC [unless the AEC that he headed was likewise being ruined by ecclesiastical laws]. If anything, this misstatement is probably not so much a lie on his part as it is a Freudian slip revealing where his thoughts were increasingly moving at the time. He concluded, "Above all, clergy and laity should not be persuaded into leaving such things [the Canons] to the experts. The experts may well be wrong."[329] In June, the Board of Directors of the FCC unanimously agreed to call a "Second Congress of Concerned Churchmen," in which representatives of "all church bodies with an Anglican ethos," would be invited to take part in the organizing committee. The supposed purpose of the second congress was to commemorate the fifth anniversary of the first congress in St. Louis.[330] However, the St. Louis Congress had specifically refused (apparently at the FCC's urging) to recognize the vagante bishops of the other Continuing bodies. Obviously, the second congress was designed for different purposes, perhaps to unify some of the various Continuing bodies (once labeled vagantes) into an Anglican church organized along more Broad-church lines. Such a possibility had been suspected by the ACC bishops, who in their discussions during the September, 1981 meeting of the College of Bishops in Liberty, New York, dismissed the proposed congress as unnecessary, even though Bishop Harvey and Mr. Berry had argued on its behalf. The bishops passed a resolution stating that the FCC representatives to the new congress, even if they were also members of the ACC, would not be speaking on behalf of the ACC.[331]

The proposed second congress accompanied a wider impulse within the overall Continuing Movement toward unity among the various jurisdictions. In the Spring of 1981, Bishop Clavier of the AEC and Bishop de Catanzaro of the Anglican Catholic Church of Canada, announced that they had informally agreed that their two bodies were in communion with each other since they found, "no essential differences in doctrine, discipline, or worship separating the major jurisdictions of the Continuing Anglican Church in North America." They also announced that they would not ask their Synods to officially agree to intercommunion until all of the jurisdictions in the Anglican Continuum were involved in ecumenical talks.[332] In May, three Anglican Rite parishes in the Polish National Catholic Church met in Spartanburg, South Carolina, to discuss their Church's recent decision to forbid the parishes from using the Anglican rite. Lead by Fr. Robin B. Connors, they agreed to associate as the English National Catholic Church, and to ask for episcopal oversight from the ACC. Shortly thereafter, Connors announced that a meeting was to be held in late August, in Spartanburg, in order to bring the Continuing Anglican bishops together and discuss the possibilities of union.[333] In June, members of assorted Continuing Anglican bodies met in Arlington, Virginia to discuss forming a unification movement. From this meeting came an announcement that the AEC and the Anglican Episcopal Church of North America had agreed to work together with the goal of merging in 1982. Bishops Clavier (AEC) and Walter Adams (AECNA) announced that both churches would form committees to iron out the details, and would meet in joint synod in 1982 to make the final decision.[334]

    Different interpretations of the August Spartanburg meeting would lay the groundwork for future difficulties in bringing the ACC into the wider movement for unity among Continuing Anglicans. In a report issued to the ACC College of Bishops in September, Bishops Lewis (Chairman of Ecumenical Relations) and Rutherford stated that the meeting lacked substance, and that the main topic of conversation was a resolution proposed by some of those bishops present that they exchange certain episcopal actions. According to the report, it was agreed that no such actions should be undertaken on an official basis.[335] According to Clavier, a statement was written "together" (did this include Bishops Lewis and Rutherford?) proposing the formation of an informal council in which all the Continuing bishops could meet and discuss the conditions that would have to be met in order to achieve union. The statement also called (informally) on the bishops present in Spartanburg to commit to consulting with and informing one another in matters such as ordinations, consecrations, or the transfer of a parish into another jurisdiction. The statement also included an (informal) agreement among the bishops not to invade each other's jurisdictions or dioceses. Clavier implied that the ACC bishops were the only obstacles to the implementation of what was termed by some the "Spartanburg Agreement." He also claimed, probably correctly, that the ACC bishops present in Spartanburg had informed him that the orders of his ministry and church were the primary obstacles to intercommunion between the two bodies. He concluded that there was little point at that time in continuing ecumenical discussions with the ACC.[336] What Clavier failed to mention was that no one present in Spartanburg, including himself, had signed the document.[337]

The most problematic statements made by Clavier regarding the Spartanburg meeting dealt with Bishop Lewis of the ACC. According to Clavier, Bishop Pagtakhan had been approached with the suggestion of arranging a service of "mutual recognition of ministries," and he had agreed that such an action would promote unity within the Continuing Movement. Lewis was supposedly asked for his opinion as to how such conditional consecrations would be received by the ACC, and he is said to have responded, in only a private opinion, that such an action would promote unity.[338] If this is true, it means that Lewis was acting as a kind of double agent within the ACC, saying one thing to his College of Bishops and another to the other Continuing bishops present in Spartanburg, or he was acting rather erratically.

The push for unity that had begun in Spartanburg reached its peak in the controversial consecration service held in San Diego, California, on September 26, 1981. This appears to have been the direct result of the discussions held in Spartanburg. Bishops Pagtakhan, Sergio Mondala, and Lupe Rosete of the PICC were reported to have conditionally consecrated, or "regularized the Orders of" three bishops of the American Episcopal Church, and three of the Anglican Episcopal Church. The AEC Bishops were Clavier, Walter H. Grundorf, and G. Raymond Hanlan. The AECNA Bishops were Primus Walter H. Adams, John Hamers, and Frank Benning. After the service, the six American bishops issued a statement claiming that they had no doubts as to the validity of their previous Orders, but had decided to be conditionally re-consecrated in order to ease the consciences of churchmen who were concerned about the validity of episcopal Orders, which were a significant barrier to unity within the wider Continuing Movement.[339] This portion of the statement was plainly meant for the bishops of the ACC.

The ACC College of Bishops first discussed the San Diego consecrations at their September meeting, and the tenor of their discussions was rather skeptical. To begin with, the ACC bishops discussed an issue that was not revealed in the Phalanx's accounts of the consecration service, which had most probably been obtained from Bishop Clavier, namely, that three bishops of the Anglican Rite Jurisdiction of the Americas (Kennaugh, G. Wayne Craig, and Ogden Miller) were also consecrated in San Diego. The ACC bishops were puzzled as to the purpose of such a consecration service, but they seemed willing to wait until more information was available. However, comments by some the bishops indicated that they were not inclined to approve of the action taken by Pagtakhan. Bishop Falk questioned the procedures by which the orders were regularized. Canon Stahl explained that for such a process to be valid it would require the regularization of all steps, from baptism through the episcopate if needed, and that it had to be done for each individual case. Falk also questioned the seriousness of the intent of those involved, and Bishop Burns stated that it was his opinion that the consecrations did not change the fact that all involved were vagantes.[340]

Complicating matters further was the unreported (by the Southern Phalanx of which Bishop Clavier was an increasingly important component) nature of the relationship that actually existed between the Anglican Rite Jurisdiction of the Americas and the American Episcopal Church. Before the AEC and AECNA had agreed in June of 1981 to work toward a merger, the AECNA had proposed an agreement of amity and intercommunion with the ARJA in May. The proposal had been accepted by the Archdeacons of the ARJA in July, and by the AECNA on August 9, only a few weeks before the Spartanburg meeting. From the ARJA's point of view, the purpose of the San Diego consecration service was to help unify all three bodies. However, attempts at contacting Clavier in regard to formalizing the ARJA's participation in the future merger of the AEC and AECNA seemed to flounder. In late October, Bishop Clavier wrote to the bishops of the ARJA and informed them that they were welcome to informally participate in talks between the AEC and AECNA, but that the AEC had not formally decided that it would be in intercommunion or unity with the ARJA. The topic became moot from the ARJA's point of view when Clavier informed them in late November that it was too late to introduce another jurisdiction into the process (of AEC-AECNA union).³⁴¹ Thus, the group that Clavier had worked with in order to gain conditional consecration or regularization of his orders (supposedly for the purpose of securing wider unity in the Continuing Movement) was now considered to be outside of the unity process. It is interesting to note that Clavier, perhaps the most outspoken advocate of greater unity in the Continuing Movement, appears to have never initiated any future talks with the ARJA. One is tempted to agree with the cynical interpretation of many within the ARJA that Clavier had used Pagtakhan and the ARJA in order to attain regularization of the AEC's orders, and that afterwards, he discarded the ARJA. A possible reason for this may have been that Pagtakhan and the ARJA were never highly regarded by anyone in the Phalanx, whereas Clavier appears to have become something analogous to their pet.

The first critiques made by the ACC of the San Diego consecrations were rather limited in scope. A December editorial in *The Trinitarian* questioned the jurisdictions of the ARJA bishops, and dismissed the AEC and AECNA bishops as vagantes, and raised the question of the "faith and morals" of these bishops who, it was claimed, had not had their backgrounds checked as had those of the ACC. The Phalanx responded by reprinting the ACC editorial, and then printed three critical responses. Bishop Clavier again repeated his claim that Bishop Lewis had agreed that the San Diego consecrations were a good idea. Fraser Barron's critique was the most detailed, and the most serious since it came from someone who was still a member of the ACC. Barron stated that, if anything, the AEC and AECNA orders were more valid than the ACC's, since Anglican orders were not recognized by Rome, while the AEC and AECNA's Old Catholic orders, though irregular, were recognized. He also repeated Clavier's claim regarding Lewis' foreknowledge of the San Diego service. What is most curious about Barron's repetition of this claim is that he had knowledge of it at all. Unless he was physically present when Lewis allegedly consented to the consecration service, it means that Barron had to have gotten his information either directly from Clavier or indirectly from the Phalanx. Perhaps this is why Barron so strongly denied another claim made in *The Trinitarian* editorial, namely, that the FCC had taken a leading role in the ecumenical discussions within the Continuing Movement. The ACC editorial had made the claim in order to illustrate the point that only the Church can finalize an intercommunion or merger agreement, and not individual participants in ecumenical discussions, many of which were largely organized and manned by members of the FCC. However, the adamancy of Barron's denial, which seems out of proportion to the nature of the charge, is more suspicious than convincing.[342] After reading Barron's letter, one can't help but conclude that the writer probably already had one foot in another ecclesiastical door. Exhibiting an ever-increasing hostility toward the ACC, *The Christian Challenge* followed the critiques of the ACC editorial immediately with another critique (by the anonymous Bishop Hobeau), of those (like the ACC) who fretted over questions of validity and jurisdiction.

The movement toward merging the various Continuing Anglican bodies continued apace, with the FCC Congress Committee meeting in Deerfield Beach, Florida, the home of Bishop Clavier. The Committee agreed to develop a plan for promoting mutual evangelism to bring more people into the Continuing Movement, with reportedly no concern as to which body new members would join. It was boasted that there were eight jurisdictions represented at the gathering, including the ACC, but upon closer inspection this was misleading. The ACC representatives were the aforementioned Lewis E. Berry, and Louis E. Traycik, president of the FCC, both of whom were members of the Diocese of the Southwest.[343] Four members of the FCC began 1982 by calling for a Convocation of

Continuing Anglicans to bring together members, and former members, of the ACC in order to discuss options for unifying the dispersed bodies of the Anglican Continuum. According to William C. White, who organized the Convocation, it was the Steering Committee's hope that "all those involved will come to an agreement on membership in a continuing Church body." He claimed that there was no intent to establish a new church body, but that the Convocation would only be a temporary place for disaffected parishes to associate until they could make their choice as to which group to affiliate with.[344] When it is recalled how much abuse was heaped onto Pagtakhan when he formed his umbrella jurisdiction for disgruntled Continuers, the attempt by the Phalanx to form such an umbrella-type of "association" borders on either gross hypocrisy or convenient amnesia. In April of 1982, the FCC met in Fort Worth, Texas, and "endorsed the aims" of the Convocation for Continuing Anglicans, even though it had essentially been organized by members of the FCC in the first place.[345]

    Perhaps feeling the pressure from the organizational efforts being undertaken by the smaller Continuing bodies, the ACC College of Bishops issued a letter in January of 1982, expressing their admiration for the other groups, and a desire that there be intercommunion among all Continuing Anglicans. The letter ended by declaring the bishops' willingness to enter into discussions to achieve such an end.[346] This all seems rather curious since the bishops had seemingly dismissed the orders and intentions of the other groups only a few weeks earlier. Whatever the ACC's motivation, be it fear of losing members or genuine concern for unity among Continuing Anglicans, the AEC bishops responded with their own letter in which they announced that they would form a commission for the purpose of conducting ecumenical discussions with the ACC.[347] Despite these hopeful signs, the delicate nature of the foundations for future unity between the two groups would be exposed when the ACC's Diocese of the Southwest took it upon itself to announce in February of 1982 that that it was in full communion with the other groups.[348] Though it was never commented on in the Phalanx-tinged publications, this action by the DSW appears to have been essentially schismatic and, if nothing else, proved that the leadership in the diocese already viewed themselves as being something other than a part of the ACC. The Convocation for Continuing Anglicans, which followed the aforementioned FCC meeting in Fort Worth by a day, disappointed its organizers in that it was unable to develop any concrete plan for achieving greater unity. About half of the participants signed a declaration expressing the sentiment that God is the head of the Church, and not the bishops.[349] However, the night before the Convocation, representatives of the AECNA and ARJA signed a formal agreement to confer with one another over the next five years regarding the adoption of a set of Canons that would combine the insights of both churches.[350]

While all of these ecumenical discussions and meetings were underway, the Phalanx managed to keep a steady barrage of criticism going against the ACC, possibly in the hopes of undermining it. Dorothy Faber criticized the development of a form of church government in which the bishops have the power, rather than the laity and clergy sharing power within the Synod. Echoing the refrain of the Phalanx, she complained that the ACC had been turned into something not envisioned by the St. Louis Congress and the *Affirmation*. Pinpointing the precise nature of the problem, Faber wondered if the ACC was to be "in fact, Anglican."[351] She later accused the ACC of being overpowered by its clergy. As evidence for this, she claimed that there were two diocesan Standing Committees that were never allowed to meet because their bishops saw no use for them. She also claimed that the ACC's focus on the Eucharist, which took up the majority of time during a worship service, was really a means of covering up poor preaching.[352] The establishment of the Holyrood Seminary in New York was criticized on many fronts, from those who thought no seminary was needed at all, to those who criticized how the funds were spent, and those who rejected the bishops playing the primary decision making role in the whole affair.[353] But the issue that agitated the Phalanx to no end continued to be the pesky ACC Canons.

The most thorough critique of the ACC Canons came from Fraser Barron, who commented that there were too many of them, that many of them were nearly incomprehensible, and most importantly, that they had established a body that was dominated by bishops.[354] The most stinging critique came from Dr. Robert M. Strippy. Strippy called the ACC "the immensely amplified hobby of one overarching individual [Fr. Andrew Stahl] whose learning is almost equal to his conceit, but more than enough to cow those among the clergy and the episcopate who are theologically limited." In typically graceless, and quasi-humorous Strippy fashion, he continued by calling *The Trinitarian*, which had recently been elevated to the status of official publication of the ACC, "the grouchy little Sunday-school leaflet…a penny broadside now elevated into the official voice of the Anglican Catholic Church – a noteworthy example of mediocrity rushing in to fill the vacuum." He also sneered that the Canons had more lines than the ACC had members, and that the Canons had been "concocted and enticed down the throats of those on the episcopal bench and in the Provincial Synod" in an intellectually dishonest fashion.[355] Srippy's critique, which seemed designed as much to malign as to analyze, appeared in June of 1982, just in time to be digested by delegates to the fourth Synod of the ACC in Kansas City, Missouri.

The Kansas City Synod was held from June 9 to 12, 1982, and resulted in yet another split or schism within the ACC, with the Diocese of the Southwest and Bishop Harvey walking out during the Synod's final session. Although the Phalanx tried to maintain that the walkout came as an unexpected shock to the rest of the delegates, it appears that many ACC churchmen had anticipated the schism all along. In retrospect, how could they not have? The previous year's controversy over Harvey's letter to the Diocese of the South had seemingly been put on hold, for both Harvey and Lewis Berry were still present at the meetings of the College of Bishops that followed, but it is doubtful that this issue wasn't on everyone's mind. Then, in February of 1982, the DSW had acted on its own authority to proclaim itself as being in intercommunion with the other Continuing groups, even though the ACC was only beginning the process of investigating such a possibility. Adding fuel to the fire in March, Harvey issued his "Other Side of the Moon" pastoral letter for the diocese, which accused the rest of the ACC of denying the laity their proper role and status within the church's structure, which resulted in a doctrine of episcopal supremacy, rather than the classically Anglican doctrine of episcopal primacy.[356] Although Harvey's message was rather pedestrian in its insights, and monotonous in its repetition of what the Phalanx had already stated many times before, it was still seen to be of such monumental importance to the Phalanx that they reprinted it for the wider Church in both the *Anglican News Exchange* and *The Christian Challenge*, both being released just in time to be read by the Kansas City delegates.

Then in late May, Harvey issued his blockbuster letter throughout the DSW and DOS, accusing the entire College of Bishops of assorted violations of the ACC Constitution and Canons. However, he vented most of his venom toward Bishop Burns, the Vicar General of the DOS, who had supposedly coerced that diocese into electing Knutti as its first bishop. Apparently, Burns revealed during the Kansas City Synod that he was seeking legal advice as to whether he should bring suit against Harvey. This revelation, revealed on the final day by Lewis Berry, supposedly shocked the delegates, since it seemed beyond the pale for a bishop to sue a fellow bishop.[357] However, the contents of Harvey's letter were never reprinted or reported on in any specific detail by the publications of the Phalanx. This is probably because they feared that repeating Harvey's charges might make them legally liable as well, and since this fear was strong enough to require editorial silence, the letter against Burns probably was, at the very least, too close to being libelous for the Phalanx to risk duplicating. That Harvey sometimes wrote letters that were questionable as to their utility (or propriety) is admitted in a diatribe against the treatment of the DSW written by Perry Laukhuff. Although Laukhuff had first considered Harvey's letter to have been a mistake, he changed his mind when he reportedly saw the vulgar and un-Christian behavior of Bishop Burns at the Synod.[358]

The delegates from the DSW, and their influential Phalanx friends from around the country, appear to have found every major item on the Synod agenda to be worthy of a bitter debate. Fr. Carroll Simcox called for the dissolution of the Holyrood Seminary. Fraser Barron criticized the report of the Ecumenical Commission, claiming that it was too arrogant and judgmental towards other Continuing groups. A resolution was passed stating that the Synod considered the need for union with other Continuing Anglican bodies to be urgent. And of course, the canons were repeatedly criticized as moving the ACC toward a Papal idea of supremacy for the Metropolitan. When the delegates of the DSW had finished their protest against the ACC, they announced their departure from the ACC and their desire to seek unity with other Continuing bodies. The ACC Synod, with the little time it had left, proposed that the next Provincial Synod consider the Constitution and Canons before it dealt with any other business, and that the Constitution and Canons Committee consult with Canonical experts from other parts of the Anglican Communion to receive suggestions for improvement or amendment of the ACC documents. The Synod also stated that anyone should be allowed to attend the meetings of the Constitution and Canons Committee.[359] Quizzically, the Synod had effectively agreed to do what the delegates from the DSW had wanted (move toward a critical examination of the Canons), yet by the time this was done, the Southwestern agitators had already withdrawn. Some interpreters did not think it would have mattered, no matter what had transpired during the Synod. According to one Kansas City delegate, "When we got to Kansas City they had their secession movement all worked out, and they knew exactly what they were doing. Strippy, and Harvey, and Simcox, and the Trayciks, they were all together. I think that this was a long term plan."[360]

    Meanwhile, the movement to create a larger, more broad-based Continuing Anglican body, continued to gather steam. The merger between the AEC and the AECNA became official in late May of 1982, during a joint synod of the two bodies held in Seattle, Washington. The new, enlarged church adopted a set of Canons, which were reportedly drafted by a committee comprised of members of each body, and retained the name of the larger group (the AEC]. Bishop Clavier was reportedly elected to be the Primus of the enlarged AEC, while Bishop John M. Hamers of the old AECNA was named the Episcopal Vice President.[361] However, the Seattle unification Synod still could not avoid being beset by yet another schism. The

Primus of the AECNA, Bishop Adams, along with Bishops Graham Lesser and Thomas Kleppinger, decided to reject the merger between the two bodies, and continue the AECNA under its prior structure. Although the reason for their hesitation in merging with the AEC is not clear, there were AECNA churchmen who claimed that Clavier had arrived with his own set of Canons, stating flatly that he was going to be the top bishop.[362] Another possibility is that the dissenting AECNA bishops were not comfortable with the manner in which the ARJA had been dealt with in the unification process. One of the first things that the dissenting bishops did after the Seattle Synod was to announce that they were seeking to be in intercommunion with the ARJA.[363] The AEC claimed, probably correctly, that the majority of the AECNA parishes had joined the AEC, but the dissenting AECNA bishops disputed the claim.[364]

It was not only the infusion of a large portion of the AECNA into its fold that enlarged the AEC, but also the absorption of some ACC parishes and members into the AEC. Shortly after the Kansas City Synod, four parishes in the Diocese of the South joined the AEC.[365] Soon thereafter, Fr. Carroll Simcox, a member of the DOS, joined the AEC, becoming the editor of its official publication, *Ecclesia*.[366] In September, the Diocese of the Southwest voted to repeal its prior ratification of the ACC Constitution and Canons, and established a unity commission to begin the process of ecumenical discussions for the purpose of a possible merger with another Continuing Anglican body.[367] The ACC bishops responded to these developments by renewing their commitment to hold ecumenical discussions with the AEC, and issuing a plea (in August of 1982) to the DSW to reconsider their departure. The bishops also expressed their condolences over the death of Dorothy Faber, who had died on June 28, and asked the faithful to pray for her.[368]

The ACC College of Bishops met in October of 1982 and addressed several issues that were causing concern for many of their churchmen. They named Bishop Falk to be the chairman of a Survey Committee to submit the ACC Constitution and Canons to authorities outside of the church for the purpose of criticism and suggestions. They also stated that they hoped that the DSW would one day be reunited with the ACC. More importantly, they announced their acceptance of informal intercommunion with other Continuing Anglican groups. The bishops stated that it was acceptable for ACC members to receive communion in the parishes of other Continuing bodies when no ACC parish was available, and vice versa. However, the bishops tempered their otherwise conciliatory and ecumenical gathering with a sobering reaffirmation of the authority of the office of bishop, stating that it was, "God given, neither bestowed nor withdrawn by mortal assemblies."[369]

On October 29, 1982, Fr. Herman Nelson was consecrated to be the Bishop of the ARJA Diocese of St. John the Evangelist. The consecration took place during a joint Clericus of the ARJA and the remnant of the AECNA, and included bishops from both groups as consecrators. A joint newsletter for the two groups was also proposed.[370] The move toward unity between the bodies, which had been strong before the inclusion of the AEC into the talks, seemed to be gaining strength once again. However, the unification of the two Continuing Anglican bodies suffered several serious blows. Bishop M. Dean Stephens, who had been one of the consecrators of Bishop Nelson, joined the ACC shortly thereafter.[371] Then Bishop Lesser left the AECNA in order to join the Diocese of Christ the King.[372] The ARJA and AECNA held a joint synod from June 1 to 3, 1983, in Columbus, Ohio. Bishop Craig, who had been chosen to replace Bishop Kennaugh as the Archbishop of the ARJA, promised to resign, once the two bodies had finalized their merger, so that both bodies could participate in the election of an Archbishop. The joint synod also appointed commissions to discuss the issues of Holy Orders and Canons for the two bodies, and it was agreed that each would jointly fund a new publication, *The Evangelist*. Also, Fr. Robert G. Wilkes was consecrated by bishops of both bodies to be a bishop in the AECNA.[373] However, once again, the hopes of the ARJA for greater unity were dampened. On June 8, 1983, in Indianapolis, Indiana, the AECNA bishops met with bishops of the ACC and Bishop de Catanzaro (who would die soon after) of the ACCC, and signed a statement in which the three bodies declared themselves to be in amity with each other. The AECNA bishops also agreed to initiate steps toward unification with the ACC, and vice versa.[374]

The former ACC Diocese of the Southwest continued its independent existence for most of 1983. In March, Bishop Harvey (who was retiring), with the assistance of Bishops Clavier and Hamers of the AEC, consecrated Fr. H. Edwin Caudill of Texas to be the new bishop of the diocese.[375] The relationship between the DSW and the AEC continued on its inevitable course, with the AEC's Provincial Standing Committee inviting the DSW to participate in the preparation of a Constitution and Canons for the potentially unified body.[376] The ACC College of Bishops followed suit by declaring the seat in the College held by the DSW to be vacant, thus putting an end to any small possibility of reunion.[377] On November 11, 1983, the DSW held what it thought to be its last synod as an independent jurisdiction, voting to accept the resolution proposing unity with the AEC. The final approval of the merger would have to wait until the next synod of the AEC, which wouldn't be held until October of 1984.[378]

The ACC held its fifth Synod in Orlando, Florida, in October of 1983. Bishop Falk was chosen to be the first

ACC bishop to hold the position of Metropolitan. The bishops of the AECNA were present to witness the Synod vote to approve intercommunion between the two bodies, and Bishop Adams told the delegates that he considered the ACC Constitution and Canons to be "undoubtedly Anglican and Catholic." A debate over the powers of the office of Metropolitan, which had been initiated by a Phalanx front known as the "Charlottesville Group," resulted in the Canons being amended to better clarify the limitations of the Metropolitan's authority. Several other suggestions by this group were reportedly incorporated into the Canons as well.[379] Whether the ACC was trying to sooth the sting of their critics, or genuinely trying to right their ship, the exhibition of a relatively peaceful process of Canonical amendment probably resulted in many hesitant churchmen deciding to stay within the Church.

Even though the focus of this chapter has been on the ACC, AEC, AECNA, and ARJA, there were other important events developing in the wider Continuing Anglican Movement. In early 1981, several of the parishes that had been involved in legal battles with the Episcopal Church regarding property ownership, heard the final decisions in their cases. Three of the original four parishes in the Los Angeles area to secede from the Episcopal Church were ruled by the California Court of Appeals to be the legal owners of their parish property.[380] However, the United States Supreme Court refused to overturn a New Jersey Supreme Court decision declaring the Episcopal Church to be the owners of the property of two parishes that had seceded there.[381] The experiences of these breakaway parishes had great symbolic power in the wider Continuing Anglican Movement, but most Continuing churchmen had to leave their Episcopal Church parish property behind. During the early years of the Movement, it was the norm for "parishes" to meet in private homes, rented office space, rented facilities from other church groups, funeral parlors, banks, restaurants, and any other venue that could be found for the right price. Many Continuers spent years worshipping in such challenging environments, slowly saving enough money to purchase their own parish building.

Another development during this time was the solidification of the Diocese of Christ the King, while the Diocese of the Southeast continued to decline steadily. The DSEUS held its synod in May of 1981, and a major focus of the meeting involved trying to tabulate how many parishes were still affiliated with the diocese. The DSEUS had apparently been reduced to 8 or 9 parishes.[382] Part of the reason for the decline seemed to have stemmed from the missionary visits made by Bishop Morse for the purpose of convincing Bishop Watterson's parishes to join the DCK. The relationship between the two bodies had been strained after a priest in the DSEUS, Fr. Frederick Preuss, had been chosen by Morse to be a Suffragan Bishop for the DCK. Watterson and his remaining supporters issued statements to Morse, asking him to recognize that Preuss was not in good standing, and had not received the necessary letters of dismissal. Apparently, under the advice of his supporters, Morse determined that he was Canonically at liberty to accept the deposed priest as his new Suffragan.[383] Morse concentrated his energies on improving the seminary of his diocese, St. Joseph of Arimathea Anglican Theological College, in Oakland, California, and on establishing resources from which his diocese could become more stable, as well as intellectually invigorating. In 1982, Morse purchased a church in Washington, D.C., and transformed it into the Episcopal Heritage Center, at which Synods, conferences, and other activities could be held.[384] Also around this time, the DCK established what were called New Oxford Houses, the purpose of which was to provide worship, service, and teaching to college students. The New

Oxford Houses were originally established at UC Berkeley, Yale, and Alabama University.[385] While improving the infrastructure of his diocese, Morse continued to solidify his reputation as the most stubborn and isolationist of the Continuing bishops. When the FCC began soliciting for parish information to be included in a directory for Continuing and traditionalist Anglican parishes, a letter was sent by Morse throughout the DCK, urging his flock not to become involved. The reason given for this stance was that the FCC Directory would include groups who were not part of the St. Louis Movement, and that such groups were lead by vagante bishops. The implication was left that there was to be no possible connection or association with these illegitimate groups.[386]

Another significant development was the shift in tone exhibited by the new editor of *The Christian Challenge*, Dorothy Faber's son-in-law, Louis Traycik, the acting president of the FCC. In his year end message, in which he admitted that he had been part of the dissident group that had departed after the Kansas City Synod, Traycik offered his best wishes to the ACC which, in his opinion, was beginning to take some positive steps toward reforming itself. He wished the ACC well, and gave the impression that the last split in the ACC had probably been for the best from the point of view of both High and Low-churchmen. He ended his message by encouraging Continuing Anglicans to develop a more charitable and relaxed attitude toward one another.[387] This seeming shift in tone may also explain why a Foundation for Christian Theology board member [Dr. Don Gerlach] who happened to champion the cause of the ACC, was chosen to write the report on the 1983 Orlando Synod. The spirit within the Continuing Anglican movement at the end of 1983 can be seen as one of relative calm or peace. In Orlando, the ACC had held its first synod in which no schism had occurred.

The DSW had ended up where it had probably always longed to be, in a Broad-church-style Continuing Anglican body (the AEC) that had originated on similar southern soil. The DCK was confident in its own self-sufficiency, and growing. Of course, the ARJA and the DSEUS under Watterson were experiencing difficulties, but they were also much smaller components of the Continuing Movement.

The total number of members and parishes within the Continuum, as the period covered in this chapter drew to a close, were estimated in a survey by Louis Traycik. The AECNA was estimated to have 6 parishes and no more than 500 members. The ARJA was estimated very roughly to have 15 parishes and perhaps as many as 700 members. The United Episcopal Church founded by Bishop Doren was thought to have about 6 congregations and 500 members. The Anglican Catholic Church of Canada was credited with around 20 congregations and 500 members. The DCK contained as many as 40 parishes and perhaps around 2,000 members. The DSEUS had about 10 parishes and 500 members. The DSW was said to have 24 congregations and 1,200 members, and when added to an earlier estimate for the AEC of approximately 3,000 members, the upcoming merger would create a body with over 4,000 members. The ACC was credited with 110 parishes and over 4,000 members. The Anglican Orthodox Church was said to have between 7 and 20 congregations, and between 1,300 to 2,600 members.[388]

Chapter 10
1984-1987

The merger of the Diocese of the Southwest into the American Episcopal Church in late 1983 marked the beginning of a period of relative calm and stability in the Continuing Anglican Movement. The Southern Phalanx, which had spent the previous few years either trying to reform or attack the Anglican Catholic Church (ACC), and which had primarily joined its fate with that of the DSW and AEC, had now created the Low to Broad-church structure for which they had worked so hard. The Phalanx influenced publications became, relatively speaking, more conciliatory and less hostile when referring to the ACC. The bishops of the ACC also appeared to be adopting a more conciliatory position toward the other Continuing Anglican bodies. If there was one dominant theme that defined the Continuing Anglican Movement during the mid-eighties, it was the belief that the unification of the Movement, or a large portion of it, was realistically possible.

The AEC, under the leadership of Bishop Clavier, had always stressed the need for ecumenical relations among all traditionalist Anglicans, no matter whether they were inside or outside of the official Anglican Communion. The AEC had engaged in five years of discussion with ECUSA about the possibility of coming to some kind of unity agreement. In June of 1983, the AEC issued a petition to Presiding Bishop Allin of ECUSA, seeking to receive recognition as a member in the official Anglican Communion. The Presiding Bishop was to be given "pastoral oversight," although Bishop Clavier stressed that the AEC would remain an autonomous body. The proposal called for the AEC to become a jurisdiction within another jurisdiction (ECUSA) within the Anglican Communion. Clavier noted that the *Affirmation of St. Louis* had stated that the Continuing Church would consider itself in communion with the See of Canterbury and all faithful Anglicans. It is interesting to note that Clavier justified his position by referring to a document that is binding for the ACC, and not the AEC, which probably sheds light on where his thoughts were at that time, namely, the ACC. In September of 1983, ECUSA's House of Bishops unanimously recommended that the proposal be sent to the Committee on Reconciliation.[389]

The first meeting was held in January of 1984 in New York. Discussions continued throughout the first half of the year, and finally resulted in the drafting of an agreement between the representatives of the two bodies. The AEC delegation included Bishops Clavier, Hamers, and Caudill; and the ECUSA delegation was lead by Bishop William C. Wantland of Wisconsin. The draft agreement stated that both bodies recognized their common identity in the formula offered by the Chicago-Lambeth Quadrilateral, and in the 39 Articles of Religion found in the Prayer Book. Each church also recognized the independence of the other, and that no member of either body was required to agree on all matters of doctrinal opinion, sacramental devotion or liturgical practice. Each body agreed to continue in dialogue with the other. ECUSA's House of Bishops met in early October and unanimously adopted the draft agreement. The AEC Synod was held in late October, 1984, in Deerfield Beach, Florida. With delegates representing the Anglican Episcopal Church of North America (AECNA) and the DSW, the Synod voted to accept the agreement for further review, upon which the Synod would vote to ratify the agreement at the 1986

Synod.[390]

Beyond the agreement with ECUSA, the AEC Synod witnessed more important accomplishments. The DSW and AECNA were formally merged into the AEC, and a set of Canons was adopted for the newly enlarged body. The structure of the AEC was to be based on the synod model, with Houses of Bishops, Clergy, and Laity. The House of Bishops was to have only "teaching authority" on spiritual matters.[391] This provision to limit Episcopal authority drew a sharper line between the AEC and ACC, and no doubt pleased the Southern Phalanx to no end. The final completion of the merger of the DSW into the AEC occurred on November 11, in Fort Worth, Texas, when the last independent synod of the DSW voted unanimously to merge into the AEC.[392]

While the AEC continued to expand in 1984, the ACC experienced another relatively calm year. The negotiations to bring the three remaining AECNA bishops into the ACC continued under a plan in which the remnant AECNA would be accepted as a non-geographical diocese [to be called the Diocese of St. Paul] within the ACC. The AECNA bishops were invited to attend the meetings of the ACC College of Bishops prior to the official merger of the two bodies, which could not be finalized until the ACC ratified the merger during their Provincial Synod in 1985.393 In October, the AECNA bishops presided over their own Synod in Tucson, Arizona, in which they voted to join the ACC.[394]

The only conflict during the year involved the expansion of the AEC and ACC into India. Although the details of the conflict are beyond the parameters of this study, the basic disagreement between the two bodies centered on the question of authority in the region, with the ACC claiming it was the legitimate ecclesiastical presence in India, where a group of dissident Indian Anglicans had recently been formed, and the AEC countering that it should also have a presence in India since two Indian bishops had been consecrated by the AECNA bishops who had merged into the AEC. Beyond the jurisdictional squabble between the two largest Continuing bodies, a most interesting statement, referring to the AEC's actions in India, was issued by Archbishop Falk of the ACC: "Our attention has been drawn to attempts by people *posing as Anglicans* [emphasis mine], but in league with the destroyers of Anglicanism, to intrude themselves into the affairs of this Diocese. It is therefore our directive and command that no member of this Diocese…shall…entertain in person, or by any other means, any officer or other member or representative of the North American ecclesial body styling itself the 'American Episcopal Church.'"[395] Archbishop Falk's estimation of the AEC, though disdainful in 1984, would change drastically within a few short years.

In February of 1985, Bishop Herman Nelson resigned from the ARJA, taking some clergy and parishes in the southern states with him.[396] If this wasn't troubling enough for the ARJA, Bishop Pagtakhan traveled to the United States in March of 1985, and announced that the ARJA had "outlived its purpose." He also reported that he was no longer communicating with the ARJA's bishops. Confusing matters within the Continuum even further, Pagtakhan presented a letter from Supreme Archbishop Ga of the Philippine Independent Catholic Church, which declared Pagtakhan to be the PICC's official representative in the United States. Apparently, the PICC was undergoing a schism of their own in which Archbishop Ga had been ousted but was still claiming to be the head of the church. Thus, the apparent schism between Bishops Ga and Pagtakhan, which had been assumed by most Continuers, had now been replaced by one in which the two prelates were in league with each other.[397] Despite these difficulties, the ARJA managed to bring five new parishes into its fold when the Pro-Diocese of Reconciliation agreed to a merger of the two bodies. The Pro-Diocese was led by Bishop Harold Lawrence Trott, who had resigned as Primus of the AEC in 1980, and taken his parish in Albuquerque, New Mexico with him. Trott called his parish the Jurisdiction of Christ the King. In 1983, the Jurisdiction of Christ the King merged with the Catholic Apostolic Church of America, and the small new body was named the Pro-Diocese of Reconciliation. The Catholic Apostolic Church of America had been inactive for several years prior to 1977, but had been reactivated by James B. Gillespie and Gordon Wiebe in order to provide a home for disgruntled Episcopalians.[398] Also accepted into the ARJA that year was Bishop Larry L. Shaver, a former bishop of the AEC [who apparently led a body known as the Society of Augustinian Reconstructionists], and his parish in Merryville, Indiana.[399]

The ACC College of Bishops and the Anglican Catholic Church of Canada issued statements early in 1985 expressing that each was in "full sacramental communion" with the other, with all Anglican jurisdictions that maintained the male priesthood, and with the Diocese of Christ the King.[400] The ACC held its sixth Provincial Synod in October, in Cincinnati, Ohio, and there were no squabbles or defections. The AECNA bishops [Adams, Robert G. Wilkes, and Thomas Kleppinger], and their parishes, were officially accepted into the ACC as the Diocese of St. Paul.[401] Although Bishop Morse had not responded to the ACC's declaration that they were in communion with the DCK, the relationship between the two bodies had apparently improved enough to allow for the first shared consecration between them. In January of 1986, Bishop Mote, with the approval of the ACC College of Bishops, joined Bishops Morse and Woolcock (of the ACCC) in consecrating Fr. John Thayer Cahoon Jr. as a bishop for the DCK.[402]

The DCK continued to flourish at this time, helped in part by the incorporation of most of the remaining parishes of Bishop Watterson's diocese into the DCK.[403] In 1984, Watterson and his family had converted to the Roman Catholic Church after "a year of study," claiming that the problem of doctrinal and ecclesiastical authority had not been adequately resolved in the Continuing Movement. At the time, Watterson was undertaking further preparation in the hopes of becoming a Roman Catholic priest.[404]

Considering the previous tensions between the ACC and AEC, and the recent proclamation by Archbishop Falk of the ACC that the AEC was a body "posing" as Anglicans, the major event that occupied the Continuum in 1986 probably came as quite a surprise to many Continuing churchmen at the time. A meeting of several traditionalist Anglican leaders, including members of many of the Continuing bodies (including the AEC and ACC) and those still within the official Anglican Communion, was held in Fairfield, Connecticut, in March of 1986. The gathering, known as the Fairfield Symposium, had been organized by a group calling itself the Foundation for Anglican Tradition, for the purpose of bringing together traditionalist Anglicans from around the world to discuss the possibility of establishing full communion among traditionalist jurisdictions. The Symposium achieved little of lasting consequence, resulting only in a generic statement of common faith and principles which, in a sign of just how futile the gathering would prove to be, was issued in two versions, one for "Evangelical" and one for "Catholic" Anglicans. The moderator of, and most prominent participant in, the Symposium was the Bishop of London, Graham Leonard. However, Archbishop Falk and Primus Clavier also took important steps during the Fairfield event.

Clavier proposed that the bishops of the Continuing Anglican churches call a "Congress" in order to form a united body, and that they be willing to resign their sees, if the Congress was able to create such a body, in order to create a less contentious Continuing Church. This proposal, which can be interpreted as either a melodramatic ploy or an example of saintly self-denial for the benefit of the Continuum, no doubt secured Clavier's image in many Continuer's eyes as the leading ecumenicist of the Movement. Archbishop Falk also began to move in a more ecumenical direction, stating that the ACC was willing to meet with the other Continuing bodies in order to discuss the issues that separated them, particularly the problem of jurisdictions encouraging or accepting the transfer of allegiance by clergy from one Continuing jurisdiction to another. He proposed that the Continuing jurisdictions agree to limit the transfer of priests, bishops, laity, and parishes from one group to another.[405] Although neither of the their proposals would come to fruition, an important, but unrecognized, change had taken place within the larger Continuing Movement. The ACC bishops, and particularly Archbishop Falk, had suddenly become more open to the establishment of relations with the Continuing bodies (especially the AEC) from which they had previously remained aloof.

The explanation for the ACC's change of attitude toward the other Continuing groups (that is, those other than the DCK and ACCC) seems rather obvious in retrospect. *The Christian Challenge* reported that there was speculation at the time that the ACC was trying to protect itself from losing members to other jurisdictions, as Bishop Tillman Williams of the ACC's Diocese of the South was rumored to be transferring to another jurisdiction, along with anywhere from six to twelve parishes from his diocese.[406] However, this explanation seems less than complete since the ACC had, as often as not, been the beneficiary of such jurisdictional transfers. The most probable reason that the ACC moved in a different direction during 1986 was that most of the Continuing Movement (excepting perhaps the DCK) had come to the conclusion that there was a good possibility that the establishment of a much larger, worldwide Continuing Movement was just around the corner. The reason that Bishop Leonard of England, as well as bishops from Africa and Australia, had traveled to the Fairfield Symposium was that the movement to ordain women had spread to other parts of the Anglican Communion. On top of this, ECUSA was moving inevitably toward consecrating the first female bishop in the history of Anglicanism. Many Continuers no doubt envisioned a potential mass exodus from Anglican churches around the world, which would occur after the Anglican mainstream began to ordain women.

Bishop Williams resigned from the ACC in March of 1986, announcing that he had been accepted into the DCK, and that he had been slandered by the ACC bishops.[407] Although the allegations against Williams seem to have never been replicated in print, several sources have anonymously indicated that he was rumored at the time to have been a homosexual, and that the monastic order he had organized (Order of St. Augustine) may have been a hotbed (no pun intended) of similar un-Christian behavior. Officially, the ACC College of Bishops had been investigating Williams for possible financial malfeasance in matters dealing with his monastic order and the Provincial Department of Evangelism, of which he was the head.[408] Many of the aforementioned anonymous sources also indicated that the financial charges against Bishop Williams, whether or not they were genuine, proved to be an easy out for the College of Bishops in what could have otherwise been an ugly confrontation over sexual misconduct.

Shortly after the controversy over Bishop Williams had been resolved, the newly established Diocese of St. Paul brought the ACC further internal problems. In early July, seven parishes and ten clergymen from Bishop Adams' diocese petitioned Archbishop Falk to be placed under the oversight of the Metropolitan, alleging several irregularities and improprieties within the Diocese of St. Paul. Among the allegations against Adams were that he had used racial slurs against some churchmen, had falsely accused and maligned others, and that he had engaged in non-Canonical actions regarding the holding of a diocesan synod and the disciplining of clergy. The process under which the protesting churchmen were to have their charges investigated called for a sixty-day period in which the College of Bishops gathered and reviewed evidence. Adams, and six of his parishes, decided to withdraw from the ACC before the process could begin.[409] For his part, Adams accused the ACC College of Bishops of reneging on their prior promise to allow the Diocese of St. Paul, and especially its bishops and clergy, to retain its special status within the ACC. Adams announced that he was reconstituting the AECNA, and that he would be its Primus.[410]

Despite these difficulties for the ACC, the movement toward reconciling the two largest Continuing Anglican bodies steadily increased its pace. A potential glitch in the process was avoided when the Foundation for Anglican Tradition, Inc. (FATI), which had organized the Fairfield Symposium, was quietly dissolved after being beset by assorted accusations, and especially financial improprieties. One of the more troubling charges revolved around the fact that FATI, which had formed a coalition with the FCC and FCT, had solicited funds from the various Continuing bodies in order to start something called the Anglican Institute for Ministry and Music. This angered many Continuers, who felt that the monies should support their own group's ministries, rather than that of a new parachurch organization. More importantly, many churchmen were also upset when it was alleged that the FCC and FCT had been involved in the solicitation project. Bishop Harvey, the then President of the FCC, quickly issued a letter in which he denied that the FCC or FCT had known that their mailing lists, which had been shared with FATI, were going to be used. Harvey also claimed that the FCC and FCT had opposed the formation of the new Institute.[411]

The speed with which the FCC distanced itself from FATI and its financial difficulties was only half of a more drastic change in strategy by the FCC. Harvey had issued another letter to the FCC constituency, with the same date as that dealing with the FATI controversy, announcing that the process for joining the organization would be greatly simplified. He further claimed that the FCC was committed to working with all groups of Continuing Anglicans, ending his letter by stressing that the current board of directors comprised representatives of all those churches rooted in the St. Louis Congress and the consecrations in Denver. Harvey then listed the churches represented on the FCC's board, including the AEC.[412] In this subtle turn of words, Harvey tried to convince as many members of the ACC as he could that the FCC was not working against them, while simultaneously intimating that the AEC was a Continuing body with ties to the Movement that had sprung from the St. Louis Congress. However, the only tie that the AEC appeared to have had with the St. Louis Movement was that it had accepted into its fold the Diocese of the Southwest, which had been aligned with the ACC, but never spiritually *of it*.

The realignment of the FCC and the Phalanx would prove to be somewhat of a moot point, since Archbishop Falk seemed to have already fallen under the spell of the potential glories of an enlarged traditionalist Anglican Communion that he saw prefigured in the Fairfield Symposium. At the end of 1986, both Falk and Clavier had traveled to England in order to strategize with traditionalists across the pond, including Bishop Leonard of London.[413] Falk and Clavier continued to have informal meetings with each other throughout 1987, which culminated in Clavier being invited to attend the ACC Synod. More importantly, the two prelates issued a joint proposal, approved by the bishops of both bodies, to Bishop Eric Kemp of Chichester, England, in which they asked him to oversee the process by which the two groups could become jurisdictionally united.[414] Little known at the time was that Falk's participation in the unification process often misrepresented the degree to which many other of the bishops and laity within the ACC were willing to compromise in order to form ties with the AEC and Clavier. For instance, during the excitement over the Proposal sent to Bishop Kemp, Falk stated that he didn't think anyone doubted "the sacramental validity" of the ordinations or consecrations performed by either group.[415] This seems strange since Falk had stated only a few years earlier that the AEC was "posing" as an Anglican body. It is difficult to determine whether Falk was engaging in wishful thinking, or perhaps was reflecting what he had perceived to be a substantial change in opinion by many ACC members toward Clavier, but within a few short months there would certainly be much contention regarding Clavier's fitness to hold the episcopal office, and therefore to be united with the ACC.

The seed for later troubles was planted when an anonymous six-page letter was mailed to many Continuing churchmen across the United States, issued under the moniker of a mysterious, probably pseudo, organization calling itself the "Center for Anglican Research."[416] The letter publicized, for the first time to many in the wider Continuing Movement, the longstanding allegations of moral and ecclesiastical wrongdoings and improprieties committed by Clavier [discussed earlier in Chapter 3] prior to, and in the aftermath of, his short tenure with the Anglican Orthodox Church. Although the letter would be largely ignored by the Phalanx, it would prove to be a major thorn in the side of the unification process between the ACC and AEC, as many within the ACC began to have second thoughts about joining hands with Clavier and the AEC. The grassroots movement within the ACC against the unification process gained strength largely outside the purview of the parties most actively involved in the negotiations, namely, Falk and Clavier, and the Phalanx. As this discontent was brewing, the lead players in the unification process were continuing their activities in the hopes of consolidating their positions in what they imagined to be a much larger Anglican Continuum that lay just around the corner. Falk traveled to Australia and received an official declaration of intercommunion from Bishop John Hazelwood of the Diocese of Ballarat, thus making the ACC the first Continuing church body to enter into intercommunion with a diocese in the official Anglican Communion.[417] In a similarly optimistic vein, Clavier and other AEC representatives held another meeting with representatives of ECUSA to discuss ways in which the two bodies could eventually establish a relationship of intercommunion.[418]

Meanwhile, as Falk and Clavier were building bridges with mainstream members of the Anglican Communion, the smaller Continuing bodies were witnessing important developments in their own right. The newly reconstituted AECNA consecrated Fr. Robert Voight as its new bishop, with Bishop Adams being assisted in the consecration by Bishop Knight of the United Episcopal Church, and Bishops Craig, Kennaugh, and Trott of the Anglican Rite Jurisdiction of the Americas. As a result of the gathering to consecrate Voight, Archbishop Craig of the ARJA composed a proposal to unite the three bodies.

However, this unity proposal eventually failed when both the UEC and AECNA accepted the newest proposal by Bishop Leonard of London, which called for all traditionalists to unite under his jurisdiction. This proposal, known as "Proposal 3," was drawn up in May of 1987 at a meeting held in Rosemont, Pennsylvania. Unfortunately for Bishop Leonard and many of the Continuers who hoped that his stature could unify the Continuum, he had ordained 70 women as deacons only two months before Rosemont gathering, and this essentially resulted in the death of the unification meetings between Continuers and mainstream Anglican traditionalists that had seemed so promising after the Fairfield Symposium.[419] The ARJA's refusal to join the UEC and AECNA in accepting Proposal 3 effectively put the unity talks between the three bodies on hold until September of 1988, by which time Leonard's proposal had fizzled out, thus relieving the UEC and AECNA of their troublesome commitment to it. The bishops from the three bodies did not completely unite their jurisdictions, but rather committed to work together for the furtherance of Continuing Anglicanism under the banner of an organization called the Confederation of Anglican Episcopal Bishops.[420]

The growth of ecumenical relations with other smaller Continuing bodies must have come as a relief to the ARJA, which had experienced some setbacks during the prior year. First, in December of 1986, Bishop Lesser took his parish with him into an independent existence. Then in April of 1987, Bishop Shaver of Indiana took his parish out of the ARJA to seek affiliation with ECUSA. Although it was alleged that Shaver had resigned due to a dispute over his desire to consecrate a husband-wife clergy team, it appears that he and his parish had decided that they wanted to use the 1979 Prayer Book and move closer to the Episcopalian mainstream, and thus no longer felt comfortable in the Continuing Movement.⁴²¹ Negotiations with the Diocese of Northern Indiana later in the year failed to bring Shaver back into ECUSA.⁴²² Even more troubling for the ARJA, sometime during 1986, Bishop Pagtakhan consecrated Fr. Thomas Gore as the Bishop of the Americas for the PICC, with parishes in California and Texas, in a jurisdiction to be known as the Anglican Rite Diocese of Texas, thus marking the logical culmination of Pagtakhan's earlier disavowal of the ARJA.⁴²³

Two other small Continuing bodies were formed during this period as well, both deriving from a small jurisdiction known as the United Episcopal Church of America (not to be confused with Bishop Doren's United Episcopal Church, U.S.A.). The UECA had been founded by Bishop Richard C. Acker sometime in 1976 due to the decline of the jurisdiction for which he had been consecrated a bishop (the United Episcopal Church – Anglican/Celtic).⁴²⁴ As was mentioned in Chapter 3, Acker had been affiliated with the AEC for a short time during the early 1970s, but had withdrawn in order to join the UECAC. Acker consecrated Fr. Charles Edward Morley to succeed him as Archbishop of the UECA in 1984 and, after Acker's death, Morley disbanded the UECA in 1986 to form a new church body; the Traditional Protestant Episcopal Church (TPEC). Bishop Acker had ordained another minister in 1984, John Riffenbury, who had in turn been consecrated a bishop by Archbishop Edward Marshall of the Evangelical Episcopal Church in 1985. The uncertain state of affairs that existed within the UECAC after Acker's death led Riffenbury to form a new body, the United Anglican Church, shortly afterward.⁴²⁵

Chapter 11
1988-1991

The movement toward unifying the ACC and AEC, lead by the charismatic Bishops Falk and Clavier, continued to gather momentum during 1988 and 1989, or so it seemed to many in the AEC and the Southern Phalanx. Bishop Falk was able to spearhead a decision by the ACC's College of Bishops in January of 1988 to appoint two committees to work on an eventual merger with the AEC. One committee, known as the Ecumenical Relations Committee, was to be comprised of clergy and laity representing each body, while the other was to be comprised of three bishops from the ACC-Canada (Woolcock, Crawley, and Mercer) and two English representatives [Bishop Anselm Genders and an eminent Anglican theologian, Fr. E.W. Trueman Dicken]. The first committee was to work on practical issues such as jurisdictional and Canonical revisions, as well as how the question of validating the holy orders of each body would be solved, while the second committee was to give an independent evaluation as to the process of solving any disputes over the validity of either body's holy orders. Bishop Clavier had also secured the AEC's acceptance of these committees.[426]

Recognizing that there were powerful forces within the ACC who were hesitant to join ranks with Clavier and the AEC, Bishop Falk initiated a campaign to educate the laity and clergy as to the benign character of the unity talks. In editorials distributed throughout the ACC's parishes he eschewed the severity of the warnings against any "hasty unity plans" that he was receiving from assorted diocesan synods and Standing Committees. Unfortunately for Falk, he was not very sophisticated in tempering his biases while trying to educate the ACC as to why they should join with the AEC. For instance, while referring to one such warning he had received from a Standing Committee, he couldn't help but sneer at its request that the doctrine of the Seven Ecumenical Councils of the "undivided and primitive church" be one area where each body should be in agreement, sarcastically dismissing it, "Undivided and Primitive until 787 -? Really -?" This statement came one paragraph after he had questioned why the opponents of the unity talks were not content with such bare minimum requirements as agreement on the Creeds, the Chicago-Lambeth Quadrilateral, the *Affirmation of St. Louis*, and "the Seven Ecumenical Councils."[427] This kind of double-speak, where the Ecumenical Councils are affirmed in one paragraph but denigrated in another, would become increasingly more frequent as the unity juggernaut continued on its path, and the opponents of the unity talks would become increasingly more suspicious of the whole process, and especially of Falk's intentions.

By the middle of 1989, the lines between the pro- and anti-unity camps within the ACC had become even more sharply drawn. An ACC bishop wrote to the College of Bishops regarding the unity negotiations, stating that he felt "that if we are not to come to complete disaster, the least we must do is rein in the Archbishop," and warning that a failure to do so would result in the ACC disappear[ring] in a cloud of schism."[428] The intensification of the anti-unity campaign within the ACC seems to have resulted largely from the appointment of a committee in February of 1989 to establish an international structure to be called the Traditional Anglican Communion (TAC). This body was to have originally consisted of an international College of Bishops with a primate at their head, and a complete synod system that would include legislative functions based on an internationally-binding Constitution and Canons. This plan would eventually be pared down to a proposed concordant between the participating national churches that would include only the international College of Bishops and the titular primate.[429] Even though the plans for the TAC had been quickly modified, many within the ACC were becoming more convinced that Falk was trying to set up an international alliance that would operate independently of the ACC, and which could eventually supplant the ACC.

In October of 1989, the ACC's Provincial Synod met in Denver to consider, most importantly among other issues, whether or not to accept the draft concordant for the TAC, and whether to continue talks with the AEC regarding an ecclesiastical merger. As it would turn out, this Synod proved to be the last hurrah for those proponents of ACC-AEC unity who were hoping for a smooth transition to a larger scale Continuing Anglican body in the United States. The Synod delegates approved the TAC concordant as it had been amended, and they approved the continuation of the negotiation process with the AEC. The main media coverage of the gathering came from the Phalanx's sardonic hatchet-man, Dr. Robert Strippy. The general tenor of Strippy's analysis was that the Synod had been a triumph for the forces of unity, and that this was due in large part to the talents of Falk, who was glowingly described as being "definitely in command of his ecclesiastical ship." This reveling in the ability of the Archbishop to manipulate an ACC synod by virtue of the powers of his office stands in marked contrast to the Phalanx's usual hostility to such a concentration of power in the hands of a single bishop, and was instructive as to how politicized and petty the controversy would become.

Strippy praised Falk for his denial of a clerical delegate's request (this cleric most assuredly being Fr. Andrew Stahl) to have the discussion of the AEC unity proposal held in private, as well as Falk's criticizing the cleric for wanting to hold clandestine meetings. This would prove ironic (though unknown to most churchmen who remained in the Phalanx's orbit) since Falk himself would allegedly soon enough take advantage of such clandestine meetings when dealing with ecclesiastical dirty laundry. Nevertheless, the only setback for the unity forces at the Synod occurred when Bishop Chamberlain of New England, the main supporter of Falk's unity plans among the ACC College of Bishops, had his supposedly impromptu motion to immediately adopt a resolution to declare unity with the AEC (on the spot) passed over by the delegates.[430]

An underlying theme of Strippy's analysis, and one that dominated the critiques made by the proponents of the unification process, was that the anti-unity camp was a small group of hardliners and obscurantists who were making harsh and elitist demands on the AEC. One fact that went largely uncommented upon at the time was that the AEC representatives were making some harsh demands of their own. Whereas the ACC unity opponents were being accused of trying to foist their Canons on the AEC, the AEC representatives were themselves stating that the ACC Canons would most probably have to go. In a report on the meetings of the Unity Commission held in 1989, a proponent of unity stated that the ACC Canons were being described as "…too detailed and as reflecting a spirit of legalism which is pre-Anglican and un-Anglican in character. It was indicated that strong elements in the AEC [members of the Southern Phalanx might be meant here] could not accept the ACC canons under any circumstances and that it would be necessary to seek Canons from some agreed orthodox Province of the Anglican Communion."[431]

The key turning point in the fortunes of the unity

movement came when the Ecumenical Committee of the ACC met in Des Moines, Iowa on July 20, 1990. Bishop Clavier appeared before the Committee to answer questions regarding the validity of his, and by extension, the AEC's orders, as well as issues regarding his fitness for the office of bishop. The opponents of the unity process asked Clavier many pointed questions about his past ecclesiastical career, including a request of him to verify whether he had listed a certain [allegedly] diploma-mill college on his curriculum vitae when applying to the Catholic Apostolic Church in 1966. His quixotic response to this request was reportedly to look over the document, which allegedly was in his handwriting and contained his signature, and state, "I guess you will have to get a handwriting expert to determine the validity of the document." This strangely inappropriate response was either an ill-advised attempt to avoid an uncomfortable aspect of his past or, at least, a reflection of the degree of acrimony that was settling over the meeting.

More troublesome for Falk and Chamberlain was the focus of the anti-unity group on a videotape of the controversial San Diego re-consecrations that had taken place in 1981. It became obvious that most of the consecration service had been deleted during the ceremony, and that the words and actions of consecration were questionably irregular. After much arguing about what constituted a valid consecration and Holy Orders, the committee ended in a standstill, but only after a motion had been derailed by Falk which would have stated that the Committee had "withheld" recognition of the AEC's orders until further notice. The Committee eventually decided to state that they did not yet have an established criterion for determining a valid consecration, and that further review of the San Diego consecrations, and the regularization of the orders of the AEC clergy, was still needed.[432]

Of the seventeen members of the Committee, ten

decided against recommending the recognition of the AEC's orders to the next Provincial Synod. What happened next depends on whose version of the events one accepts. The anti-unity members of the Committee quickly issued a report written by one of their members, Mrs. Mary Buerger, which is largely the basis for the previous description of the meeting. Falk and his supporters countered that the committee had never made a decision regarding the validity of the AEC's orders because they were not empowered to do so. The pro-unity camp issued their own document within a few days, which limited itself to "corrections" of the anti-unity group's report. This counter-report had the dubious distinction of arguing that the minority group had agreed to go along with the issuance of the final "unable to decide" report only because the wording of the report admitted that it was actually "unable" to decide – that is, the Committee was claimed to be simply stating that it did not have the authority to make any decision. The pro-unity forces claimed that only bishops were qualified to make decisions regarding the validity of orders.[433] Bishop Falk's position would be clarified in his report to the College of Bishops in early August. He correctly noted that the Committee had been unable to come to a conclusion regarding the minimum criteria for determining the validity of Holy Orders, but he also criticized the Committee members for coming to the meeting inadequately prepared to discuss how to define such questions. He also impugned some of the Committee members for their statements that they feared a union with Clavier, as being evidence of their prejudice and unfitness to serve on such a body. His report concluded by offering for his fellow bishops' consideration the same criterion for determining a valid consecration as he had unsuccessfully put forward during the Des Moines meeting.[434] Unfortunately for Falk and his supporters, the College of Bishops failed to reach a decision in favor of accepting the validity of the AEC's orders.

The fact that the ACC was probably not going to accept a plan for unification with the AEC any time in the near future became crystallized at a gathering of Continuing Anglican leaders held in Victoria, Canada for the purpose of establishing the TAC. At this meeting, the TAC was officially brought into being, and Falk was elected to be the new communion's first Primate.[435] However, Clavier and the other AEC bishops only participated as observers, since the ACC was still dragging its feet in terms of officially recognizing the AEC. The ACC viewed the establishment of the TAC as a triumph for the growth of the Continuing Movement, but the AEC and the Phalanx viewed the Victoria meeting as the last straw in a series of rebuffs from the bishops of the ACC. The reason for the renewed bitterness was that the pro-unity forces had tried to have the Victoria gathering vote to approve the AEC for membership in the TAC, and, once again, the ACC bishops declined to go along with the "winds of change." Once again, the task of skewering the opponents of unity fell to the ever-resourceful Dr. Strippy, who took great pleasure in attacking the ACC priest (obviously referring to Fr. Stahl once again), who was portrayed as manipulating the "invertebrate" ACC bishops "like a marionette," mesmerizing them with his "largely self-taught and imaginatively arcane scholarship." The opponents of unity within the ACC were described as being both ignorant and selfishly clinging to their positions of power.[436]

Matters began to deteriorate more rapidly after the Victoria meeting. The ACC's College of Bishops met in Indianapolis, in January of 1991, and announced that they had finally adopted, by a vote of 9-2, an official position regarding the acceptance of the AEC's orders. They described their position as relying on precedent, rather than on formulating any new criterion for evaluating the validity of another church body's Orders.[437]

Even though the proverbial writing seemed to be on the wall, Falk either continued to politic for unification with the AEC, or he began laying the groundwork for a future withdrawal from the ACC, according to which side is recounting the events. He began circulating to strategically placed priests, without the knowledge of his fellow bishops, drafts of a pro-unity proposal that he was encouraging them to put forward at their diocesan synods leading up to the Provincial Synod in October of 1991. Falk appears to have been hoping to circumvent any perceived attempts at squashing the discussion of the unity proposal within the local dioceses by having these churchmen who were sympathetic to his cause bring the issue to a vote within the local synods, thereby hoping that a groundswell of lay support could be harnessed at the upcoming Provincial Synod. He was also quite possibly establishing connections by which a potential withdrawal from the ACC on his part could lead to the greatest possible success. His memo concluded with the rather questionable request of his contacts to report back to him as to how the discussions within the local synods had transpired.[438]

Despite Falk's best efforts, 7 out of the nine ACC diocesan synods passed resolutions supporting a resolution that had been recommended by the College of Bishops, which called for all unity negotiations with the AEC to be undertaken strictly within the limits and conditions set forth in the ACC Canons and Constitution.[439] This proposed resolution was drawn up during another meeting of the College of Bishops held in Indianapolis, in April of 1991.[440] This much can be ascertained, but accusations of nefarious conduct by the ACC bishops began to fly soon after the second Indianapolis gathering of the College of Bishops. According to the ACC version, Falk knew of the meeting, but did not attend.[441] According to his supporters, the meeting was held in secret, without Falk or Bishop Chamberlain being invited to attend.[442] With the acrimony between the two parties now escalated to a hopeless level, Falk and Clavier issued a joint "Call For Unity" in conjunction with a similar document issued by the bishops of the ACC-Canada. The "Call" was issued for all Continuing Anglicans interested in unity to attend the AEC Synod in Deerfield Beach, Florida, in October of 1991, for the purpose of possibly establishing a new, united Continuing body.[443]

    Soon after the issuance of the "Call For Unity," Falk quickened the pace of his behind the scenes maneuvering. Just as the majority of the laity within the Continuing Movement had been unaware that he had seeded resolutions into local diocesan synods, and that he had attempted to monitor the debates held on these resolutions, they were also largely unaware that he was taking allegedly disgruntled parishes in the Diocese of the South under his wing. In July of 1991, two parishes from Florida and North Carolina contacted Falk with requests to be placed under the jurisdiction of the Patrimony, the stated reasons revolving around internal parish disputes that had not been handled properly by the diocesan bishop, William Lewis.[444] However, just as likely, the real issue could have centered upon a desire by these churchmen to accompany Falk in what was no doubt perceived as an inevitable coming split in the ACC.

    In June, Falk had completed his report as chairman of the Ecumenical Relations Department, which was to be presented to the delegates of the upcoming ACC Provincial Synod. Interestingly, he made no mention of his previous argument that the Committee was not empowered to make any decision regarding the validity of the AEC's orders, and he instead gave an accurate account of how the Committee had been unable to reach any agreement on the matter. He ended his report, no doubt in the full knowledge that there was no realistic hope for such an outcome, recommending that his criterion be accepted, and that, if three-fourths of the delegates approved of his criterion, the AEC's orders would be officially recognized by the ACC.[445] In the meantime, Falk continued to establish his independence from the ACC while working to finalize the organization of the TAC. In a meeting held in Deerfield Beach, Florida, in June of 1991, Falk and Bishop Connors of the ACC met with Clavier, Fr Frank Pannitti and Fr. Walter Crespo of the AEC, to discuss selections for potential bishops and priests to serve the TAC in South America. An ACC priest from Colombia, Fr. Victor Manuel Cruz-Blanco, tried to convince Falk that some of the candidates were unfit for their office, and noted that one of them had been denied the priesthood in the ACC due to some alleged moral misconduct while studying as a Roman Catholic seminarian, only to be ordained later into the AEC. Falk withdrew into a private meeting with Clavier and Connors, eventually returning to inform Fr. Cruz-Blanco that the questionable candidates would be accepted into the TAC since, it was declared, the South American region was henceforth under their control. The next day they informed the Colombian priest that he was no longer to refer to himself as the Vicar-General of Colombia, that he was no longer to write letters to any of his fellow priests, and that all of his candidates for the priesthood were to be handed over to Fr. Crespo's supervision.[446] Not surprisingly, there was no mention of these events, nor even the troubling behavior of the TAC bishops [who had allegedly held a "clandestine meeting" after all], in the Phalanx orbit. As if to cement his standing as a renegade in the eyes of many within the ACC, Falk then issued a letter that not only dismissed the accusations against Clavier, and called for ACC Provincial Synod delegates to vote for unity, but recommended that they read an accompanying letter that had written by an ACCC priest. While mostly engaging in a critique of the anti-unity forces within the ACC, the letter from the ACCC priest also included a highly derogatory opinion regarding Fr. Stahl: "I, for one, have little desire to be in communion with a Church [ACC] in which Andrew Stahl is ultimately victorious. Having seen his conduct at Bp. DeCatanzaro's consecration, and having learned that he behaved the same way in Victoria last year, I can but conclude that he is not merely psychotic but demonic. I can think of no other explanation for the manner and degree of influence that he exerts on some of the U.S. Bishops."[447]

Each of these actions by Falk eventually came to the knowledge of the other ACC bishops, and they finally brought official charges against him in August of 1991. All of the above mentioned actions by Falk were listed as evidence of the overall charge that he was inciting schism within the ACC. In a striking example of how the Phalanx molded (some would say distorted) the news that Continuing churchmen were receiving at the time, all of the charges against Falk were reported, but few of the specific details that gave the charges against him their force were included. Thus, the letter that had smeared Fr. Stahl, and that had been distributed by Falk, was mentioned, but churchmen were only informed that the letter made "uncomplimentary" remarks about Stahl, and not that it had stated that he was demon-possessed. Likewise, Continuing churchmen were left with the impression that Falk had taken some of Bishop Lewis' parishes under his care *after* he had been inhibited by the ACC bishops, when, in fact, he was alleged to have been interfering inside of Lewis' diocese *prior* to the inhibition.[448] Overall, the coverage gave the impression that Falk was being accused of frivolous violations because he was working to bring unity to the Continuing Movement, despite the fact that the evidence suggests there was reasonable suspicions within the ACC that Falk was engaging in rather questionable schismatic activities after he realized that his plans of bringing the full ACC into his unity scheme were doomed. In other words (to many within the ACC), his actions gave the appearance of covert machinations of a man who was trying to take as many as he could from his old ecclesiastical body before he bolted for another.

The trial of Archbishop Falk, to be held in September of 1991, would never be completed as envisioned. One of the bishops seated as a judge had to excuse himself early on the day of the trial due to the death of his mother, thus leaving the court with too few bishops to hold a Canonically valid trial. A compromise was finally reached in which Falk was allowed to take his diocese with him out of the ACC.[449] Falk attended the Deerfield Beach meeting in October, at which the Diocese of the Holy Trinity, a reported 70 percent of the Diocese of the South, and a smattering of parishes from both the ACC and other Continuing bodies merged with the AEC to form the Anglican Church in America (ACA), the long anticipated new, enlarged Continuing body. After the formation of the ACA, the schismatic ACC bishops joined with the AEC bishops and several others from around the world in a consecration service that was undertaken to ease the minds of all involved regarding the validity of the new body's Orders. Falk was elected to be the Primate of the ACA, and Clavier was elected as its Metropolitan of the Eastern Province.[450]

The ACC had held its Provincial Synod in Charlotte, North Carolina, a few days after the aborted trial of Falk, and elected Bishop Lewis to be the new Metropolitan. As was expected, the Synod also voted to reject the proposal to unite with the AEC. The Phalanx, voicing itself through the pages of a journal that was supposed to be for "all" Continuing churchmen, described the overall outcome of the events as a "massive purge," and summed-up the new ACC as a more Catholic church in which, "the 1928 Book of Common Prayer seemed to have been replaced by the Missal; the Holy Communion by the Mass; quiet prayer and meditation by the rosary; the humble dress of the clergy by fancy frock according to rank and importance."[451]

The fact that the ACC bishops may have had legitimate concerns about the character of Clavier was never considered seriously within the orbit of the Phalanx. Thus, when a scandal involving Clavier and his priests emerged only a few weeks before the Deerfield Beach conference, it was reported in the secular press, but somehow escaped the attention of the Phalanx publications as a serious story. The scandal involved Fr. Crespo and his priests in New Jersey, who were charged with defrauding the government by helping illegal immigrants falsify their documents. Although Clavier dismissed Crespo and the other priests involved, evidence emerged during the investigation that Clavier had unknowingly consecrated a priest who had been a bigamist, but then had only mildly disciplined the priest for concealing the impropriety from his bishop. Worse still, Clavier had "supported" a priest who had been placed in a mental hospital for sexually assaulting young boys. All of these issues were viewed by his detractors as providing evidence that Clavier was not capable of making sound moral decisions regarding the priests under his authority. Clavier dismissed his opponents as being "anti-sinner" and too harsh in their judgments of others.[452]

In retrospect, and with a decade of historical distance with which to view the events surrounding the formation of the ACA, it becomes apparent that many of the arguments either for or against greater unity within the Movement were ultimately of only secondary importance. Although the facts may disturb many Continuing churchmen, and may provide ammunition for critics of the

Movement within the Anglican mainstream, there seems to be little doubt that the greatest hindrance to a more unified Continuing Anglican witness was the perpetual cycle of conflicts between individual leaders within the Movement, shared among the episcopate, the clergy, and certain influential-wealthy lay members (the Phalanx). Although these conflicts were no doubt influenced by issues of doctrine, worship, and ecclesiastical order; they seem to have been guided even more by personal drives toward the aggrandizement or maintenance of power.

One of the strongest arguments made by the advocates of the proto-ACA was that the ACC had accepted the AECNA bishops without any quarrelling over their also having received the questionable 1981 re-consecrations in San Diego. The ACC's defense of their actions in the case of Bishops Adams and Kleppinger was that they were not aware at the time of just how serious the nature of the irregularities were, but this rings hollow when it is remembered that the San Diego consecrations had been criticized and dismissed by Continuing churchmen from the very beginning. The real reason that the ACC bishops focused so much attention on the San Diego consecrations appears to have been their realization that they needed some kind of concrete evidence to justify what was essentially their intuitive dislike and distrust of Clavier. Furthermore, many of the opponents of the unity movement were clearly never going to unite with Clavier and the AEC, and their participation in unity discussions gives the appearance of a cynical ploy to string along pro-unity factions within their church until more evidence could be gathered against Falk and Clavier. Seen in this light, Falk and Clavier's more deceptive actions can at least be seen more sympathetically as comprising an interplay with forces that were probably not acting in good faith.

Having mentioned these negative actions within the

ACC, it is only right to keep in mind that the pro-unity movement had much about it that strikes one as being as much of an assault on the ACC [as it was then constituted] as it was the simple movement toward a stronger Continuum, as it was then portrayed by the Phalanx. Little known at the time was that the pro-unity forces often acted in a manner that was anything but harmonious in intent. A telling example of this fact can be seen by examining the case of All Saints, an ACC parish in Charlottesville, Virginia. When certain influential members of this parish failed in their efforts at reforming the ACC's Canons, they led the parish out of the ACC in 1985. After obtaining a priest who would serve them while they existed as an independent parish, they eventually made overtures to the AEC, and a meeting was arranged with Clavier. However, when the parish priest returned with a negative report on the AEC Primus, he was forced to resign within a few months. After a subsequent parish vote to join the AEC, the dissenting members of All Saints formed St. David's parish, and re-affiliated with the ACC.

That a parish had left one jurisdiction for another was certainly nothing new in the world of Continuing Anglicanism. However, what made the Charlottesville events symbolically important was that All Saints parish would become a beacon of the pro-unity movement. Clavier moved to Charlottesville to become the rector of All Saints, thus joining ranks with parishioners who were often leading figures within the Phalanx, such as Perry Laukhuff. The FCC itself was based in nearby Arlington, Virginia. Furthermore, during this period Robert Strippy would relocate from New Orleans to All Saints in Charlottesville, and the *Christian Challenge* would change its address from Texas to Washington, D.C., only 120 miles from Charlottesville. Thus, by the late 1980s, a concentration of the most influential advocates of the pro-unity movement (due to their leadership in the Phalanx media network) had settled in Northeast Virginia. Yet these same pro-unity advocates operated in a daily ecclesiastical environment where jurisdictional harmony was anything but the norm. Perhaps most tellingly, when the unity talks between Clavier and Falk were at their peak, Falk made several visits to Charlottesville, where the All Saints parish extended him the warmest welcomes, but, reportedly, he never once paid a visit to the ACC's St. David's parish.[453]

While such questionable activities were being undertaken by pro-unity forces in places like Charlottesville, and in relative obscurity in terms of the wider Continuum, another potentially salient development had occurred within the AEC that was likewise editorially ignored by the Phalanx. The AEC's Diocese of the Southwest, only a few years after having left the ACC over the issue of its Canons, left the AEC for similar reasons. During 1988 and 1989, the DSW's Bishop, H. Edwin Caudill, withdrew from the AEC with as many as twenty parishes over alleged attempts by the AEC's leadership, including Clavier, to interfere in the affairs of the DSW. The DSW had once again reconstituted itself as an independent entity.[454] Shortly after this, Bishop Frank Benning of the Diocese of the South likewise led a couple of parishes out of the AEC. This Diocese of the South would, along with the newly independent DSW and the western parishes of the AECNA that had refused to accept the merger with the AEC in 1984, form a new Continuing body shortly after the meeting at Deerfield Beach, calling itself the Anglican Church in the United States.[455] During the course of the 1990s, this small group would also be known as the American Anglican Church. However, as far as most readers of the Phalanx publications were concerned, these developments were largely unknown. Thus a new Continuing body, with close to thirty parishes, and which had been formed from out of discontent within the AEC, was largely ignored by a Phalanx that was busy trying to convince members of the ACC to join ranks with the supposedly less contentious and more tolerant AEC. None of these facts speak well for the honesty of intentions among many of the most forceful advocates of unity.

Beyond all of the examples of hypocrisy and veiled intentions among members of both parties leading up to the formation of the ACA, perhaps the most convincing evidence that the debates were often settled outside the realm of substantive differences can be seen by examining both bodies shortly after the dust from the Deerfield Beach meeting had settled. In an evaluation of the Continuing Anglican Movement that appeared at the end of 1994 in *The Christian Challenge*, it was noted that the ACC contained a large number of parishes that were Evangelical or Low-church in their emphasis, and, conversely, that there were many parishes in the ACA that were Catholic or High-church in their worship. Remember that this same journal had intoned in the heated aftermath of the Deerfield Beach meeting that the ACC appeared to be dominated by missal worship and rosaries, and that many within the ACC considered the ACA to be nothing more than another Protestant denomination. Even more tellingly, the evaluation of the other smaller Continuing bodies showed that most of them also accepted many of the same doctrinal and liturgical standards, such as the 1928 Prayer Book and the *Affirmation of St. Louis*, and yet remained separated.[456]

Chapter 12
1992 – 1996

The immediate aftermath of the Deerfield Beach meeting was a cooling-off period between the newly formed ACA and the ACC. The ACC denounced the bishops of the Continuing Canadian and Australian churches for their participation in the consecration service in Deerfield Beach, and after unsuccessfully demanding that the foreign bishops repent of their actions, broke off relations with both bodies. However, the ACC attempted to rebound from its image as the anti-unity Continuing church body by beginning a series of dialogues with other churches. The most fruitful of these talks was with the UECNA, in which the bishops of both churches signed an intercommunion agreement in early 1992, and each church officially ratified by the end of 1993.[457] Another interesting ecumenical endeavor involved a series of official dialogues with the Orthodox Church in America in 1995.[458] The talks were aimed at developing closer ties between the two bodies, and possibly of recognition of the ACC by the OCA, but they would eventually fail to produce the desired results.

Despite these ecumenical activities by the ACC, any hope for a future reconciliation with churchmen in many of the other Continuing bodies was effectively terminated with the 1995 release of a document by the ACC College of Bishops outlining their official position regarding any proposals for expansion of the unification of the Continuing Movement. Although the document was quite intricate in laying out the bishops' theological and historical justification for their position, most of its critics would focus on its insistence that only the ACC, the DCK, and the UECNA could legitimately claim to be the representatives of continuing Anglicanism in the United States.[459] The ACC bishops had not developed this position in total isolation from the rest of the traditionalist Anglican world, for in 1993 the chairman of Ecclesia, one of the more influential traditionalist Catholic organizations in the Church of England, had recommended the ACC as the only legitimate choice among Continuing church bodies for those English churchmen who could no longer remain within the mainstream church.[460] *The Christian Challenge* devoted two issues to the subject of the bishops' statement, inviting representatives from assorted Continuing bodies and traditionalist organizations to pan the document, but the general attitude among most Continuing churchmen seems to have been one of indifference since most of those who were critical of the bishops' position had already left the ACC, or had never held any real desire to be affiliated with it in the first place.[461]

  The only substantive conflict between the ACC and ACA during this period occurred at the level of the local parish, where individual churchmen and clergy used vestries and other means in attempts to persuade parishes to change their allegiance. The most visible instance of these largely underground developments occurred in Los Angeles, where Fr. Gregory Wilcox led his ACC parish, St. Mary of the Angels, into the TAC in 1993. St. Mary of the Angels had been one of the original parishes to secede from the Episcopal Church in the 1970s, and was a venerable example of the ornate, Anglo-Catholic parishes of another time in Episcopalian history. The transfer was claimed to have been provoked by the ACC's interference in the parish's attempts at establishing ecumenical contacts with other Continuing Anglicans. After Bishop David A. Seeland of the ACC unsuccessfully tried to stop the departure of the parish from his diocese, he then began a series of legal challenges to the property of the seceded parish, which were concluded in 1995 with the court ruling in favor of Fr. Wilcox and St. Mary of the Angels.[462]

The victory of the ACA in the St. Mary of the Angels matter could not overcome the major events that would shake the ACA in 1995. In developments that some members of the ACC could have gloated that they had predicted would occur, Bishop Clavier resigned from the ACA amid allegations of sexual misconduct. Although the charges against Clavier were never revealed fully in the publications of the Southern Phalanx, the secular press reported that Clavier had been charged by ten women in Florida of either sexually abusing them or trying to force them to have sex with him. He reportedly would invite female parishioners into his office and then "come onto them." He was further reported to have told them that they should be "honored for Jesus Christ to want your body."[463] The scandal began in the middle of 1994 when some women reported Bishop Clavier's alleged misconduct toward them to lower-level church officials, who then forwarded the information up the ACA hierarchy. By late 1994, Clavier became aware that his fellow bishops were investigating the allegations against him, but claimed that he was not informed as to the details of the charges. He then began to delay the proceedings by insisting that a lawyer be allowed to accompany him during a meeting that was to be private between himself and Bishop Falk. Then, when Falk attempted to phone Clavier to discuss the allegations before the primate's scheduled trip to England, Clavier mysteriously disappeared, reportedly leaving even his wife and children wondering where he had gone. Clavier then issued a letter in which he resigned his office in the ACA.

Bishop Clavier later wrote a letter stating that he had left, and had resigned, in despair of having been given no opportunity to defend himself appropriately. He then sent the ACA bishops a letter stating that he was rescinding his earlier resignation. This request was denied by a 6 to 4 vote of the ACA bishops, and Clavier was formally deposed from the ACA. In yet another letter that followed, Clavier continued to stress his innocence, but claimed that he had experienced a "burnout," and apologized for the pain he had caused members of the ACA.[464]

As the 6 to 4 vote indicates, there was not a united opinion within the ACA regarding the necessity of Clavier's resignation and subsequent deposition. There were some who thought Clavier was the victim of small group of churchmen who were out to get him, and there were others who thought that Bishop Falk had maneuvered the situation against Clavier.[465] However, Falk continued to emphasize that Clavier's exodus was a serious loss for the ACA, and it was also reported that Falk was "staggered by the news" of the charges against Clavier.[466] Even worse than the psychic effect that Clavier's fall from grace had on those ACA activists who had expended so much energy defending him, was the material loss that the ACA was to suffer as a consequence of the events. The Standing Committee of the ACA's Diocese of the Eastern United States became the de facto authority in the diocese until a replacement for Clavier could be elected. In the months following Clavier's departure, disputes began to arise over decisions being made by the Standing Committee. Within a short time, over half of the dioceses' parishes withdrew from the ACA, and eventually formed yet another Continuing Anglican body known as the Anglican Province in America (APA], electing Bishop Walter Grundorf as its new leader.[467] Interestingly, many of those who went with the APA tended to be comprised of original members of the AEC, and those who remained in the newly shrunken ACA tended to have been those who were originally affiliated with the old ACC.

Also of note, Clavier's son, Mark, would become a priest under Bishop Grundorf and the APA.

While the ACC and ACA continued to tread through the same old waters of occasional spurts of growth, followed by devolutions into schism, the biggest news within the world of Continuing Anglicanism revolved around the entry of new groups into the fray. Two groups in particular quickly developed in terms of garnering widespread attention and membership: the Episcopal Missionary Church (EMC) and the Charismatic Episcopal Church (CEC).

The EMC began when the largest and most influential organization working on behalf of orthodoxy within the Episcopal Church at that time, the Episcopal Synod of America, established what was called the Missionary Diocese of the Americas (MDA) in 1991. The MDA had initially been formed as a way to force ECUSA to allow disgruntled parishes (that were not content to remain under the authority of bishops who were perceived to be doctrinally unsound) to place themselves under the authority of other bishops who were deemed to be doctrinally orthodox. Controversy immediately erupted within the Episcopal Church over the establishment of what was an essentially alternative diocese within the church. However, before this controversy could bring any serious jurisdictional or legal clashes, the See of Canterbury in November of 1992 voted to officially ordain women to the priesthood, causing the MDA to announce its existence as a body separate from the official Anglican Communion. The MDA changed its name to the Episcopal Missionary Church, and chose a retired Episcopalian bishop, A. Donald Davies, to be its leader.

The EMC quickly expanded, and began contacting all of the already existing Continuing bodies in the hopes of signing intercommunion agreements. Most of the smaller bodies would eventually sign such agreements, including the ARJA, which reportedly dissolved into the EMC shortly thereafter. However, the ACA and ACC did not immediately sign any agreements with the EMC. By the end of 1994, the EMC had expanded into four dioceses, and was reported to have approximately 40 parishes and 2,000 members.[468]

The growth of the Charismatic Episcopal Church (CEC) would prove to be even more impressive than that of the EMC. During the late 1970s a group of Evangelical ministers and intellectuals began to re-evaluate the role of tradition and liturgy in their own religious journeys. This initial investigation was more popularly known by the creation of a group calling itself the Evangelical Orthodox Church, led by such noted Evangelical figures as Peter Gilquist and Jack Sparks, that would eventually join the Antiochan Orthodox Church in 1987. However, other Evangelical congregations that grew from this investigation into more ancient Christian forms began to use the Episcopalian model of liturgy and doctrine. The result was the establishment of the CEC in 1992 with three parishes and one Archbishop, Randolph Adler. From such small beginnings the CEC would expand to a claimed 200,000 members in over 1,000 parishes worldwide.

The CEC represents a kind of antithesis to the story of the other Continuing Anglican bodies in that its doctrinal and liturgical positions are eclectic in the extreme. The church accepts the use of all of the standard Western liturgies (Roman Catholic, Orthodox, and Anglican), but primarily uses the 1979 Prayer Book, which is claimed to provide a better representation of ancient liturgical practice than other Anglican prayer books. It shares with more Catholic-minded Continuing churchmen the emphasis on the historic episcopate and the seven sacraments, including an emphasis on the real presence in the Eucharist, but also emphasizes that the individual parishes have a more prominent role in the overall decision-making processes of the wider communion. Most uniquely, in accordance with the tenets and practices of the modern charismatic movement within the 20th century Evangelical world, room is left open during the otherwise structured liturgy for the "manifestations of the spirit," such as speaking in tongues and spontaneous revelation.[469]

Chapter 13
1997-2001

Just as the Biblical writer had intoned that there was "nothing new under the sun," so did the Continuing Movement bear witness to this metaphysical truth by continuing to metaphorically spin its wheels as it approached the new millennium. Bishops continued to wage ecclesiastical and doctrinal wars against each other as their followers often continued to scratch their heads at the seeming foolishness of it all. Groups and men who had either been open or closed to proposals for unity within the Movement on "serious doctrinal grounds" seemed to reverse themselves at the drop of a hat. And, as if to prove the old adage that lessons are never really learned until they are learned for oneself, traditionalists within the ECUSA rediscovered the impulse to forge out on their own in defiance of official authorities within the Anglican Communion.

The prize for the most bizarre series of events to occur within this period, by far, must belong to the bishops of the ACC, who seemed to have gathered together all of the experience that they had gained over the years in political machinations and back-stabbing (either as perpetrators or victims) in order to engage in one grand orgy of an ecclesiastical purge. On the surface level, the problem had begun to build during 1996 when Suffragan Bishop John Charles was elected to be the Bishop Ordinary of the Missionary Diocese of New England, even though he was planning to continue in his duties as the Dean of Holyrood Seminary, which, on Canonical grounds, appeared to create a conflict of interest in terms of the residency requirements for holding either position.[470] As the enthronement of Bishop Charles in New England was being defeated on Canonical grounds, a simultaneous problem had arisen when a book by Fr. Mark Haverland, one of the bright young lights of the ACC, published a small book entitled *Anglican Catholic Faith and Practice*. Fr. Haverland's book, which was designed to be an introductory and explanatory text for enquirers, had the misfortune of offending the doctrinal sensibilities of a few of the more stringently Catholic-minded bishops when it referred to the Marian doctrines (such as her ever-virginity) as being matters of "pious opinion," rather than doctrine to be required for belief. This assertion from Haverland had sprung from his maintenance of the classic Anglican position that nothing could be considered doctrinally binding unless it could be proven from Scripture.[471] No doubt, the reason that Haverland's book came under such close scrutiny was due in large part to the fact that he was the obvious heir apparent to be the replacement for Archbishop Lewis (who had announced that he would retire in October due to poor health) as the Bishop Ordinary in the Diocese of the South.[472]

The intensification of the theological divide within the ACC's College of Bishops reached its boiling point after Haverland was elected as the Bishop Coadjutor of the Diocese of the South in April of 1997. Bishops Kleppinger, Seeland, and McNeely (the "Catholic party" in the USA) refused to give their consent to the election, thus leaving Haverland without the required number of confirmations to be consecrated. The first report of these events to appear in the wider church was in the pages of the official church publication, *The Trinitarian*, and problematically left readers with the impression that the three dissenting bishops were in the wrong by focusing on how much pastoral damage had been done by their actions (having supposedly left the diocese without a desperately needed bishop). Even more problematically, after quoting Bishop Seeland's contention that he had withheld his consent because the bishops had not met in person to discuss the confirmation, the article noted that Seeland himself had been confirmed without such a personal meeting among the bishops in 1993, thus editorially painting a picture of Seeland as being somewhat of a hypocrite.[473] Although such editorial license is common in articles, it is a rather rare occurrence in an official church publication, especially when directed toward a bishop who had not yet faced any official charge of impropriety, and shows that an irreparable divided had developed within the College of Bishops.

After the article was distributed throughout the ACC, the bishops met in Athens, Georgia, on July 19 and 20 of 1997, apparently to argue before the Provincial Court as to which bishop was the Senior Bishop Ordinary, and thus to act as the presiding bishop in the event of the death or sudden resignation of Archbishop Lewis, who was seriously ill at the time. The accounts of what transpired during this meeting contradict one another, with the Catholic party stating that the "non-decision" of the court had temporarily reiterated that Bishop Kleppinger would continue to sit as the Senior Bishop Ordinary, as the Catholic party had claimed that he had at several points during the preceding year when Archbishop Lewis' illness had prevented him from performing the duties of his office during meetings of the College of Bishops. The other party claimed that an agreement had been reached in Athens that had left the decision regarding which bishop had seniority to the Provincial Chancellor, who had supposedly decided that Bishop Cahoon, of the "Comprehensive" party (as they were derogatorily labeled by the Catholic Party) was the temporary Senior Bishop Ordinary. What is clear is that another agenda had been revealed during the Athens meeting, in that the Catholic party had tried to have the court decide on an official doctrinal position paper that had been composed in the hope of forcing the other bishops to clarify the Catholic nature of their dogmatic beliefs. The plan was for the court to reach its decision on the basis of which claimant to the position of senior bishop was more doctrinally sound. The Provincial Court had declined to consider the document, which had been composed by Bishop Alexander Price of New Zealand, and had been reportedly inspired by a message from the Virgin Mary challenging Bishop Price to clarify the ACC's teaching regarding the Marian doctrines. Ominously, the Virgin's message had also foretold an eminent schism in the ACC.[474]

The Virgin's prophecy would soon be proven accurate when the bishops gathered at Holyrood Seminary on August 4th to discuss the issues that had been causing friction among them. The Catholic party had tried to place a motion on the agenda to censure the editor of *The Trinitarian*, John Omwake, for the negative article about them. When the other bishops failed to place the item on the agenda, Bishop Seeland moved it anyway, and it was defeated by a five to four vote. Then Bishop Bromley moved a counter resolution of commendation for Mr. Omwake for the accuracy of his article, which won by another five to four vote. At this point the events that ensued become "hazy" when filtered through the different interpretations of the bishops. An argument ensued in which Bishop Deyman either provoked Bishop McNeley by waving a pen in his face, which angered Bishop McNeley to the point of knocking the pen out of Deyman's hand, *or*, Deyman had been assaulted by way of an open-handed slap from McNeley, which was only obstructed by Deyman's defensive reflex to move his hand (which was clutching the pen) in front of his face to block the blow.

The counter interpretations continued regarding the events that followed the "brawling bishops" incident. The

Catholic party claimed that Bishops Deyman and McNeley had quickly apologized to each other and been reconciled. The other party claimed that Bishops Seeland and McNeley sat in a corner after the incident and talked about how they were going to go to their cars and bring back a gun with which they could settle the argument. The Catholic party claimed that these comments were made in jest, as a way of easing the tension in the room after the confrontation. The following day, Bishops Seeland, McNeley, and Hamlett signed a document (under a proviso in the ACC Canons) certifying that Archbishop Lewis was medically incapacitated from fulfilling the obligations of his office. On August 6, Archbishop Lewis suspended Seeland from his position as the President of Holyrood Seminary, and Seeland responded by informing his Archbishop that he didn't have the authority to suspend him. Later in the day, Bishops Mote, Stephens, and Bromley visited Archbishop Lewis in the hospital, and later signed a letter certifying that he was mentally competent to perform the duties of his office. Archbishop Lewis then sent a letter to many prominent people in the church, including within Bishop McNeley's diocese, informing them that McNeley was under inhibition and excommunicated. The Catholic party claimed that this was done before McNeley had been informed of his inhibition, thus implying that Lewis was trying to sabotage McNeley's diocese. On August 21st Archbishop Lewis then sent a letter throughout the church announcing that all of the renegade bishops had been inhibited for allegedly trying to take over the ACC. The accused bishops responded that Lewis did not have the authority to inhibit his fellow bishops, and further complicated matters by claiming that they doubted that Lewis' actions were his own, and that he was thus being manipulated by the other bishops in order to purge the ACC of its more stringently Catholic elements. Lewis then announced in September that the upcoming

Provincial Synod, which was to be held in Allentown, Pennsylvania, in Bishop Kleppinger's diocese, had been moved to Norfolk, Virginia, and was to be overseen by the designated Senior Bishop Ordinary, John Cahoon. Kleppinger, claiming to be the legitimate Senior Bishop Ordinary by precedent, announced that the "real" ACC Provincial Synod would be held as scheduled in Allentown. Consequently, in October of 1997, there were two rival ACC Provincial Synods, overseen by two rival claimants to the position of the Senior Bishop Ordinary.

Within the basic framework of these scandalous events, dozens of accusations of nefarious conduct and intentions were alleged by and against partisans of each side. Without going into all of these in mind-numbing detail, it will simply do to point out that each side acted in ways that were hardly becoming of the office of a bishop. Each side had serous concerns about the other. The Catholic party claimed that there were parishes in the majority bishops' dioceses that were not celebrating the Eucharist every Sunday, and that these same bishops were trying to change the ACC Canons so as to allow children to take Communion prior to their having been Confirmed. They also claimed that the majority bishops were refusing to discipline the South African church (due to its having so many members) for its allowing the laity to administer the Eucharist, as well as allowing girls to be acolytes. The majority bishops likewise claimed that Bishop Hamlett was attempting to have the Gregorian Canon of the Mass replace that of the Prayer Book, and that Bishop Price had composed his own service, including his own version of the Nicene Creed. The fact that the substantive difference between the two groups centered on such theological disagreements should have allowed for these men to either work their differences out within the College of Bishops, or to agree to part as amicably as possible so as to do as little damage as was necessary to their flock. The bishops chose instead to make a power grab for as much of the machinery and property of the institutional church as they could before the inevitable breakup.

    The Catholic party was clearly an outvoted minority within the College of Bishops. Rather than being content to try and change their situation by way of persuasion, or, if they had such serious theological doubts about their fellow bishops, trying to negotiate their way out of the ACC in a more peaceable manner, they chose instead to try and manipulate the system in order to temporarily improve their position within the College of Bishops, and to remain in the national church. The move to declare Archbishop Lewis incapacitated was clearly drawn up in advance, and was only used as a kind of after-the fact stratagem by the Catholic party to remain a powerful force within the College of Bishops. Bishop Hamlett, who was probably the most articulate and serious advocate of the stringent Catholic position, seemed to be the one bishop who had truly grasped the essentially theological and doctrinal nature of the disagreements, but even he was not above attempting to manipulate the events through misrepresentation. For example, he had written to Archbishop Lewis that he had only signed the incapacitation document when he had learned that Archbishop Lewis had, on August 6th, cancelled the scheduled meeting of the Holyrood Board of Directors. Hamlett claimed that he had assumed that Archbishop Lewis must either be incompetent, or that he was not really the one making such decisions, since the trip to the above mentioned meeting was too expensive of a journey for Hamlett to have made to only be cancelled so abruptly. The problem with this excuse was that Hamlett appears to have signed the incapacitation papers the day *before* the meeting had been cancelled by Archbishop Lewis. Regardless of the conditions leading up to the controversy, the Catholic party would have looked better if they had brought up the issue of Archbishop Lewis' incapacity before the August meltdown at Holyrood, rather than after the fact as they did.

The actions of the majority of ACC bishops were likewise questionable. The article in *The Trinitarian* was obviously biased and intended to poison the well of lay opinion against the three bishops who had denied their consent to Haverland's election to the episcopate. The inhibition and excommunication of McNeley, based as they were on only a few eyewitness accounts, which were obviously contested by other eyewitnesses, gives the appearance of a pre-determined outcome. At the very least, the speed with which the discipline was handed out was far too hasty, and, in the worst case scenario, looks like an attempt to do as much damage to McNeley within his diocese as was possible in order to strengthen the claim to legitimacy of the majority bishops in his diocese. Furthermore, a claim by the majority bishops that the minority bishops had no basis for declaring Archbishop Lewis incapable of performing his duties, since none of them had actually seen him in more than six months, was deceptive. The Catholic party claimed that Archbishop Lewis was *physically* unable to perform his duties, which was obviously true since he was confined to a nursing home during the period in question, and the ACC Canons required the relatively consistent physical presence of the Archbishop at certain official meetings of the church. The standard for competency was never whether the Archbishop was mentally capable enough to delegate his instructions through his representatives to the wider church, which was the claim of the majority bishops, but whether the Archbishop could preside in person at enough of the required meetings of the church. The position of the majority bishops on this account was basically a smokescreen designed to withhold from the wider church the fact that the Catholic party was correct in the most technical sense (this of course is irregardless of the moral sense of the catholic party's position).

When all of the smoke had settled from the controversies of 1997, the Catholic party had essentially formed a new church, declaring Bishop Hamlett as the new Archbishop. Thus, the ACC had lost most of its Dioceses of the Resurrection, Pacific and Southwest, and Holy Trinity and Great Plains, as well as those in England and New Zealand. During the Allentown Synod a series of doctrinal pamphlets, known as *The Allentown Tracts*, were distributed in order to clarify the more thoroughly Catholic doctrine and theology of the new body. Among the most important topics covered, the Marian doctrines (including the Assumption) and the role of "Holy Tradition" were clarified and asserted as essential doctrine. In general, *The Allentown Tracts* contain the language and spirit of Eastern Orthodox interpretations of the faith. It was alleged at the time that Bishop Hamlett, being based in England, was chosen in order to make the collection of the newly broken-away church's funds and property by the majority ACC more difficult in American courts. A court case, brought in New Jersey, ensued in which the majority ACC would win recognition as the legal claimant to the name, "Anglican Catholic Church," and in which the dissident body was banned from using the words "Anglican" and "Catholic" in any combination in any new name chosen to designate the group. Quizzically, the newly established group eventually began to call itself the Holy Catholic Church – Anglican Rite (HCC-AR), which was technically a violation of the legal order. However, as of 2001, the ACC had taken no action to challenge the new name chosen by the dissident group. While the secular courts were busied with the decision as to which rival group was the legitimate ACC, each body, for good measure, held ecclesiastical trials in which they found the other side guilty of violating an assortment of Canonical and Constitutional laws.

The final chapter in the whole affair occurred in 1999 when the majority of the American delegates to the HCC-AR Provincial Synod in Kansas City discovered upon their arrival that Archbishop Hamlett and Bishop Price had decided to separate the foreign wing of the new church from the American dioceses, supposedly due to the failure of the American bishops to act quickly enough to enforce the teaching of strict Catholic doctrine within their dioceses. This newest split had apparently been precipitated by renewed allegations that Archbishop Hamlett was planning to enforce the use of the Gregorian Canon of the mass on all of the parishes within the HCC-AR. Bishops Hamlett and Price returned home, the three American bishops chose Bishop Kleppinger to be the temporary, acting Archbishop of the (American) HCC-AR, and each body seems to have effectively agreed to leave the other alone. Many people within both groups maintain that no official split has occurred, and that the bishops may eventually reunite into a more unified structure once again in the near future.[475] However, the 2001/2002 FCC Directory of traditional parishes was listing Hamlett's group as the Holy Catholic Church – Western Rite.

While the ACC was undergoing perhaps the most bitter internal dispute in its history, the other Continuing bodies, including the newly pruned ACC, appeared to be moving into a period of improved communication and cooperation. In 1998, the Anglican Province of America (APA) signed an intercommunion agreement with the Reformed Episcopal Church (a 19th century Evangelical body formed in reaction to the importation of the Catholic liturgical revival from England to the Episcopal Church),[476] and the ACA House of Bishops adopted a resolution of "understanding" between itself and the ACC in recognition of each group's adherence to the Lambeth Quadrilateral and the *Affirmation of St. Louis*.[477] Although the ACC did not immediately reciprocate the action of the ACA bishops, talks were begun between the ACA's Archbishop Falk and the ACC's Archbishop Cahoon. During 1999, Cahoon also participated in exploratory ecumenical talks with the Charismatic Episcopal Church, the APA, and Forward in Faith (FIF) of England.[478] Perhaps the most symbolic sign of a general thawing of opinion toward other Continuing groups by the ACC was its decision to offer its health care coverage to any clergy in a Continuing body who requested it.[479]

The yearning by many members of the individual Continuing bodies for a greater unity among them seemed to take a great step forward in May of 1999 when a meeting was held in Bartonville, Illinois. Called by an "ecumenical, orthodox, Benedictine" community of monks, the gathering included most of the leading bishops from the Continuing bodies, as well as four traditionalist bishops from ECUSA. The ACA's Archbishop Falk was joined by three other bishops of the TAC, Presiding Bishop Davies of the EMC, Bishop Deyman of the ACC, Presiding Bishop Grundorf of the APA, three bishops from the Anglican Rite Synod in the Americas,[480] and bishops from the Anglican Orthodox Church and American Anglican Church. These Continuing bishops were joined by ECUSA's Bishops Keith Ackerman, Jack Iker, Edward MacBurney, and Donald Parsons. The purpose of the meeting was to foster greater unity of purpose among traditionalist Episcopalians and Anglicans, and to begin the process of exploring the possibilities of establishing institutional unity among them. The result of these initial discussions was another gathering held in October, in which most of the above mentioned Continuing prelates signed Articles of Fellowship which endorsed each group sending representatives to the Synods of other groups, limiting the transference of laity and clergy between bodies, and promising to gather for ecumenical meetings at least once a year. The ECUSA bishops only sent a letter expressing support for the Articles of Fellowship.[481]

The participation of ECUSA bishops in the Bartonville meeting signified a major shift of emphasis within the world of the Continuing Anglicans, many of whom had expressed little hope for rapprochement with the official Anglican Communion. However, the latest events within ECUSA and the Anglican Communion had created an environment in which many Continuers began to see (once again) hopeful signs for renewal and reform within the mainstream church they had departed from. The great shift occurred during the 1998 Lambeth Conference, when a block of African, Asian, and Latin American primates joined American and English conservative primates to issue a strong reaffirmation of traditional sexual morality, including a condemnation of the practice of homosexuality and pre-marital sex. This action was taken in large part to stem the tide of what was seen by many of the primates as a dangerous shift in the church's moral teaching. During the late 1980s and early 1990s, ECUSA had adopted what was essentially a policy of local autonomy in regard to allowing homosexuals to be ordained to the priesthood, and this gay-rights movement was poised to gain official recognition from the wider church. The decision reached at Lambeth was a rebuke of the prevailing liberalism of ECUSA in regard to sexual morality, and, more ominously, included intimations that some means for disciplining the American church may have to be devised should it continue to violate the wider communion's teaching on sexual morality.[482]

While the rebuke of the movement to loosen the standards of sexual morality within Anglicanism gained most of the attention in the immediate aftermath of the

Lambeth conference, another resolution issued by the mainstream prelates offered an olive branch to the Continuing churchmen, calling for the Archbishop of Canterbury to initiate discussions with all of the groups who had been disaffected by the Anglican Communion, with the suggested goal of beginning a process that would bring most of the groups claiming an Anglican heritage back into communion with the Anglican mainstream.[483] Seemingly buoyed by the world bishops' endorsement of a plan to renew orthodox teaching in the Anglican Communion, the Episcopal Syndo of America (ESA) emerged shortly thereafter with a new identity, calling itself Forward in Faith in North America (FIFNA), thus aligning itself with the body based in England. FIF had already signed intercommunion agreements with the TAC (1994) and EMC, and FIFNA now joined in the agitation by FIF to have a separate province for traditionalist Anglicans established if the worldwide communion could not adequately purify itself of radical theology and sexual morality.

    The possibility of the formation of a separate "orthodox" province became more conceivable when six primates from Africa, Asia, and Australia stated in April of 1999 that they were committed to "take action" should leaders within ECUSA continue to announce their intentions to not pay heed to the warnings issued at the 1998 Lambeth Conference.[484] The predominate line within ECUSA in the immediate aftermath of the Lambeth gathering had been to deny that the foreign bishops had the authority to infringe in the affairs of the American dioceses. Throughout 1999, one ECUSA diocese after another denounced the decision reached at Lambeth as an intolerant affront to the "progress" that had been achieved in United States, thus challenging the traditionalist foreign primates to back up their threats of discipline with action.

    Several traditionalist organizations working within

ECUSA, including FIFNA and the American Anglican Council (AAC), had formed an umbrella organization called First Promise, which, throughout 1999, had petitioned and met with the traditionalist foreign prelates to discuss possible means for addressing the "urgent situation" of traditionalists within ECUSA. In October of 1999 several of the foreign primates had visited the United States, at the request of Presiding Bishop Griswold, to investigate the American situation for themselves. Shortly thereafter, the prelates issued a report criticizing ECUSA for ignoring the voice of the worldwide Anglican majority. Then, after it had become apparent that little of immediate practical substance was to come of the warnings by the foreign prelates, two of them moved independently to give substance to their threats.

In Singapore, in January of 2000, Primates Moses Tay of South East Asia, Emmanuel Kolini of Rwanda, and John Ruchyahana of Rwanda, consecrated two American priests, Charles H. Murphy of South Carolina and John H. Rodgers of Pennsylvania, for the purpose of providing "temporary" episcopal oversight to traditionalist churchmen within ECUSA. These actions were sharply criticized by Presiding Bishop Griswold, Archbishop Carey, and most bishops in the Anglican Communion. Perhaps because they had felt so little harmed by the first Continuing movement, the potential for another one did not seem to faze ECUSA's leadership, who led the 2000 General Convention to adopt a non-committal set of resolutions that essentially maintained the status quo of allowing bishops to decide whether gays would be ordained in their dioceses. The immediate result of this "rebellion" by ECUSA was the announcement by the consecrating bishops of Singapore that Bishops Murphy and Rodgers were no longer considered to be interim figures. The foreign prelates announced the formation of yet another Continuing Anglican church, to be known as the Anglican Mission in America (AMIA). Before the end of the year, more than 25 parishes had affiliated with AMIA, and as many as 50 more parishes were expected to do likewise in the coming months.[485] In January of 2001, AMIA and FIFNA leaders announced that they would work together for the establishment of an orthodox province within the United States. Notably, however, FIFNA did not officially endorse the action of the AMIA in consecrating bishops when it did, and chose instead to focus on finding foreign bishops to consecrate a bishop for FIFNA. The stated purpose of this policy was to gain the wider approval and acceptance of the Anglican Communion at large.[486]

The reaction to the formation of the AMIA within the world of the older Continuing bodies was mixed. The APA joined the REC in initiating discussions toward an intercommunion agreement with the new body, but the ACC and many of the other groups tended to stress that ECUSA's problems were far more serious than a failure to discipline its bishops and clerics for not upholding traditional morality. One bishop from a smaller Continuing body also anonymously informed this author that, even though some Continuers may be initially intrigued by the AMIA, "they will sour on it when they discover that most of its parishes are charismatic, holy-roller types of churches." Furthermore, some Continuers expressed to this author that they expected the AMIA bishops to assert their unique position as the "legitimate" traditionalist body in the United States, and thus seemed to contain little hope for any larger re-union effort with other traditionalist Episcopalians or Continuing churchmen.

As the Continuing Movement moved into the new millennium, it found itself largely where it had started more than twenty-five years earlier. For the most part, mainstream Episcopalian traditionalists were either leaving the church altogether, or hoping to form a more "legitimate," institutionally secure, orthodox body, rather than opting for the

Continuing alternative.[487] The Continuum remained not much larger within the United States than it had been shortly after its peak years in the late 1970s and early 1980s. And of course, the problems of disunity, schism, and episcopal shenanigans continued. In 1999, two EMC bishops joined the DCK. This was followed by the resignation of EMC Presiding Bishop Davies in February of 2000, and then by the withdrawal of Bishop Jon Lidenauer and his Diocese of the West. The new group apparently planned on extending a Haitian group, known as the Christian Episcopal Church, into the United States. The new Presiding Bishop of the EMC, William Millsaps, reportedly claimed that Bishops Davies and Lidenauer left only after they found out that there were going to be charged with assorted Canonical violations and other improprieties. The accused bishops were to be charged with illicitly regularizing the episcopal orders of two bishops who had recently left the ACA due to a controversy over their having been consecrated improperly (with no other consecrators and now prior announcement of the service) by a retired ACA Bishop, Charles Boynton, who had since also left to join the EMC. The other group claimed that there was simply no confidence in Bishop Millsaps' leadership ability, and they also accused him of invading Bishop Lidenauer's diocese.[488]

Unity efforts, and dreams of more peaceable relations between the Continuing jurisdictions, continued apace as well. In 2001, the Traditional Episcopal Church (TEC), which had been formed in 1992 by Bishop Richard Melli (a former bishop in the American Episcopal Church and the TPEC), merged with a body known as the Anglo-Catholic Church in the Americas to form another Continuing group: the United Anglican Church (UAC). After this merger, the UAC began negotiations with the ACA's Archbishop Falk in the hopes of joining the Traditional Anglican Communion. Falk and the TAC continued to work for the unification of the Continuum, even inviting Bishop Morse of the APCK and Bishop Grundorf of the APA to a meeting of the ACA in February of 2002.[489] The TAC had even contacted the bishops of the hyper-Catholic Holy Catholic Church – Anglican Rite about joining its ranks and, inexplicably, the HCC-AR was rumored to be seriously considering the proposal.[490]

    Perhaps the most fitting conclusion to this study involves the final fate of Fr. Anthony Clavier, who was the symbol of either the well-intentioned Continuing churchmen who was hounded out of the Movement by closed-minded forces, or the archetype of the vagabond bishops who manipulated and harmed the Movement for their own personal vanity and gain. Clavier had been serving a parish in Arizona for the American Anglican Church, but in November of 1999 he was received as a priest into the Diocese of Arkansas in ECUSA.[491] His new Bishop, Larry Maze, was supportive of the liberalized policies toward homosexuals prevalent in the national church. Although promising not to become involved in any controversial issues within his new church, by June of 2000 his name was associated with a group of conservative and liberal churchmen within ECUSA called the New Commandment Task Force, which had the stated purpose of "preserving the unity of the Church without insisting on the uniformity of our theological beliefs."[492] He was also passing himself off as a wizened veteran of the dissident traditionalist impulse, warning those within the Episcopal Church who were contemplating the AMIA option of the inherent pitfalls of such a course.[493]

Conclusion

THE STATUS AND FUTURE OF CONTINUING ANGLICANISM

Most observers of the Continuum, whether inside or outside of it, have interpreted the Movement in largely negative terms. The reaction of mainstream Episcopalians has been one of near total silence for more than two decades, and traditionalist Episcopalians have likewise ignored the Continuum almost as consistently as their fellow churchmen. However, with the recent development of the Anglican Mission in America, and the resulting spirit of optimism among disgruntled Episcopalians that an "orthodox" jurisdictional haven is eminent, tentative olive branches are being extended to the Continuers.

Fr. Peter Toon, an influential Evangelical churchmen and former President of the Prayer Book Society, recently broke the ice in a commentary on the Continuing Movement. In an attempt to explore the means by which a new orthodox jurisdiction could form a working relationship with the Continuing Churches, Toon listed the major weaknesses of the Movement. Although making the usual observations that episcopal jockeying for power had overridden the dedication to shepherd souls, and that bishops had vainly run amok, he also added that Catholic churchmen could be blamed for their attempt to force their churchmanship on their fellow Continuers. This last observation reflected his overall critique that the basic mistake committed by the Continuers involved their departure from authentic Anglicanism. Authentic Anglicanism, according to

Toon, is reflected in its comprehensiveness, which is its ability to differentiate between essentials and non-essentials, and results in a tolerance of belief and practice in non-essentials. Furthermore, authentic Anglicanism should recognize that the Bible is the foundation upon which dogma and the interpretations of the Ecumenical Councils were built.[494]

It is difficult to imagine that Toon, one of the most thoughtful and articulate of traditionalists who have remained in the Anglican mainstream, actually thinks that his suggestions will make an impact among Continuers. First of all, it is doubtful that the Catholic portion of the Continuum (Anglican Catholic Church, Province of Christ the King, and Holy Catholic Church – Anglican Rite) will be willing to embrace his Low-church theological framework. His upholding of the classic Anglican principle of unity in essentials, diversity in non-essentials, and making the distinction by recognizing the supremacy of the Bible, is precisely the kind of muddled doctrinal reflection that the High-Church Continuers were trying to escape from. More problematically, there would appear to be a wide gulf between the orthodoxy of mainstream Episcopalians, most of whom have accepted the concept of women holding Holy Orders, and the more classically Anglican Continuers (Anglican Church in America, Anglican Province in America, Episcopal Missionary Church, Charismatic Episcopal Church, and other smaller bodies). Even if such a difficult difference could be worked out between the disgruntled and ex-Episcopalians, a further problem remains in that many Continuers have never forgiven the former for failing to follow them into the Continuum. Many Continuers think that those traditionalists who remained in the Episcopal Church were rather cowardly, being unwilling to give up their comfortable positions and well-endowed parishes, and have viewed them rather suspiciously for too many years. Bridging such a gulf of distrust will probably be more difficult than the likes of Toon imagine.

Those outside of both the Continuum and Anglicanism, but who share a concern for renewing orthodoxy in contemporary Christianity, have likewise declared the Continuing Movement to be a failure at worst, a disappointment at best. In a 1989 issue of *Touchstone*, a journal dedicated to "ecumenical orthodoxy," Michael Gallo described the Continuing Movement as, at best, "on the periphery" of Anglicanism. While correctly noting that the old divide between High and Low-churchmen had played an important role in the difficulties experienced within the Continuum, he also observed that the Movement largely suffers from an image problem, giving the impression of being composed of "reactionaries" and "sectarians." Worse still, the Continuum "has attracted some rather unusual and highly exotic types; characters of the ecclesial twighlight, the conspiracy hunters, the weird and wonderful, the fantasizing egos." Although Gallo admits that all religious groups contain such elements, he argues that they have stood out more in the Continuum than in other groups. The Continuers were further scored for their overly obsessive concentration on the regularity of their Holy Orders, for their attempts at constructing Canons that address every problem, and for their inability to compromise with each other.[495]

Although many Continuers would agree with some of Gallo's points, the general consensus within the Movement has been that their problems have stemmed from political infighting – motivated by both theological and personality conflicts. In general, Low-church Continuers interpret their separation from the High-Churchmen in terms of theological and liturgical differences, and the schisms within the Low-Church Continuing groups to be the result of personality conflicts. The High-

Church Continuers likewise see theological reasons for their separation from the Low-Churchmen, and blame their own schisms on clashes of personality and vanity. A typical example of the self-criticism that is found inside the Continuum is a recent piece by Fr. Mark Clavier of the Anglican Province in America. The junior Clavier opines that the Continuing Movement has shown no growth during the 1990's, has not done as it should and focused on preaching the Gospel, and finally, sums up the feeling of so many Continuers, "Our movement has, from the start, been plagued by conflicting personalities, weak jurisdictional structures, and widely differing definitions for Anglicanism."[496] Of course, there are those in the Continuum who now seem to prefer to define themselves a part of worldwide Catholicism, rather than the Continuing Anglican Movement. These Catholic Continuers define the problem on an inability, or unwillingness, of many of those Low-churchmen who left the Episcopal Church to be instructed in genuine Catholicism. The development of this alternative interpretation can be seen in Fr. Thomas McDonald's *A Time To Stand*, which was originally published in 1997 with the subheading, "Written especially for Those Who Have Chosen To Continue The *Traditional Anglican Church* [emphasis mine]. In 2001, he released an addendum to *A Time To Stand*, with a new subhead: "Written especially for Those Who Have Chosen To Continue The *Teachings and Practices of the Church Fathers and the Seven Ecumenical Councils of the Undivided Church* [emphasis mine again].[497] Nonetheless, this ultra-Catholic position is certainly not widespread.

As the above criticisms reflect, and as the opinions and actions of most Continuers demonstrate, the future of the Continuum (as of this writing) does not appear to be very bright by contemporary standards of measurement.

The unity and harmony that most Continuers seek (either among themselves or with the Anglican/Episcopal mainstream) will most probably only result from the kind of theological, doctrinal and liturgical compromises that many Continuing churchmen despise. If these contemporary unity options prevail (such as portions of the Continuum joining with the Anglican Mission in America to be a traditionalist jurisdiction within the mainstream Anglican Worldwide Communion), they will necessarily entail a compromise or repudiation of the separatist option taken by the first Continuers, since these Continuers will once again be in communion with jurisdictions that ordain women to the priesthood and episcopate.

If unity efforts among Continuing ecclesiastical bodies should happen to prevail, these too would probably entail compromises between High and Low-churchmen that would not bode well for the future of the Continuum and/or traditionalist Anglicanism. Although many observers have viewed the doctrinal conflicts between Catholic and Protestant churchmen as the greatest weakness of the Continuing Movement, one could make the obverse argument that such doctrinal confrontations are precisely the kind of self-evaluation and criticism that Anglicanism has always needed. Perhaps one of the biggest mistakes among traditionalists Anglicans, both in the past and the present, has been to assume that the deterioration of the Anglican and Episcopal churches was/is the result of their church capitulating to the "modern" secular and sinful culture. When one examines the basic foundations of the sinful culture that is alleged to have infested contemporary Anglicanism (its pluralism, relativism, and hyper-individualism, to name a few), it becomes apparent that many of these supposedly secularly derived blights have close parallels to the foundations of the kind of comprehensive, "unity in essentials, diversity in non-essentials" approach that is the mark of the classic Anglican position. After all, the conflicts that accompanied the Protestant Reformation were based on some rather serious doctrinal disagreements, but the Anglican "compromise" was the only Reformation era solution to assert that the conflicts were essentially not necessary. What else can be implied from the classic Anglican position that Catholics and Protestants can inhabit the same ecclesiastical body. Regardless of whether this was the best solution, it is difficult to avoid the conclusion that a church that allows (for example) its members to either view the Eucharist as a symbolic memorial meal, or as the Grace-bearing very Body and Blood of Christ, is an essentially pluralistic and relativistic body. Taking such an observation into consideration, it may do Continuing and traditionalist Anglicans well to examine their own theological presuppositions, rather than continuing to view their internal problems as the result of interference from alien sources.

Perhaps it will be in the Continuum, where doctrinal and theological issues are taken very seriously, that the mainstream Anglican Communion may receive some much needed helpful instruction on how to genuinely express itself as an "orthodox" ecclesiastical body, being *in* the world, but not *of* the world. Perhaps it is best that either the High or the Low-church position should prevail within the Continuum, rather than the Broad-church option, whose legacy very well may be the kind of mushy-brained heterodoxy that Continuers and traditionalists oppose.

Appendix A
THE AFFIRMATION OF ST. LOUIS

The Continuation of Anglicanism
 We affirm that the Church of our fathers, sustained by the most Holy Trinity, lives yet, and that we, being moved by the Holy Spirit to walk only in that way, are determined to continue in the Catholic Faith, Apostolic Order, Orthodox Worship and Evangelical Witness of the traditional Anglican Church, doing all things necessary for the continuance of the same. We are upheld and strengthened in this determination by the knowledge that many provinces and dioceses of the Anglican Communion have continued steadfast in the same Faith, Order, Worship and Witness, and that they continue to confine ordination to the priesthood and the episcopate to males. We rejoice in these facts and we affirm our solidarity with these provinces and dioceses.

The Dissolution of Anglican and Episcopal Church Structure.
 We affirm that the Anglican Church of Canada and the Protestant Episcopal Church in the United States of America, by their unlawful attempts to alter Faith, Order, and Morality (especially in their General Synod of 1975 and General Convention of 1976), have departed from Christ's One, Holy, Catholic, and Apostolic Church.

The Need to Continue Order in the Church
We affirm that all former ecclesiastical governments, being fundamentally impaired by the schismatic acts of lawless Councils, are of no effect among us, and that we must now reorder such godly discipline as will strengthen us in the continuation of our common life and witness.

The Invalidity of Schismatic Authority
We affirm that the claim of any such schismatic person or body to act against any Church member, clerical or lay, for his witness to the whole Faith is with no authority of Christ's true Church, and any such inhibition, deposition or discipline is without effect and is absolutely null and void.

The Need for Principles and a Constitution
We affirm that fundamental principles (doctrinal, moral, and constitutional) are necessary for the present, and that a Constitution (redressing the defects and abuses of our former governments) should be adopted, whereby the Church may be soundly continued.

The Continuation of Communion with Canterbury
We affirm our continued relations of communion with the See of Canterbury and all faithful parts of the Anglican Communion.

Wherefore, with a firm trust in Divine Providence, and before Almighty God and all the company of heaven, we solemnly affirm, covenant and declare that we, lawful and faithful members of the Anglican and Episcopal Churches, shall now and hereafter continue and be the unified continuing Anglican Church in North America, in true and valid succession thereto.

FUNDAMENTAL PRINCIPLES

In order to carry these declarations, we set forth these fundamental Principles for our continued life and witness.

PREFACE

In the firm conviction that "we shall be saved through the grace of the Lord Jesus Christ," and that "there is no other name under heaven given among men by which we must be saved," and acknowledging our duty to proclaim Christ's saving Truth to all peoples, nations and tongues, we declare our intention to hold fast the One, Holy, Catholic and Apostolic Faith of God.

We acknowledge that rule of faith laid down by St. Vincent of Lerins: "Let us hold that which has been believed everywhere, always and by all, for that is truly and properly Catholic."

I. Principles of Doctrine

1. The Nature of the Church

We gather as people called by God to be faithful and obedient to Him. As the Royal Priestly People of God, the Church is called to be, in fact, the manifestation of Christ in and to the world. True religion is revealed to man by God. We cannot decide what is truth, but rather (in obedience) ought to receive, accept, cherish, defend and teach what God has given us. The Church is created by God, and is beyond the ultimate control of man.

The Church is the Body of Christ at work in the world. She is the society of the baptized called out from the world: In it, but not of it. As Christ's faithful Bride, she is different from the world and must not be influenced by it.

2. The Essentials of Truth and Order

We repudiate all deviation or departure from the Faith, in whole or in part, and bear witness to these essential principles of evangelical Truth and apostolic Order:

Holy Scriptures

The Holy Scriptures of the Old and New Testaments and the authentic record of God's revelation of Himself, His saving activity, and moral demands – a revelation valid for all men and all time.

The Creeds

The Nicene Creed as the authoritative summary of the chief articles of the Christian Faith, together with the Apostles' Creed, and that known as the Creed of St. Athanasius to be "thoroughly received and believed" in the sense they have had always in the Catholic Church.

Tradition
The received Tradition of the Church and its teachings as set forth by "the ancient catholic bishops and doctors," and especially as defined by the Seven Ecumenical Councils of the undivided Church, to the exclusion of all errors, ancient and modern.

Sacraments
The Sacraments of Baptism, Confirmation, the Holy Eucharist, Holy Matrimony, Holy Orders, Penance and Unction of the Sick, as objective and effective signs of the continued presence and saving activity of Christ our Lord among His people and as His covenanted means for conveying His grace. In particular, we affirm the necessity of Baptism and the Holy Eucharist (where they may be had) – Baptism as incorporating us into Christ (with its completion in Confirmation as the "seal of the Holy Spirit"), and the Eucharist as the sacrifice which unites us to the all-sufficient Sacrifice of Christ on the Cross and the Sacrament in which He feeds us with His Body and Blood.

Holy Orders
The Holy Orders of bishops, priests, and deacons as the perpetuation of Christ's gift of apostolic ministry to His Church, asserting the necessity of a bishop of apostolic succession (or a priest ordained by such) as the celebrant of the Eucharist – these Orders consisting exclusively of men in accordance with Christ's Will and institution (as evidenced by the Scriptures), and the universal practice of the Catholic Church.

Deaconesses
The ancient office and ministry of Deaconess as a lay vocation for women, affirming the need for proper encouragement of that office.

Duty of Bishops

Bishops as Apostles, Prophets, Evangelists, Shepherds and Teachers, as well as their duty (together with other clergy and laity) to guard and defend the purity and integrity of the Church's Faith and Moral Teaching.

The Use of Other Formulae

In affirming these principles, we recognize that all Anglican statements of faith and liturgical formulae must be interpreted in accordance with them.

Incompetence of Church Bodies to Alter Truth

We disclaim any right or competence to suppress, alter or amend any of the ancient Ecumenical Creeds and definitions of Faith, to set aside or depart from Holy Scripture, or to alter or deviate from the essential Pre-requisites of any Sacrament.

Unity with Other Believers

We declare our firm intention to seek and achieve full sacramental communion and visible unity with other Christians who "worship the Trinity in Unity, and Unity in Trinity," and who hold the Catholic and Apostolic Faith in accordance with the foregoing principles.

II. Principles of Morality

The conscience, as the inherent knowledge of right and wrong, cannot stand alone as a sovereign arbiter of morals. Every Christian is obligated to form his conscience by the Divine Moral Law and the Mind of Christ as revealed in Holy Scriptures, and by the teaching and Tradition of the Church. We hold that when the Christian conscience is thus properly informed and ruled, it must affirm the following moral principles:

Individual Responsibility

All people, individually and collectively, are responsible to their Creator for their acts, motives, thoughts and words, since "we must all appear before the judgment seat of Christ…"

Sanctity of Human Life

Every human being, from the time of his conception, is a creature and child of God, made in His image and likeness, an infinitely precious soul; and that the unjustifiable or inexcusable taking of life is always sinful.

Man's Duty to God

All people are bound by the dictates of the Natural Law and by the revealed Will of God, insofar as they can discern them.

Family Life

The God-given sacramental bond in marriage between one man and one woman is God's loving provision for procreation and family life, and sexual activity is to be practiced only within the bonds of Holy Matrimony.

Man as Sinner

We recognize that man, as inheritor of original sin, is "very far gone from original righteousness," and as a rebel against God's authority is liable to His righteous judgment.

Man and God's Grace
We recognize, too, that God loves His children and particularly has shown it forth in the redemptive work of our Lord Jesus Christ, and that man cannot be saved by any effort of his own, but by the Grace of God, through repentance and acceptance of God's forgiveness.

Christian's Duty to be Moral
We believe, therefore, it is the duty of the Church and her members to bear witness to Christian Morality, to follow it in their lives, and to reject the false standards of the world.

III. Constitutional Principles

In the constitutional revision which must be undertaken, we recommend, for the consideration of continuing Anglicans, the following:

Retain the Best of Both Provinces

That the traditional and tested features of the Canadian and American ecclesiastical systems be retained and used in the administration of the continuing Church.

Selection of Bishops

That a non-political means for selection of bishops be devised, adopted and used.

Tripartite Synod

That the Church be generally governed by a Holy Synod of three branches (episcopal, clerical, and lay), under the presidency of the Primate of the Church.

Scriptural Standards for the Ministry

That the apostolic and scriptural standards for the sacred Ministry be used for all orders of Ministers.

Concurrence of all Orders for Decisions

That the Constitution acknowledge the necessity of the concurrence of all branches of the Synod for decisions in all matters, and that extraordinary majorities be required for the favorable consideration of all matters of importance.

Re-establishment of Discipline

That the Church re-establish an effective permanent system of ecclesiastical courts for the defense of the Faith and the maintenance of discipline over all her members.

Constitutional Assembly to be Called

That our bishops shall call a Constitutional Assembly of lay and clerical representatives of dioceses and parishes to convene at the earliest appropriate time to draft a Constitution and Canons by which we may be unified and governed, with special reference to this Affirmation, and with due consideration to ancient Custom and the General Canon Law, and to the former law of our provinces.

Interim Action

In the meantime, trusting in the everlasting strength of God to carry us through all our trials, we commend all questions for decision to the proper authorities in each case: Episcopal, diocesan, and parochial, encouraging all the faithful to support our witness as subscribers to this Affirmation, and inviting all so doing to share our fellowship and the work of the Church.

IV. Principles of Worship

Prayer Book – The Standard of Worship

In the continuing Anglican Church, the Book of Common Prayer is (and remains) one work in two editions: The Canadian Book of 1962 and the American Book of 1928. Each is fully and equally authoritative. No other standard for worship exists.

Certain Variances Permitted

For liturgical use, only the Book of Common Prayer and service books conforming to and incorporating it shall be used.

V. Principles of Action

Intercommunion with other Apostolic Churches
   The continuing Anglicans remain in full communion with the See of Canterbury and with all other faithful parts of the Anglican Communion, and should actively seek similar relations with all other Apostolic and Catholic Churches, provided that agreement in the essentials of Faith and Order first be reached.

Non-Involvement with Non-Apostolic Groups
   We recognize that the World Council of Churches, and many national and other Councils adhering to the World Council, are non-Apostolic, humanist and secular in purpose and practice, and that under such circumstances, we cannot be members of any of them. We also recognize that the Consultation of Church Union (COCU) and all other such schemes, being non-Apostolic and non-Catholic in their present concept and form, are unacceptable to us, and that we cannot be associated with any of them.

Need for Sound Theological Training
   Re-establishment of spiritual, orthodox and scholarly theological education under episcopal supervision is imperative, and should be encouraged and promoted by all in authority; and learned and godly bishops, other clergy and lay people should undertake and carry on that work without delay.

Financial Affairs
   The right of congregations to control of their temporalities should be firmly and constitutionally recognized and protected.

Administrative Matters

Administration should, we believe, be limited to the most simple and necessary acts, so that emphasis may be centered on worship, pastoral care, spiritual and moral soundness, personal good works, and missionary outreach, in response to God's love for us.

The Church as Witness to Truth

We recognize also that, as keepers of God's will and truth for man, we can and ought to witness to that will and truth against all manifest evils, remembering that we are as servants in the world, but God's servants first.

Pensions and Insurance

We recognize our immediate responsibility to provide for the establishment of sound pension and insurance programs for the protection of the stipendiary clergy and other Church workers.

Legal Defense

We recognize the immediate need to coordinate legal resources, financial and professional, for the defense of congregations imperiled by their stand for the Faith, and commend this need most earnestly to the diocesan and parochial authorities.

Continuation, Not Innovation

In this gathering witness of Anglicans and Episcopalians, we continue to be what we are. We do nothing new. We form no new body, but continue as Anglicans and Episcopalians.

NOW, THEREFORE, deeply aware of our duty to all who love and believe the Faith of our Fathers, of our duty to God, who alone shall judge what we do, we make this Affirmation.

Before God, we claim our Anglican/Episcopal inheritance, and proclaim the same to the whole Church, through Jesus Christ our Lord, to whom, with the Father and the Holy Ghost, be all honor and glory, world without end, Amen. [1977][498]

Appendix B

THE SOUTHERN PHALANX

The use of the term "Southern Phalanx" has been undertaken only after careful consideration. In the course of researching this book, it became apparent that the conflicts between High and Low-churchmen could not be adequately explained by focusing only on the ideological and theological disagreements between the rival factions and individual churchmen. A pattern of interpersonal networking and politicking obviously dominated both groups. However, a conceptual problem emerged in that the network (really networks) of High-churchmen tended to operate and be limited *within* denominational boundaries, whereas the most important network of Broad Low-churchmen (the Phalanx) worked both within and *independently* of the assorted Continuing church bodies. Consequently, although it was sensible to speak of a High-church or Catholic *party* (within the context of a particular denomination or organization), such a term did not adequately encompass the often supra-denominational activities of the Broad Low-church network that comprised the Southern Phalanx.

The original draft of this book used the term "FCC Phalanx" to describe the actions of the Broad Low-church network that was later labeled as the Southern Phalanx. The original decision to focus on the FCC (Fellowship of Concerned Churchmen) was largely based on the assertion of many High-church Continuers that the FCC was the primary thorn in their side. However, upon further reflection, I decided that the FCC was not as uniformly antagonistic to the plans of the High-church parties as it was accused of being. Furthermore, another organization (the Foundation of Christian Theology) seemed to be just as involved in opposing the goals of the High-church parties as was the FCC.

The FCC and FCT were the two organizations that primarily either organized, publicized, and/or interpreted the Continuing Movement. Both organizations were dominated by, though never completely beholden to, a Protestant [Broad to Low-church) understanding of Anglican identity. Importantly, both organizations published periodicals that were read and respected within all of the Continuing church bodies. High-churchmen focused much of their resentment on the FCC and FCT, blaming both for sowing seeds of dissension within the Continuum. The challenge I faced as a historian was how to describe the actions of this group of elite Protestant churchmen who almost always acted under the organizational or editorial cover of the FCC and/or FCT, while at the same time making it clear that these organizations were not always institutionally responsible for the opposition to the Catholic (High-church) parties. My solution was to describe the Broad Low-church network that usually worked within the FCC and FCT as the Southern Phalanx. In this sense, the Southern Phalanx should be seen as a coalition of elite Protestant churchmen who usually used the FCC and FCT to spread their message throughout the Continuum.

The use of the term "Southern Phalanx" should not be interpreted as a smear of churchmen who lived in the southern United States, nor as an insinuation that all southern churchmen hold the Protestant or Low-church theological position. The designation was chosen in part in imitation of an historical term (Hackney Phalanx) that was used to describe an early coalition of High-churchmen within the Church of England in the late 18th and early

19th centuries. Just as the use of the term "Hackney Phalanx" allowed historians to employ a geographic designation to discuss a particular group of persons who promulgated a theological position, so too does the use of the term "Southern Phalanx" allow for a differentiation between the general Broad Low-church theological position, and the particular coalition of churchmen who acted within the FCC and FCT (as well as through other channels) to influence the Continuing Movement. The geographic designation reflects the fact that most of the members of the Southern Phalanx either lived in, moved to, or published in periodicals based in, the South. The designation allows for a distinction between the Broad to Low-church Protestants scattered across the various Continuing church bodies, and the specific group of elite Broad Low-churchmen who made up the constituency of the Southern Phalanx.

Notes

1. See Appendix B for a discussion of the choice of the term "Southern Phalanx."
2. *Anglicans Online*, an impressive internet website that offers an array of information and links on all things Anglican, noted in its introduction to the "Not in Communion" page that it no longer included descriptions of the assorted Continuing groups due to their having been sued by a Continuing bishop who felt slandered by the website.
3. "Snippets and Tippets," *US Anglican*, December 2001, p. 40.
4. David L. Holmes. *A Brief History of the Episcopal Church.* (Valley Forge, PA: Trinity Press, 1993), p. 57.
5. Thomas C. Reeves. *The Empty Church: The Suicide of Liberal Christianity.* (New York, NY: Free Press, 1996), p. 11.
6. K.L. Billingsley. *From Mainline to Sideline: The Social Witness of the National Council of Churches.* (Washington, DC: Ethics and Public Policy Center, 1990), p. 45.
7. C. Gregg Singer. *The Unholy Alliance: The Definitive History of the National Council of Churches and its Leftist Policies - from 1908 to the Present.* (New Rochelle, NY: Arlington House, 1975) p. 202-203.
8. Billingsley, p. 158.
9. Ibid., p. 50, 67, and 161.
10. HUAC (in another incarnation) was first formed during the 1920's as an investigative arm of the United States Congress in order to investigate anti-American or potentially traitorous groups. It had been used by the

Roosevelt Administration during World War II in order to harass radical right-wing and Nazi-sympathizer groups. However, it gained in visibility, and controversy, during the early years of the Cold War.

11. Some examples of this literature include Edgar C. Bundy's *Collectivism in the Churches* (1960), James DeForest Murch's *The Protestant Revolt* (1967), and Edmund and Julia Robb's *The Betrayal of the Church* (1986). The Air Force Manual incident helped to spark the anti-communist career of Rev. Billy James Hargis, who continued to "hunt" for communists into the 1980's. For information on both the Air Force Manual controversy and the career of Billy James Hargis, see John George and Laird Wilcox's *American Extremists: Militias, Supremacists, Klansmen, Communists, and Others.* (Amherst, NY: Prometheus Books, 1996), p. 173-185.

12. David E. Sumner. *The Episcopal Church's History: 1945-1985.* (Wilton, CT: Morehouse, 1987), p. 40.

13. The information on PECUSA involvement in civil rights activism and the formation of the GCSP is gathered from Sumner, p. 38-42.

14. The information on the Alianza controversy was gathered from John W. Ellison's "J'ACCUSE - The Alianza," *The Living Church*, February 1, 1970, p. 8-10; and from "Silk Hats and Brown Berets," *The New American*, February 19, 1996, p. 33-34 [no author listed].

15. "General Convention Report," *The Living Church*, September 28, 1969, p. 8.

16. Ibid., p. 5-9.

17. "...About South Bend," *The Living Church*, October 19, 1969, p. 12.

18. Carrol Simcox. "South Bend: One Man's Opinion," *The Living Church*, October 5, 1969, p. 9.

19. Sumner, p. 50.

20. John W. Ellison, "Let's Crucify The Church," *The Living Church*, October 4, 1970, p. 27.
21. "Missouri: PB Raps FCT," *The Living Church*, November 16, 1969, p. 6.
22. "General Convention Opens," *The Living Church*, November 1, 1970, p. 7. Additional information on the GCSP and the Black Manifesto was gathered from Sumner, p. 46-59; and *The Christian Challenge*, November-December, 1999, p. 10-12.
23. L. William Countryman, "Authority and Crisis in the Church," *The Living Church*, June 21, 1970, p. 3.
24. Ibid.
25. Holmes, p. 159-160.
26. Actually, Pittenger would also join in the political radicalism that was in vogue in the 1960s and 1970s by becoming one of the first influential churchmen to campaign for the ordination of homosexual priests.
27. Singer, p. 232.
28. "Part I: 1962-1974," *The Christian Challenge*, November-December, 1999, p. 8.
29. Ibid.
30. Robert Prichard. *A History of the Episcopal Church.* (Harrisburg, PA: Morehouse, 1991), p. 258.
31. William Stringfellow and Anthony Towne. *The Death and Life of Bishop Pike: An Utterly Candid Biography of America's Most Controversial Clergyman.* (New York, NY: Doubleday, 1976), p. 149, 202, 322, and 327.
32. Reeves, p. 184-185.
33. James DeForest Murch. *The Protestant Revolt: Road To Freedom For American Churches.* (Arlington, VA: Crestwood Books, 1967), p. 121-122.
34. "Part I: 1962-1974," *The Christian Challenge*, November-December, 1999, p. 9.
35. Murch, p. 122.
36. Prichard, p. 259.

37. Part I: 1962-1974, Ibid.
38. Stringfellow and Town, p. 202.
39. Biographical information on Fr. Dees gathered from Donald S. Armentrout, "Episcopal Splinter Groups: Schisms in the Episcopal Church, 1963-1985," *Historical Magazine of the Episcopal Church*, December 1986, p. 295-296; and Eric A. Badertscher, "The Measure of a Bishop: The Episcopi Vagantes, Apostolic Succession, and the Legitimacy of the Anglican "Continuing Church" Movement," an M.A. thesis at Gordon-Conwell Theological Seminary, 1998, p. 22.
40. Neil R. McMillen. *The Citizen's Council: Organized Resistance to the Second Reconstruction, 1954-1964.* (Urbana, IL: University of Illinois Press, 1971), p. 114-115.
41. John George and Laird Wilcox. *American Extremists: Militias, Supremacists, Klansmen, Communists, and others.* (Amherst, NY: Prometheus Books, 1996), p. 275-277.
42. C.H. Simonds. "The Strange Story of Willis Carto: His Fronts, his friends, his philosophy, his Lobby for Patriotism." *National Review.* September 10, 1971, p. 982.
43. Ibid.
44. Willis Carto's is one of the darkest stories in modern American history. He was the leading supporter, champion, and publisher of Francis Parker Yockey's *Imperium*, which is considered to be the "bible" of the modern Neo-Nazi movement. Carto also founded the National Youth Alliance (an organization designed to introduce young people to neo-Nazi ideology) in 1972. An early leader in the organization, William Pierce, would go on to earn infamy by authoring the *Turner Diaries*, a terrorist fantasy about the overthrow of the American government. Timothy McVeigh, whose bomb killed over a

hundred people at the Oklahoma City federal building in 1994, admitted that he had modeled his attack on the one described in Pierce's book. Carto also solidified his infamy when he established the Institute For Historical Review, which regularly publishes pseudo-scholarly articles and books that deny the historical reality of the Nazi Holocaust of the Jews.

4. Rev. James Parker Dees. *The US Supreme Court Destroyers! Some Observations and Conclusions.* (Los Angeles, CA: Christian Nationalist Crusade, no date.), p. 12.
46. "Censure in North Carolina." *Living Church.* February 22, 1959, p. 8.
47. Ibid.
48. "Reply From Mr. Dees." *Living Church.* March 15, 1959, p. 3-4.
49. James P. Dees. "Should Christians Support Integration?" in *Essays on Segregation,* edited by T. Robert Ingram. (Houston, TX: St. Thomas Press, 1960), p. 37.
50. Ibid., p. 41-42.
51. "Mr. Dees Leaves Church" *Living Church,* December 1, 1963, p. 7.
52. Ibid.
53. Armentrout, p. 296.
54. Ibid.
55. See "Separation" *Living Church,* March 11, 1962, p. 9; "Schism" *Living Church,* August 19, 1962, p. 4.
56. "Mr. Dees Leaves Church" p. 7.
57. "Followers for Mr. Dees" *Living Church,* February 16, 1964, p. 7.
58. Melton. *Encyclopedia of American Religions.* (NY,NY: Triumph Books, 1991) p. 107.
59. The current Presiding Bishop of the SEC, Huron C. Manning, confirmed the relationship between the AOC

and SEC in a phone interview, April 5, 2001.
60. "Dees Consecrated." *Living Church.* April 19, 1964, p. 9-10; Melton, p. 270.
61. Ibid.
62. Rt. Rev. James P. Dees. "Content With Validity" *Living Church.* May 24, 1964, p. 5.
63. J. Gordon Melton. *The Encyclopedia of American Religions: Volume 1.* (Tarrytown, NY: Triumph Books, 1991, p. 107.
64. Bishop Huron C. Manning. Telephone interview with author. April 5, 2001.
65. Melton, p. 100.
66. Armentrout, p. 297-298.
67. Ibid., p. 299.
68. "Our History: A Dynamic Beginning." *Episcopal Orthodox Christian Archdiocese of America* Website, http://eoc.orthodoxanglican.net /html/history.html.
69. Mark F.M. Clavier. *The Early Years of the American Episcopal Church and the Diocese of the Eastern United States.* Posted on the Website of the Diocese of the Eastern United States, Anglican Province of America.
70. Melton, p. 102.
71. Armentrout, p. 301.
72. M.F.M. Clavier, Ibid.
73. See Appendix B for an overview of the debate over Vagante episcopal orders.
74. M.F.M. Clavier, Ibid.
75. Ibid.
76. Melton, p. 96.
77. A Majority Report of the Department of Ecumenical Relations of the Anglican Catholic Church. *Resource Document On Ecumenical Relations, 1991.* June 14, 1991, p. 46.
78. "Russell G. Fry, Jr. to Archbishop Louis W. Falk," Vigil of the Feast of the Nativity, 1987.

79. Ibid., p. 45-46.
80. Ibid., p. 26.
81. M.F.M. Clavier, Ibid.
82. Russell G. Fry, Ibid.
83. A Majority Report..., p. 22 and 45.
84. Louis Molyneaux. "The Rise of Anthony Clavier: A Chapter in Parenthesis in the History of the Continuing Church Movement in North America," *The Glastonbury Bulletin* no. 66 (June 1983): p. 180.
85. Anthony F.M. Clavier. "Is Pelagius Right?" *Living Church.* May 6, 1973: p. 4.
86. Anthony F.M. Clavier. "AEC and BCP." *Living Church.* September, 5, 1971: p. 4.
87. Armentrout, p. 301.
88. These are independent groups that are recognized by the Episcopal Church, and are in communion with PECUSA, such as the Philippine National Catholic Church or the Polish National Catholic Church.
89. M.F.M. Clavier, Ibid.
90. Armentrout, p. 302.
91. "Convert Unconverted." *Living Church.* November 7, 1976: p. 6.
92. A Majority Report..., p. 22.
93. "AEC Bishop Joins PTHE EPISCOPAL CHURCH" *Living Church.* July 11, 1976: p. 6-7.
94. Fry, Ibid.
95. Anthony F.M. Clavier. *The American Episcopal Church.* (Brotherhood of the Servants of the Lord, 1975), p. 16.
96. Armentrout, p. 304.
97. Ibid., p. 305.
98. The accounts of these smaller groups are drawn from the contradictory reports on these groups made by Armentrout, p. 305; Melton, p. 100; and M.F.M. Clavier. While correlating these three accounts it became obvious that dates and names did not line up correctly.

Consequently, I have reconstructed these accounts to the best of my ability. Any mistakes are simply the result of the sketchy nature of source material regarding these groups.

99. Anthony F.M. Clavier. "The Problem of Schism." *Living Church*. February 23, 1975: p. 4.
100. "Two American Breakaway Bodies Plan Union." *Living Church*. August 3, 1975: p. 5.
101. Armentrout, p. 305.
102. "Two American Breakaway…," Ibid.
103. Melton, p. 108.
104. Armentrout, p. 299-300.
105. "ACU Committee Resigns," *The Living Church*, February 14, 1971, p. 8.
106. "The Other Side," *The Living Church*, March 14, 1971, p. 5.
107. Donald S. Armentrout (2). *Episcopal Splinter Groups: A Study of Groups Which Have Left the Episcopal Church, 1873-1985.* (Univ. of the South, TN, 1985), p. 30.
108. Murch, p. 126.
109. "News in Brief," *Living Church*, June 27, 1971, p. 13.
110. Lester Kinsolving. "The Coup That Impends: Episcopal Extremism," *Nation*, January 23, 1967, p. 108. The John Birch Society was an extremely conservative political education organization that was frequently assumed by many liberal or left-wing commentators during the 1960s to be a dangerous, potentially neo-fascist, enemy of the social and political order.
111. "A Plea to Convention," *Living Church*, September, 6, 1970, p. 11.
112. "SPBCP Membership Exceeds 17,000," *Living Church*, June 10, 1973, p. 12-13.
113. Sumner, 19-21.
114. All of these arguments can be found in *The Certain Trumpet*, July 1972, number 3.

115. Armentrout (2), p. 26.
116. Ibid., p. 22.
117. Ibid., p. 20.
118. "The Vote Was No," *Living Church*, October 28, 1973, p. 7-8.
119. Sumner, p. 21.
120. *Christian Challenge*, November-December 1999, p. 14.
121. Armentrout (2), p. 21.
122. Ibid., p. 22.
123. George W. Rutler. "In Philadelphia a Storm of Reaction," *Living Church*, August 25, 1974, p. 6.
124. Sumner, p. 22-23.
125. Rutler, Ibid.
126. Holmes, p. 168.
127. Rutler, p. 7.
128. Sumner, p. 24.
129. "Dissension Continues," *Living Church*, July 6, 1975, p. 5.
130. "Bishop Dropped From Membership," *Living Church*, October 10, 1974, p. 9.
131. Armentrout (2), p. 34.
132. "ACU Initiates Steps Toward Ecumenical Council," *Living Church*, August 10, 1975, p. 6.
133. "No Surrender, No Desertion," *Living Church*, September 21, 1975, p. 9.
134. "ACU Leadership Undergoes Radical Shake-up," *Living Church*, February 15, 1976, p. 6.
135. "ACU Shake-up," *Living Church*, March 28, 1976, p. 5-6.
136. Armentrout (2), p. 37.
137. "Position Clarified To Bishops," *Living Church*, May 16, 1976, p. 8.
138. "CAM Repudiates Threats of Schism," *Living Church*, April 4, 1976, p. 7.
139. Armentrout (2), p. 38.

140. Robert C. Harvey. *A House Divided*. (Dumont, NJ: Canterbury Guild, 1976), p. 5.
141. Ibid., p. 10, 11, 15, and 24.
142. Ibid., p. 66.
143. Ibid., p. 70.
144. Armentrout (2), p. 39.
145. Ibid., p. 39-41.
146. "Traditional Episcopalians Push Plans For Church Congress," *The Christian Challenge*, March 1977, p. 6.
147. Ibid.
148. Armentrout (2), p. 41, and *The Christian Century*, December 22, 1976, p. 1143.
149. "Parish Takes Solemn Step," *The Living Church*, December 26, 1976, p. 5-6.
150. "Fourth Los Angeles Parish Breaks from The Episcopal Church," *New Oxford Review*, February 1977, p. 10; Armentrout (2), p. 43.
151. Reprinted in Appendix D of Fr. Thomas McDonald's *A Time To Stand: The Purpose of the ACC*. Privately published in 1997.
152. Armentrout (2), p. 43-44.
153. "Retired Bishop Ministers to Seceded Episcopal Parishes," *New Oxford Review*, May 1977, p. 14.
154. "Three California Episcopal Churches Sever Bonds with the Episcopal Church," *New Oxford Review*, April 1977, p. 12.
155. Robert S. Morse. "Editorial," *New Oxford Review*, September 1977, p. 2.
156. *The Christian Challenge*, January-February 2000, p. 9.
157. Robert C. Harvey. "On CAM/ECM: Why Catholics Who Remain in the Protestant Episcopal Church Will be a Losing, Not a Saving, Remnant," *New Oxford Review*, September 1977, p. 8.
158. "Toward FCC – "Goodwill," *The Living Church*, September 11, 1977, p. 17.

159. Badertscher, p. 25.
160. Armentrout (2), p. 45.
161. Anthony F.M. Clavier. "Here We Stand," *The Christian Challenge*, October 1987, p. 9.
162. Louis E. Taycik, "The Continuing Church Today: Part Two – the Other Churches." *The Christian Challenge*, March 1983, p. 10.
163. "Protesters Meet in St. Louis," *The Living Church*, October 9, 1977, p. 7.
164. Perry Laukhuff. "This Extraordinary Congress," *Christian Challenge*, November 1977, p. 4.
165. George W. Rutler. "Our Theological Imperative," *New Oxford Review*, October 1977, p. 9-14.
166. Carroll E. Simcox. "Our Biblical and Moral Imperative," *New Oxford Review*, October 1997, p. 15-18.
167. Thomas G. Barnes. "The Vocation and Future of Anglicanism," *New Oxford Review*, October 1997, p. 19-21.
168. "Protesters Meet...," *The Living Church*, Ibid.
169. Jean Caffey Lyles. "The Old Schism Trail," *The Christian Century*, October 5, 1977, p. 867.
170. Francis W. Read. "The St. Louis Congress and The House of Bishops," *New Oxford Review*, November 1977, p. 13.
171. Ibid.
172. Robert S. Morse. "The Long March into the Desert," *New Oxford Review*, October 1977, p. 23.
173. "Split in Episcopal Church Rated No. 1 News Story of 1977 by Religion Newswriters," *New Oxford Review*, February 1978, p. 24.
174. Lyles, Ibid.
175. David B. Reed. "The St. Louis Congress," *The Living Church*, October 16, 1977, p. 15.
176. Perry Laukhuff. "I Was At St. Louis," *The Christian Challenge*, September 1987, p. 9.

177. *Affirmation of St. Louis* as reprinted in the appendix of McDonald's *A Time To Stand*.
178. Louis E. Traycik. "The Continuing Church Today," *The Christian Challenge*, December 1982, p. 8.
179. Read, p. 12.
180. Albert A. Chambers. "Statement to the Port St. Lucie Meeting of the House of Bishops," *New Oxford Review*, December 1977, p. 7-8.
181. "Meeting at Port S. Lucie," *The Living Church*, October 30, 1977, p. 5.
182. Kenneth Briggs. "Episcopal Bishops Eke Out a Fragile Peace," *The Christian Century*, November 2, 1977, p. 996-997.
183. "Fifteen Midwest Churches Begin New Diocese for Traditional Episcopalians," *New Oxford Review*, December 1977, p. 28.
184. "The Developing Church," *The Christian Challenge*, December 1977, p. 6.
185. "Dissident Episcopalians Consider Eastern Diocese," and "Episcopalian Dissidents in Virginia Align with Anglican Church in North America," *New Oxford Review*, January 1978, p. 29.
186. Armentrout (1), p. 308.
187. Dorothy A. Faber. "The Story Behind The Consecration," *The Christian Challenge*, March 1978, p. 19.
188. "Separatist Movement Growing?" *The Living Church*, January 1, 1978, p. 8.
189. Armentrout (1), Ibid.
190. Faber, "The Story Behind The Consecrations," p. 17-18.
191. Ibid., p. 18.
192. Virginia Culver, "Anglican Secessionists Consecrate Four Bishops," *The Christian Century*, February 15, 1978, p. 151.
193. "Albert J. duBois. "Canon duBois Comments," *The

Living Church, March 19, 1978, p. 3.
194. Culver, Ibid.
195. Faber, Ibid.
196. F.J. Starzel. "Four Consecrated," *The Living Church*, February 19, 1978, p. 6.
197. As an example of the contradictory accounts as to the manner in which the DHT was formed, in an interview with Fr. Anthony Rasch, who was present at most of the early meetings of the DHT, he claimed that duBois was present at the supposedly surreptitious meeting of the DHT which elected Fr. Mote. Telephone interview with Fr. Anthony Rasch, February 10, 2002.
198. Armentrout (1), p. 310.
199. Melton, p. 106.
200. Sumner, p. 157.
201. "It Happened In Denver," *The Christian Challenge*, March 1978, p. 6.
202. COCU (Consultation On Church Unity) was a manifestation of the larger ecumenical movement within the mainline Protestant denominations. From the 1950s until the 1980s, Episcopalian leaders participated in the COCU negotiations, which sought to bring the divergent denominations under one jurisdictional and institutional umbrella.
203. Culver, p. 149-150.
204. Starzel, Ibid.
205. Richard Coombs. "One View Of The Denver Event," *The Living Church*, March 19, 1978, p. 10.
206. Carroll E. Simcox. "Another View Of The Denver Event," *The Living Church*, April 30, p. 14-15.
207. Dorothy A. Faber. "In The Wake Of Denver," *The Christian Challenge*, April 1978, p. 6.
208. "Consecrators' Roles Disputed," *The Living Church*, March 19, 1978, p. 5-6.
209. Faber, Ibid., p. 6-7.

210. The Anglican Consultative Council acts as a body that meets between the Lambeth Conferences, which are worldwide councils of Anglican Communions that gather every ten years in Canterbury, England.
211. "Bishop Howe Questions Validity of Consecrations," *The Living Church*, April 23, 1978, p. 8.
212. Thomas G. Barnes. "On The Denver Consecrations," *New Oxford Review*, June 1978, p. 8
213. Fr. George D. Stenhouse. "Background For Hot Springs: Factors in Anglican Catholic Crisis," *The Anglican Churchmen*, July 16, 1979, p. 8.
214. "Episcopal House of Bishops Cites Five Bishops Judged Defiant of Church Law," *New Oxford Review*, December 1978, p. 25.
215. Stenhouse, Ibid., 2. It is claimed by supporters of Bishops Morse and Watterson that Bishop Mote, as secretary of the meeting, inexplicably failed to take notes.
216. "According to the Papers," *The Christian Challenge*, June 1978, p. 20-21.
217. Ibid.. p. 6.
218. That is, as far as I have been able to discover. I am sure that future editions will include additional material given to me by those who feel as though they have been misrepresented. However, until that time arrives, I can remember all of the unanswered attempts to find said material.
219. Stenhouse, p. 6.
220. "The Anglican Congregations," *The Christian Challenge*, September 1978, p. 22.
221. *The Christian Challenge* (Ibid.) reported that there were nine parishes represented. Stenhouse (Ibid.) claimed there were seven parishes at the meeting.
222. The preceding section is drawn from the account of Stenhouse (Ibid., p. 7), who claims that one of the priests never served in the DSW, and that the other transferred

to Pennsylvania shortly after the Dallas Synod.
223. Dorothy A. Faber. "An Open Letter To The Bishops And Priests Of The Anglican Church In North America," *The Christian Challenge*, August 1978, p. 15.
224. Perry Laukhuff. "The Future Of The Anglican Church In North America," *The Christian Challenge*, October 1978, p. 17.
225. *FCC Newsletter*, November 1978, p. 2.
226. Stenhouse, p. 6.
227. Dorothy A. Faber. *The Christian Challenge*, December 1978, p. 5.
228. Paul W. Pritchartt. "Events and Comments," *The Living Church*, November 12, 1978, p. 11.
229. See Faber, Ibid.; Stenhouse, Ibid.; and *FCC Newsletter*, Ibid, p. 1.
230. Faber, Ibid., p. 6.
231. Ibid.
232. Stenhouse, Ibid.
233. Faber, Ibid.
234. Ibid.
235. Stenhouse, p. 7.
236. Faber, Ibid.
237. Ibid., p. 7.
238. Stenhouse, Ibid.
239. Faber, p. 5.
240. "The Dallas Synod." *The Living Church*, November 11, 1978, p. 12.
241. In 2001, during his first interview in twenty-three years, Bishop Morse remembered Mote as "an English romantic, a green fields of England type." See David Virtue. "A Lion in Winter: Archbishop Robert Sherwood Morse, a man of character, conviction, and principle." *Virtuosity* Internet News Service, December 2001, Week 2, #2, p. 2.
242. "Further Echoes From The Dallas Synod," *FCC*

Newsletter, January 1979, p. 2.
243. *FCC Newsletter*, December 1978, p. 2.
244. The word *Protestant* was dropped from PECUSA's legal name in 1979.
245. Fraser Barron. "The Continuing Church Movement: What Has Happened?" *The Christian Challenge*, March 1979, p. 10.
246. Morse would probably cringe at being labeled a Catholic Revivalist.
247. Dorothy A. Faber. "The Story Behind The Consecration," *The Christian Challenge*, January 1979, p. 6.
248. Ibid., p. 8.
249. Ibid.
250. E.J.M. LaRoque. "The New Jersey Consecrations: Canonical Questions," *The Christian Challenge*, January 1979, p. 9-10.
251. Stenhouse, Ibid.
252. "Bishop Doren Elected To Mid-Atlantic!" *Christian Challenge*, February 1979, p. 7.
253. Stenhouse, p. 7.
254. The term "FCC" in this quote could be replaced with my term "Southern Phalanx."
255. "Brickbats and Rosebuds," *FCC Newsletter*, January 1979, p. 1.
256. "Prexy's Annual Address," *FCC Newsletter*, February 1979, p. 1.
257. The claim was that only photocopies containing various errors and omissions had been circulated.
258. Stenhouse, Ibid.
259. E.J.M. LaRoque. "Episcopal Translations: The Case Of Bishop Doren In Canon Law," *The Christian Challenge*, May 1979, p. 10-11.
260. Rt. Rev. Anthony F.M. Clavier. "The Continuing Church Movement As Viewed By An Interested

Observer," *The Christian Challenge*, April 1979, p. 7.
261. Sterling Rayburn. "Letter," *FCC Newsletter*, March 1979, p. 1.
262. "The Anglican Congregations," *The Christian Challenge*, May 1979, p. 25.
263. Stenhouse, p. 8.
264. Dorothy A. Faber. "Secession In The ACC," *The Christian Challenge*, June 1979, p. 6.
265. Stenhouse, Ibid.
266. Ibid.
267. Ibid.
268. Dorothy A. Faber. "Continuing Church Movement Divides," *The Christian Challenge*, August 1979, p. 6
269. "Standing Committee Reaffirms Synod's Constitution Stand," *The Anglican Churchman*, July 16, 1979, p. 1,5.
270. Faber, Ibid., p. 6-7.
271. Catherine Seabrook. "Diocese Weathers Summer Storms," *The Anglican Churchmen*, August-September 1979, p. 1.
272. Faber, Ibid., p. 7-8.
273. Seabrook, Ibid.
274. Stenhouse, p. 8.
275. Faber, Ibid., p.8-9.
276. "Report From Nashville," *FCC Newsletter*, September 1979, p. 1.
277. "The Anglican Congregations," *The Christian Challenge*, October 1979, p. 21.
278. "Bishop Morse to Father Preuss," *Fellowship of Concerned Churchmen Newsletter*, October 1979, p. 1.
279. "The Anglican Congregations," *The Christian Challenge*, November 1979, p. 27.
280. "From A Priest In Canada," *FCC News Exchange*, November 1979, p. 1,
281. "The Anglican Congregations," Ibid.
282. Dorothy A. Faber. "The Synods In Action," *The*

Christian Challenge, December 1979, p. 6.
283. *The Anglican Churchmen*, July 16, 1979, p.1. Bishops Morse and Watterson issued a call for suggestions from throughout their dioceses in developing the content of the proposed Constitution and Canons. I have been unable to determine whether the proposed documents adopted at Hot Springs resulted or benefited from this process.
284. Faber, Ibid.
285. Ibid.
286. Ibid., p. 1.
287. Roderic B. Dibbert. *The Story of Holy Catholic Church, Anglican Rite of the Americas, 1980-1990.* (Akron, Ohio: DeKoven Foundation, 1991[?]), p. 4.
288. Dorothy A. Faber. "The Tale Of The Mythical Jurisdiction," *The Christian Challenge*, August 1980, p. 1.
289. "Dear Bishop Pagtakhan," Standing Committee, Diocese of the Holy Trinity, November 14, 1979.
290. Dibbert, p. 14. According to Fr. Rasch, there were not members of the AECNA or AEC in the Deanery.
291. Deanery of Southern California, Minutes, September 17, 1979.
292. Fr. Rasch stated that the PICC representatives actually had seat and voice in the Deanery meetings.
293. "Jurisdiction," *FCC News Exchange*, February 1980, p. 1.
294. Rev. Louis W. Falk. "Another Point of View," Ibid., p. 1-2.
295. Dorothy A. Faber. "Ecclesiastical Musical Chairs," *The Christian Challenge*, June 1980, p. 8.
296. Faber, "The Tale of the Mythical Jurisdiction," Ibid.
297. Faber, "Ecclesiastical Musical Chairs, p. 7-8.
298. Faber, "Tale of the Mythical Jurisdiction," p. 10-11.
299. Dibbert, p. 7, 11.

300. Deanery of Southern California, Minutes, April 28, 1980.
301. Dibbert, p. 6.
302. Faber, "Ecclesiastical Musical Chairs, p. 8.
303. Perry Laukhuff. "And Some Question Marks Outside The Church," *The Certain Trumpet*, April 1980, p. 3.
304. Dibbert, Ibid.
305. Dorothy A. Faber. "Confronting The Issues," *The Christian Challenge*, October 1980, p. 14-15.
306. The Clergy and Laity of the Deanery of Southern California. "An Open Letter," September 22, 1980.
307. A photocopy of this allegedly racist cartoon was included in a letter from the head of the Deanery, Fr. Anthony Rasch, to Bishop Mote on September 11, 1980.
308. Deanery of Southern California, Minutes, September 22, 1980.
309. Faber, Ibid., p. 14.
310. Robert C. Harvey. "The Indy Speedway," *The Christian Challenge*, December 1979, p. 1.
311. Robert C. Harvey. "Our House May Be Too Small – So, Too, May Be The Doorway," *The Christian Challenge*, January 1980, p. 1.
312. Robert C. Harvey. "The Spike And The Jackhammer," *The Christian Challenge*, April 1980, p. 1, 3.
313. Perry Laukhuff. "Stick To The Eternals, Not The Externals," *The Certain Trumpet*, April 1980, p. 4-5.
314. Faber, "Ecclesiastical Musical Chairs," p. 6.
315. C. Dale David Doren. "My Dear Fellow Churchmen," *FCC News Exchange*, Summer 1980, p. 1.
316. Dorothy A. Faber. "The Orphan Syndrome," *The Christian Challenge*, October 1980, p. 17-19.
317. Robert M. Strippy. "The Massive Machinery Moves – But Where?" *The Christian Challenge*, December 1980, p. 11-13.
318. Louis Falk. "The Bible Toter's Mary," *The Trinitarian*,

Trinity 1980, p. 3.
319. Letter from Fr. Anthony F. Rasch to Fr. George H. Clendenin, January 22, 1981.
320. Dibbert, p. 8.
321. Perry Laukhuff, "Another Dropout," *The Certain Trumpet*, February 1981, p. 4.
322. "The Anglicans," *The Christian Challenge*, February 1981, p. 17.
323. Laukhuff, Ibid, p. 5.
324. "The Anglicans," *The Christian Challenge*, May 1981, p. 22.
325. Dorothy A. Faber, "What Hath Been Wrought?" *The Christian Challenge*, August 1981, p. 10.
326. For instance, the June issue of *The Christian Challenge* reports on the installation service for Bishop Knutti, but makes no mention of any controversy surrounding it or anything that occurred prior. "The Anglicans," June 1981, p. 22.
327. Faber, Ibid, p. 10-15.
328. Laukhuff, "Constitution and Canons," Ibid, p. 3.
329. "The Meanderings of Bishop Hobeau: Stumbling Along," *The Christian Challenge*, April 1981, p. 15-17.
330. "Second Congress of Concerned Churchmen Scheduled for 1982," *The Christian Challenge*, August 1981, p. 14.
331. "Minutes of the College of Bishops Meeting," September 1981, p. 2.
332. "The Anglicans," *The Christian Challenge*, June 1981, p. 22.
333. "Continuing Anglican Bishops To Meet," *The Christian Challenge*, August 1981, p. 12.
334. "The Anglicans," *The Christian Challenge*, August 1981, p. 22.
335. Minutes of the College of Bishops Meeting," p. 3.
336. Anthony F.M. Clavier, "Anglican Unity – Forwards and Backwards," *The Christian Challenge*, December 1981,

p. 13.
337. Dibbert, p. 32.
338. Clavier, Ibid.
339. "The Anglicans," *The Christian Challenge*, November 1981, back cover.
340. "Minutes of the College of Bishops Meeting," p. 2.
341. Dibbert, Ibid.
342. "The Wandering Bishops Debate," *The Christian Challenge*, March 1982, p. 6-8.
343. "Congress Committee Meets," *FCC News Exchange*, November 1981, p. 1.
344. "Convocation," *FCC News Exchange*, March 1982, p. 1.
345. "FCC Annual Meeting," *Anglican News Exchange*, Special Addition, Volume 5, Number 6.
346. "An Intercommunion Gesture," *The Christian Challenge*, March 1982, p. 16.
347. "The Anglicans," *The Christian Challenge*, April 1982, p. ?, (back cover).
348. "Resolution," *FCC News Exchange*, May 1982, p. 1.
349. "The Anglicans," *The Christian Challenge*, June 1982, p. 18-19.
350. Dibbert, p. 32.
351. Dorothy A. Faber, "The Development of Polity in the ACC," *The Christian Challenge*, September 1981, p. 15-17.
352. Dorothy A. Faber, "The ACC – Some Thoughts and Afterthoughts," *The Christian Challenge*, April 1982, p. 7-9.
353. Dorothy A. Faber, "Holyrood Seminary – A Costly Mistake?" *The Christian Challenge*, October 1981, p. 6-9.
354. Fraser Barron, "The Canonization of the ACC," *The Christian Challenge*, May 1982, p. 7-13.
355. Robert M. Strippy, "A Postscript On Anglicanism," *The Christian Challenge*, June 1982, p. 11.

356. Robert C. Harvey, "The Other Side of the Moon," *The Christian Challenge*, June 1982, p. 6-8.
357. Dorothy A. Faber, "Another Split In The ACC," *The Christian Challenge*, August 1982, p. 7-11.
358. Perry Laukhuff, "A Declaration of Conscience," *Anglican News Exchange*, Special Edition, Volume 5, Number 9, p. 1-2.
359. Faber, Ibid.
360. Interview with Anonymous churchmen, March 17, 2001.
361. "The Anglicans," *The Christian Challenge*, August 1982, p. back cover.
362. Interview with Mary Buerger.
363. "The Anglicans," *The Christian Challenge*, September 1982, p. 23.
364. "The Anglicans," *The Christian Challenge*, October 1982, back cover.
365. "The Anglicans," *The Christian Challenge*, September 1982, p. 23.
366. "The Anglicans," *The Christian Challenge*, October 1982, back cover.
367. "The Anglicans," *The Christian Challenge*, November 1982, p. 23.
368. "The Traditionalists," *The Christian Challenge*, December 1982, p. 21.
369. "The Traditionalists," *The Christian Challenge*, February 1983, p. 17, 21.
370. Dibbert, p. 33.
371. "The Traditionalists," Ibid, p. 21-22.
372. Dibbert, p. 15.
373. Ibid, p. 33.
374. "Religion USA," *The Christian Challenge*, August 1983, p. 19.
375. "Religion USA," *The Christian Challenge*, May 1983, p. 18.

376. "Religion USA," *The Christian Challenge*, August 1983, p. 19.
377. Louis Traycik, "The Anglican Catholic Church: Five Years Later," *The Christian Challenge*, December 1983, p. 8.
378. "Southwest Diocese Votes For Union With American Episcopal Church," *The Christian Challenge*, December 1983, p. 14.
379. Don R. Gerlach, "The Spirit of Orlando," *The Christian Challenge*, December 1983, p. 7-8, 13-14.
380. "The Anglicans," *The Christian Challenge*, March 1981, p. 21-22.
381. "Court," *FCC News Exchange*, March 1981, p. 1.
382. "Evangelism Year Proclaimed," *The Anglican Churchman*, May-June 1981, p. 1.
383. "Bishop Morse Seeks Parishes In Southeast," Ibid, p. 3.
384. Armentrout (1), 314.
385. "The Traditionalists," *The Christian Challenge*, February 1983, p. 21.
386. "Quoted Without Comment," *Anglican News Exchange*, Special Edition, Volume 5, Number 9.
387. Louis Traycik, "Peace At Last?" *The Christian Challenge*, December 1983, p. 3-4.
388. Louis Traycik, "The Continuing Church Today: The Other Churches," *The Christian Challenge*, March 1983, p. 11, 14.
389. "American Episcopal Church Petitions Presiding Bishop," *The Christian Challenge*, January 1984, p. 13.
390. "The AEC General Synod Reviewed: Delegates Adopt Canons, Episcopal Church Agreement," *The Christian Challenge*, December 1984, p. 7-9.
391. Ibid, p. 7.
392. "Home at Last: The Diocese of the Southwest Completes Its Union With the American Episcopal Church," *The Christian Challenge*, January 1985, p. 4.

393. Louis E. Traycik, "Anglican Episcopal," *Christian Challenge*, January 1985, p. 18.
394. Dibbert, p. 33.
395. Louis and Auburn Faber Traycik, "The Continuing Church Today: Part 6: Move Into Asia," *The Christian Challenge*, October 1984, p. 8.
396. Dibbert, Ibid.
397. Sue Scofield, "Bishop Pagtakhan Speaks Out," *The Trinitarian*, April 1985, p. 3.
398. Armentrout (1), p. 315-316.
399. Dibbert, Ibid.
400. "Official Statements," *The Trinitarian*, Ibid, p. 4.
401. Sue Scofield, "Synod Meets In Cincinnati," *The Trinitarian*, November 1985, p. 1.
402. "New Continuing Bishop Consecrated In California," *The Christian Challenge*, March 1986, p. 4, 20.
403. Armentrout (1), p. 312.
404. Jeffrey Weiss. *Miami Herald*, June 11, 1984, p. 1A.
405. *The Christian Challenge*, April 1986, p. 8.
406. Ibid, plus "Bishop Williams Received," *The Christian Challenge*, April 1986, p. 24.
407. "Bishop Williams Received," *The Christian Challenge*, April 1986, p. 24.
408. "Diocese of the South Reorganizes," *The Trinitarian*, May 1986, p. 1.
409. "Diocese of St. Paul: Bishop Wilkes, Visitor and Administrator," *The Trinitarian*, October 1986, p. 12.
410. Melton, p. 62.
411. Robert C. Harvey. A letter written to FCC members and subscribers to the News Exchange. March 10, 1987.
412. Robert C. Harvey. Letter to Regular and Associate Members, and to would-be Members. March 10, 1987.
413. "Falk, Clavier Explore Prospects For Greater Unity." CC, March 1987, p. 22.
414. "ACC, AEC Petition Kemp In Search Of Jurisdictional

Unity." CC, May 1987, p. 15.
415. "Hopes High For ACC, AEC Joint Venture." CC, June 1987, p. 11.
416. Perry Laukhuff. "Calumny." CC, September 1987, p. 6.
417. "Bishop Hazelwood Declares Communion With the ACC," *Trinitarian*, July 1987, p. 1.
418. "Episcopal Church-American Episcopal Dialogue Committee Meets," CC, September 1987, p. 32-33.
419. Dibbert, p. 34.
420. Ibid., p. 34-35.
421. CC, September 1987, p. 38.
422. CC, October 1987, p. 31.
423. Dibbert, p. 9-10.
424. The UECAC is discussed in Chapter 2. See Melton, p. 270.
425. Melton, p. 269-270.
426. Louis W. Falk. "What is Really Happening Between the ACC and the AEC." *Trinitarian* September 1988, p. 8.
427. Louis W. Falk. "Metropolitan's Message: Politics and Issues." *Trinitarian* Ibid., p. 3.
428. "To the Bishops of the ACC meeting in Indianapolis," May 9, 1989.
429. CC, October 1989, p. 19.
430. Robert Strippy. "ACC Provincial Synod Focuses on Unity," *The Christian Challenge*, December 1989, p. 9-14.
431. "Report of the Commission on Unity to Provincial Synod, 1989" No author is listed on my copy, although internal references suggest it was probably written by someone very close to Bishop Chamberlain, if it in fact was not written by him.
432. Mary Buerger. "Meeting Minutes," ACC Department of Ecumenical Relations, July 1990.
433. Louis W. Falk. "Memorandum," Office of the Chairman,

Department of Ecumenical Relations, July 31, 1991.
434. Louis W. Falk. "Report to the College of Bishops," Office of the Chairman, Department of Ecumenical Relations, August 08, 1990.
435. "TAC Officially Launched," *Trinitarian*, December 1990, p. 1, 11.
436. Robert M. Strippy. "Send in the Clowns," *North American Anglican Review*, Christmastide 1990, p. 6-11.
437. John Omwake. "Bishops Issue Statement on Orders," *Trinitarian*, March 1991, p. 4-5.
438. Louis W. Falk. "Memorandum," Office of the Metropolitan, March 11, 1991. Exhibit F-1 in the ecclesiastical trial of Archbishop Falk by the ACC College of Bishops.
439. John Omwake. "7 Out of 9 Synods Back Indianapolis Resolution." *Trinitarian*, July 1991, p. 1, 5.
440. "10 Bishops Approve Proposal On Unity," *Trinitarian*, May 1991, p. 1-2.
441. Ibid., p. 1.
442. Anthony F.M. Clavier. "Bishop's Letter." May 1991, p. 2.
443. *Ecclesia*, Spring 1991, p. 1, 5.
444. From the Presentment brought against Archbishop Falk in the Provincial Court of the Anglican Catholic Church, August 9, 1991, p. 1-4.
445. Louis W. Falk. "Report of Ecumenical Relations Department to IX Provincial Synod," June 15, 1991.
446. Robert V. Preston, translator for Fr. Cruz-Blanco, in Affidavit #5779 (August 1, 1991), listed as exhibit D in transcript of the trial of Archbishop Falk by the ACC College of Bishops.
447. AEC priest's letter, dated March 9, 1991, listed as Exhibit G-2 in transcript of Archbishop Falk's trial by the ACC College of Bishops. Archbishop Falk's letter, con-

taining the above, dated May 1, 1991, listed as Exhibit G-1 in the same trial transcript.
448. "Charges Levelled At ACC Archbishop," *CC*, October 1991, p. 20-22.
449. "ACC Chooses Another Course, New Leadership," *CC*, November 1991, p. 10-11, 13, 23.
450. Louis E. Traycik. "Anglican Church of America Unites Majority of U.S. Continuing Church," Ibid., p. 10, 12.
451. "ACC Chooses Another Course...," Ibid.
452. Tim Pallesen. "Fraud charges against monks may mar bishop's attempt to unite Episcopalians," *Palm Beach Post*, September 30, 1991, p. 1A, 4A.
453. Jennie H. Merrill. "A Sad Tale of Two Parishes," *Credo*, Trinitytide 1991, p. 15-16.
454. Michael F. Gallo. "The Continuing Anglicans: Credible Movement or Ecclesiastical Dead End?" *Touchstone*, Winter 1989, p. 30.
455. Information taken from. "Memo Regarding a Sketch of Continuing Anglican History since 1977," sent to Rev. Donald Nist on August 13, 1992, p. 3-4 (author unknown).
456. Gregory J. Diefenderfer. "The Traditional Anglican Movement Today: An Update On The Continuing/Traditional Anglican Churches," *CC*, October-November 1994, p. 16-24.
457. John Omwake. "Unity, Harmony Mark Synod: UEC Pact, pension plan highlight action," *Trinitarian*, December 1993, p. 5-7.
458. John Omwake. "ACC, OCA Metropolitans meet," *Trinitarian*, April 1995, p. 1,7.
459. ACC College of Bishops. "Statement on Unity." *Trinitarian*, April 1995, p. 18-19.
460. "Ecclesia Chairman: ACC is best option." *Trinitarian*, September 1993, p. 7.
461. See "Responses to the ACC Bishops Statement on

Church Unity" in *CC*, Summer 1995, p. 12-15; and "More on the ACC Bishops Statement on Church Unity," *CC*, September 1995, p. 4-8.

462. See the following articles in *The Christian Challenge*: "Move by Priest, People, to Different Continuing Body Prompts Trial in ACC Court," October 1993, p. 12-14; Suit Filed in Case of Former ACC Parish," May 1994, p. 15-16; and "Part VII: 1994-1995," January 2001, p. 13.

463. Elaine Walker. "Archbishop Resigns Amid Abuse Charges," *Tampa Tribune*, February 5, 1995, Florida/Metro section, page 3.

464. See articles in *The Christian Challenge*: "ACA Rocked by Clouded Resignation of Clavier," March/April 1995, p. 13-16; and "Part VII: 1994-1995," January 2001, p. 12-13.

465. Stated to this author by two anonymous interviewees for this book.

466. "ACA Rocked by Clouded Resignation of Clavier," Ibid.

467. "Part VII: 1994-1995," Ibid.

468. For information on EMC, see *Christian Challenge*: "Part VI: 1991-1993," November 2000, p. 7, 9-11; "EMC Works Toward Unity With Concordant Offer," October 1993, p. 11; "Synod Reorganizes Growing EMC: Approves Mission Statement Affirming '28 Book, Stresses Outreach," January/February 1994, p. 16-17; and Diefenderfer, "The Traditional Anglican Movement Today," Ibid., p. 20-21.

469. For information on the CEC, see "Bishop Consecrated For CEC," in *CC*, January/February 1994, p. 17-18; and the CEC website at www.iccec.org/CEC_Statement.htm.

470. Fr. Michael M. Wright to the Chairman, members, and Board of Governors of Holyrood Seminary. December 17, 1996.

471. Fr. Mark Haverland. "Anglican Catholic Faith and Practice." Holyrood Seminary Press, 1996, p. 3.
472. "Abp. Lewis to Step Down in October." *Trinitarian*, February 1997, p. 6-7.
473. "Three Bishops Block Confirmation of Coadjutor," *Trinitarian*, August 1997, p. 5.
474. Alexander Price. "Background to a "Clean Break." *Anglican Catholic Times*, Volume 1, #13 (no date), p. 5.
475. The following sources were used in discussing the ACC and HCC-AR controversies: Several private letters from the individuals involved, as well as: William O. Lewis, "To the Clergy, People, and Officers of the Diocese of the Holy Trinity and Great Plains," August 10, 1997; Thomas J. Kleppinger, "Good Christian People," August 15, 1997; William O. Lewis, "A Letter From the Metropolitan to the Bishops, Cllergy, and Laity of the Anglican Catholic Church," August 21, 1997; Roger J. Hall, "An Open Letter to the Most Reverend William Oliver Lewis," August 29, 1997; Arthur David Seeland, "To the Clergy and Faithful of the Diocese of the Pacific and Southwest," September 2, 1997; Kleppinger, "Dear Brethren," September 4, 1997; John A. Hollister and Frank L. Wiswall, "In Regard to the Inhibitions of Five Bishops, August 1997 and Other Matters," September 22, 1997; Margaret Anne Pointon, "In Response to a Statement Issued by Canon John Hollister and Dr. Frank Wiswall Dated 22nd September 1997," September 25, 1997; John Omwake, "5 Bishops inhibited, face trial: Presentments follow apparent coup attempt," *Trinitarian*, October 1997, p. 5, 8; Thomas J. Kleppinger and John A. Hollister. "More on the ACC," *CC*, November 1998, p. 3-5; "News of the Weird: Tournabout is Fair Play," *CC, December 1998, p. 5;* "Majority Body Upheld as Legal ACC in Suit by "Other" ACC Group," *CC*, March/April 1999, p. 19-20;

"Summary of Deliberations: Court of Metropolitan," *Anglican Catholic Times*, Volume 1, #13, p. 3; "Ex-ACC Group, Barred From Using ACC Name, Adopts New Appellation," *CC*, Summer 1999, p. 22; "Group That Left ACC Suffers Further Mitosis," *CC*, January/February 2000, p. 24.
476. "Two Orthodox Bodies Sign Intercommunion Pact," *CC*, September/October 1998, p. 26-27.
477. "ACC, ACA Consider "Understanding," *CC*, March/April 1999, p. 30.
478. "ACC Enters Into Ecumenical Conversations," *Trinitarian*, August 1999, p. 3.
479. "ACC Offers Health Coverage To All Continuing Clergy," *CC*, November/December 1999, p. 26.
480. The Anglican Rite Synod in the Americas appears to have been formed as an attempt to continue the Anglican Rite Jurisdiction of the Americas after it had (apparently) dissolved into the EMC.
481. "Orthodox Episcopal, Continuing Bishops Make the First Serious Move Toward Unity," *CC*, Summer 1999, p. 10-15; "Continuing Leaders Adopt Articles of Fellowship," *CC*, January/February 2000, p. 13-14.
482. Robert Stowe England. "Lambeth '98: Turning Point," *CC*, September/October 1998, p. 6-17.
483. "Resolution Seeks Dialogue With Continuing Churches," *CC*, Ibid., p. 19-20.
484. Auburn Faber Traycik. "We Hear Your Cry: Six Anglican Leaders Tell Embattled U.S. Conservatives They're Committed to Action," *CC*, May 1999, p. 8-11.
485. For information on the events surrounding the formation of AMIA, see: Auburn Faber Traycik. "The Singapore Sling," *CC*, March 2000, p. 6-11; "Foreign Leaders' U.S. Visit Results in Critical Report," Ibid., p. 12, 14; Auburn Faber Traycik. "Archbishops Give Go-Ahead To Singapore Two and New Anglican Mission in

America," *CC*, September/October 2000, p. 18-22; Auburn Traycik and David Virtue. "General Convention 2000: The Bonfire of the Sexualities," Ibid., p. 11-17; and Auburn F. Traycik. "Dropping Out, Dropping In: As More Depart ECUSA, Foreign Bishops Plan Pastoral Visit to America," *CC*, November 2000, p. 16-19, 34.
486. See FIF-NA, AMIA Alliance Confirmed, As Jammed AMIA Meeting Convenes," *CC*, February 2001, p. 27; and "FIF-NA To Try for Foreign-Made Bishop," *CC*, November/December 2001, p. 27.
487. For its part, the AMiA does not consider itself to be a Continuing Church body, since it is in communion with bishops who are still members of the mainstream Anglican Communion. It remains to be seen what position the AMiA will take if the Anglican Communion removes the dissenting foreign primates from official communion.
488. "EMC Presses On Despite New Losses," *CC*, Summer 2000, p. 29-30.
489. "Snippets and Tippets," *US Anglican*, Christmas, 2001, p. 42.
490. This rumor was relayed to myself by several members of the HCC-AR.
491. "Clavier Received into ECUSA," *CC*, January/February 2000, p. 22-23.
492. "Report from New Commandment Task Force, Regional Reconciliation Meeting #2, St. Christopher's Church, Dallas, Texas, June 12-16, 2000," http://members.aol.com/newcmndment/ Dallas.htm
493. Anthony F.M. Clavier. "On the Continuing Churches of Anglicanism: by one who served 25 years as a bishop in one," posted at andromeda.rutgers.edu/~lcrew/joy109.html on August 28, 2001.
494. Peter Toon. "The Anglican Continuum – some thoughts

for its renewal." Posted at episcopalian.org/pbs1928/continu.htm. July 13, 2001.
495. Michael F. Gallo. "The Continuing Anglicans: Credible Movement or Ecclesiastical Dead End?" *Touchstone*, Winter 1989, p. 27-32.
496. Mark R. M. Clavier. "Ecumenical Report." Posted at deusonline.org/ecumenicalsynod2000.html. March 9, 2001.
497. Thomas McDonald. "A Time To Stand! – Addendum – A personal Apologetic Written Especially For Those Who Have Chosen To Continue The Teachings and Practices of the Church Fathers and the Seven Ecumenical Councils of the Undivided Church." (Self published: Orange, CA), 2001.
498. Text of the *Affirmation* is printed in McDonald, p. 19-25.